The Future of
Teledemocracy

The Future of
Teledemocracy

Ted Becker and
Christa Daryl Slaton

Westport, Connecticut
London

Library of Congress Cataloging-in-Publication Data

Becker, Theodore Lewis.
    The future of teledemocracy / Ted Becker and Christa Daryl Slaton.
        p.   cm.
    Includes bibliographical references (p.   ) and index.
    ISBN 0–275–96632–1 (alk. paper).—ISBN 0–275–97090–6 (pbk.: alk. paper)
    1. Democracy.   2. Information technology—Political aspects.   3.
Telecommunication—Political aspects.   4. Communication in politics—Technological
innovations.   I. Slaton, Christa Daryl.   II. Title.
JC423.B3   2000
321.8'01—dc21   99–055169

British Library Cataloguing in Publication Data is available.

Library of Congress Catalog Card Number: 99–055169
ISBN: 0–275–96632–1
        0–275–97090–6 (pbk.)

First published in 2000

Praeger Publishers, 88 Post Road West, Westport, CT 06881
An imprint of Greenwood Publishing Group, Inc.
www.praeger.com

Printed in the United States of America

The paper used in this book complies with the
Permanent Paper Standard issued by the National
Information Standards Organization (Z39.48–1984).

10 9 8 7 6 5 4 3 2 1

To our Nordic colleagues

Auli, Marcus, Tomas

for their inspiration, support, and friendship
throughout the years

Contents

Acknowledgments

In the 23 years that we have worked together in designing and testing new democratic processes, we have been helped, supported, and motivated by many people in many ways.

From the early days, we are deeply indebted to Alvin and Heidi Toffler, who brainstormed with us many times in tropical settings in Honolulu, in New York City restaurants, and in their home in Connecticut; Jim Dator, who served as trusted friend, esteemed mentor, and creative co-advisor in ETM projects; and Dick Chadwick, who was our original partner in the Hawaii Televote experiments.

As we became more aware of the deeds of others who dreamed and invented new means to more fully engage citizens in representative democracy, we developed enormous respect for the vision, innovativeness, and true grit of Hazel Henderson, Alan Kay, Duane Elgin, Ann Niehaus, Larry Greene, Ted Wachtel, and Ned and Pat Crosby. We are proud to count them as our allies to this very day.

More recently, as our work was welcomed by the international community, we have been fortunate to forge close professional and personal relationships in several countries. Through continuous and fruitful interaction with them, we have come to understand that we are just a small part of a strong and growing global movement toward some new form of future democracy. Those with whom we have worked the closest and developed the greatest synergy are Dick Ryan (New Zealand), Mike Hollinshead (Canada), Auli Keskinen (Finland), Marcus Schmidt (Denmark), and Tomas Ohlin (Sweden).

Then there are our parents who instilled in us the values to seek a more honest and just society: Charles Becker, who fought the good fight in Newark, New Jersey, against corruption, leading a grand jury to indict the entire City Commission for illegal kickbacks in the 1930s; Katherine Lowder whose way of life was to exude compassion for the "underdog"; Hubert L. Lowder, who showed us that working-class people had infinitely more good sense than those who ran the show. We continue our own work always mindful of what our parents stood for and stood up to their entire lives.

A major part of our work over the past five years has been our Web site, Teledemocracy Action News + Network, or TAN+N. Given the complexity of Web construction, this could not have been accomplished without the gracious and high caliber contributions of Charles Spindler, Richard Schmitz, Carlos Urbizu, Sim James, and Jody Bronaugh.

Finally, as we come to this past year that we spent writing this book, we would like to express our gratitude to our editor, Jeremy Geelan of Adamantine Press, for his encouragement on this project; Virginia Prickett for lending us her great technical expertise; and Bob Bernstein, the chair of our department, for assisting us in every way that he could.

Introduction: Our Past and Present Journey into the "Unconventional Politics of the Future"

This book began for us in January 1977 at the University of Hawaii in Honolulu. It was the first meeting of a graduate course Ted Becker was teaching for the first (and only) time, with the odd title of "Unconventional Politics of the Future." One of the graduate students in that seminar was Christa Daryl Slaton.

The required texts for the course were Becker's two most recently published books (both of 1976 vintage). Each of them was heavily larded with harsh critiques of American representative democracy. Each prescribed inventive democratic remedies: US Americard—voting by credit card—and The Random House—a randomly selected legislature.

The students grappled with the critical analysis of "the system" and imagined and evaluated novel solutions. At the conclusion of the class, however, most continued on in mainstream political activities, for example, law school, or the military. Only one chose to explore more fully "the unconventional politics of the future." Thus was born a partnership of personal political perspectives and positions that has persisted to this point in time. What began as a heady academic exercise became a fused odyssey into what has truly been, and remains to this day, "the unconventional politics of the future."

It has been a wild and woolly adventure for the two of us. We have found some true blue allies along the way. We have also joined some collaborations of convenience and made compromises to achieve some of our goals. We have been foiled at times by those who opposed our ideology and had the means to halt our experiments.

If we had to add up all the wins, losses, and ties, we think we come out on the plus side. After all, here we are in the year 2000 publishing our first book together, one that not only describes a series of real gains over the past 23 years, but how we intend to keep at it into the indefinite future.

In addition, some of what we simply imagined in 1977 are now recognizable as new but practical innovations in democratic governance. For example, "scientific deliberative polling" is not yet a "conventional" form of citizen participation, but it exists in several forms, has proved its merit, and continues to expand and be incorporated into actual politics. While voting from the home electronically may not be conventional yet, is there any doubt it will be an option in the near future?

So this book of ours is a major milestone for us. It proves to us that we were not really as beyond-the-pale as some of our colleagues and acquaintances thought we were at the outset and throughout our mutual journey. Maybe we were "slightly ahead of our time," but the times they are a changin'. After all, this book is not just about us; it is about a growing political movement that includes a lot of acclaimed people, all of whom have accomplished great things.

As we have compelled ourselves to relive this sojourn by writing this book, it has made us recapture the excitement of the discoveries and the warmth of the collaborations we have enjoyed over the years. But the best part of it is that there will be, inevitably, more unconventional politics in the future; new discoveries to be made; old alliances renewed; and new coalitions and projects tomorrow.

The Future of Teledemocracy is not just another book to us. It has been a way of life since we first met. And it will continue to be the beacon that draws us together into whatever will come.

PART I

Introduction to the New Physics and New Democratic Paradigm

As we take a quantum leap into the 21st century and envision the future of teledemocracy, we need to break free from the theoretical bondage that has defined and constrained democracy in the last few centuries. Representative democracy, which emerged from the Enlightenment, along with the revelations in scientific thinking, reached its peak in the late 18th and 19th centuries. Throughout the 20th century, demands and movements for more direct democracy have become increasingly successful in the United States. Struggles for greater economic equality have transformed political systems throughout Europe. Also during the 20th century representative democracy has been on the decline wherever it is in use. Public trust in such government is at an all-time low in the United States and on a downward slope elsewhere.

This high level of dissatisfaction is not only due to unresponsive and out-of-touch political leaders. It is, importantly, the result of the level of frustration that comes from trying to fit new knowledge and new technologies into an outdated political system, one that evolved from the theory, knowledge, and technologies of more than three centuries ago. Although the printing press and new scientific inventions, such as the telescope, greatly expanded knowledge and access to information, the world remained dominated by illiteracy, enormous discrepancies between rich and poor, transportation by boat and horse and buggy, and communication systems that took days, weeks, or even months to traverse from one person to another. At the dawn of the new millennium, however, we have instant communication, rapid transportation, and extensive education, coupled with a tottering, doddering, unresponsive representative democracy.

We will demonstrate in Part I that we are experiencing the dawn of a paradigm shift, the rise of a new worldview. During the Enlightenment, the world experienced revolutionary changes in religion, science, and government that were all connected to how we understood the world, how we studied phenomena, and how we gained new knowledge. Luther, Copernicus, Galileo, Descartes, Bacon, Newton, Hobbes, and Locke all shared a worldview that embraced reason, logic, scientific method, certainty, and cause-and-effect determinism. The political philosophers of that time were heavily influenced by the scientific method developed in the natural sciences—so much so that liberalism, the philosophy that underlies representative democracy, has been referred to as "Newtonian politics" (Landau 1961; Barber 1984; Becker 1991; Slaton 1992).

That was then. This is now. A new revolution in the natural science world has preceded many of the dramatic contemporary changes in transportation and information and communications technologies, or ICT. Quantum physics, which arose out of investigations into the microscopic world, uncovered many of the limitations of Newtonian physics and some of the fallacies of universally accepted laws of the natural universe. These new discoveries generated new hypotheses, which produced even greater discoveries and innovation.

Part I examines the relationship between the political theories, institutions, and practices that emerge from a Newtonian paradigm and those that emanate from a paradigm that incorporates aspects of Newtonian thought as well as quantum thinking and chaos theory. As Thomas Kuhn asserted, all paradigms become outdated and ineffective after a time. On the one hand, paradigms are enormously useful because they help us focus our research and give us a common language and method of study. On the other hand, they limit our understanding and our vision because they box us in. Paradigms are useful only as long as they continue to generate new hypotheses and answer more questions. They become obsolete when we become stymied in seeking answers and solutions to unresolved questions and problems.

This became abundantly clear in the natural science world several decades ago. We are asserting in this book that it has now become obvious in the social science world—and more specifically, the political science world—that the prevailing paradigm or worldview, rooted firmly in Enlightenment thought, has trapped us and prevented us from exploring new and higher ground. Chapter 1 will discuss the emergence and components of the New Democratic Paradigm, one that incorporates new ICTs that lead to a transformation of representative democracy into new forms of teledemocracy. Writings of early teledemocratic visionaries like Buckminster Fuller, Eric Fromm, Hazel Henderson, and Amitai Etzioni will be examined to demonstrate the application of ICT in creating a more direct and participatory form of democracy. The chapter will conclude with a discussion of how the New Democratic Paradigm is post-Newtonian and offers the theoretical basis for new forms, types, and styles of democracy in the future.

Chapter 2 demonstrates that there has been an enduring relationship between physics and political theory. The problem with modern political theory is that it remains unconsciously and uncritically tied to Newtonian physics and fails to consider the value in new political theories emerging out of the new physics. The chapter explores how quantum theory has been applied in both nongovernmental arenas as well as in politics and calls for a new political science and a New Democratic Paradigm based on the principles of chaos theory, quantum theory, and social energy.

Any structure made by humans—when built on an unstable, incomplete foundation—weakens over time. When extra stress is placed on it, the weaknesses produce unnerving tremors and frightening noises throughout the superstructure. Until the deeper problem is understood, no number of repairmen on the roof, in the attic, and in the kitchen will reduce the vibrating and deterioration of the base. What is needed is a radical reinforcement of the foundation—a correction of the underlying theory of all our social, economic, and political structures. Part I will begin to do that for the rickety political house in which we live—representative democracy.

1

The Emergence and Components of the New Democratic Paradigm: Historical Surges and Visions of the Future

A few years back, Francis Fukuyama attracted a lot of serious attention from a wide variety of "experts" on world affairs by trumpeting no less than that the "end of history" was at hand (Fukuyama 1989). According to this viewpoint, the sudden implosion of the Communist house of cards (at least the Marxist-Leninist-Stalinist model) meant that there were no more crucial political-economic battles to be waged, now and forever. Representative democracy and global corporate capitalism would be gloriously triumphant forever after.

Actually, this proclamation was equally fatuous to the one made earlier in the 20th century proclaiming the death of God. If this announcement of the end of political evolution were true, and tomorrow and tomorrow and tomorrow were relegated to nonideological squabbling, then the future would indeed be placid and subject only to mundane and dreary projects in social engineering. In Fukuyama's own words,

> The end of history will be a sad time. The struggle for recognition, the willingness to risk one's life for a purely abstract goal, the worldview ideological struggle that called forth daring, courage, imagination and idealism, will be replaced by economic calculation, the endless solving of technological problems, environmental concerns and the satisfaction of sophisticated consumer demands. (Fukuyama 1989, 18)

But if that is so and modern hybrids of representative democracy and the new global corporate order have sated all basic human needs and yearnings, then what accounts for the continuing military build-ups, the escalating fear of terrorism, the fall of conservative governments in Europe, the upswing in religious/political fundamentalism, and the swelling alienation of citizenries? Why all the trepidation, travail, and trembling over what the future holds for today's young and restless and for generations unborn? Why are there not jubilant celebrations throughout the world and the giddiness of victory? The reason is obvious: the truly enduring ideological vortex continues to rotate, with wide swaths of material, psychological, emotional, and spiritual destruction in its path and wake.

So, what is the internal and infernal dynamic of this eternal philosophical storm? It is the perennial and perpetual conflict between the powerful and the powerless, the have-lots and have-nots, masculine self-ordination and feminine subordination, the help-themselves and the helpless. In political-scientific terms, it is the millennia-tested war over a fairer distribution of the authoritative allocation of values and consequently a fairer deal of goods, goodies, and goodwill in every society that has ever graced this Earth. Surely the death or dearth of Soviet-style communism in the 1990s has not even begun to terminate this ageless contest—and it cannot, for it turns out to be the disappearance of only the latest superficial symptom of the disease.

Our global situation at the dawning of the third millennium is a much prettier picture than it was when the sun rose on the second millennium. But it is more like the portrait of Dorian Gray: Many governments are warring with segments of their own population; there are still deep class antagonisms everywhere; billions work and toil in poverty while a few hundred billionaires live in obscene luxury; and humankind still shamelessly exploits its sustainable natural environment. Indeed, the number and intensity of antagonisms among ethnic groups, races, classes, and nations is not much less acute and chronic today than eons ago. Thus, grave concerns remain, such as:

- the rapidly warming condition of planet Earth and the vanishing of many of its natural resources;
- the increasing domination of so-called representative governments by tiny cliques of economically powerful and well-organized interests who are, by and large, sexist, racist, and Social Darwinists at heart;
- the astronomical national debts run up by fighting the Cold War, arming the Third World, and pursuing the chimera of some "new world order" run by an imperious global oligarchy and unaccountable global bureaucracy;

- the nagging sense of isolation and despair among youth everywhere concerning what meaning and value, if any, life holds for them;

- the incapacity of people at community, local, state, provincial, national, and international levels to collaborate on solutions to these and other life-threatening maladies.

So here we are at the third millennium and 21st century, facing uniquely menacing dilemmas. Technological leaps in the past few years have truly converted our universe into a "global marketplace"—where we are a remote-control zap away from everyone else's tragedies, grudges, neuroses, xenophobia, vendettas, and dirty laundry. New high-tech gadgets have provided fabulous luxuries, dizzying speed, unconscionable indulgences, fantastic conveniences, and instantaneous access to oceans of information. But not only have they not assuaged the severe situations that confront us now and will in the immediate future, they have instead compounded them and confounded us. How can we be so brilliant and retarded at the same time?

Still, we see some encouraging signs as well, portents of a better world and enlightened transformations—a political-economic synthesis that will permit America and the rest of the world to cooperate on latent solutions rather than bicker endlessly over patent problems. One of the most promising, from our point of view, is what we discern as the most recent widespread and strongest democratic quantum leap ever in the history of humankind.

From our vantage point, then, Fukuyama was dead wrong. The ancient and future ideologial wrangling—*democracy vs. oligarchy + hierarchy*—is far from over. It perseveres with its antagonists as deeply divided as ever. Those of us on the side of a purer, future democracy see this form of governance holding many solutions to most of the aforementioned threats to human viability. Indeed, we hold this truth to be self-evident: The present and future ideological struggle will be over the emergence and growth of new forms of democracy—particularly more direct democratic mutations at all levels of governance—that integrate the new information and communications technologies (ICT), what we coined as "teledemocracy" (Becker 1981).

FAITH IN DEMOCRATIC PROGRESS

We are not certain whether there is or is not a divine fortune cookie baked by God, Jahweh, Allah, or The Force that predicts a Frank Capra, Steven Spielberg, or Walt Disney happy ending for all humankind: everyone living harmoniously here, there, and foreverafter. Was Hegel right that destiny is the unfolding of a universal idea and that we are unwitting and sometimes unwilling role players in a drama inspired by the seemingly fickle fantasies of fate? Perhaps. Are there enormous tsunamis of inevitable human progress that we catch on our minuscule surfboards—frequently getting wiped out in the tumbling turbulence? Maybe so. Is the world inexorably moving toward maximum violence and malevolence only to be rescued at the abyss by the Second Coming of the Messiah? Who really knows?

Our work does not focus on a comprehensive and ironclad theory of human *destiny* that drives our thinking and action. We are not historical, scientific, or biblical determinists. What we do have, though, is the Enlightenment's faith in some degree of continued improvement in the human condition throughout history, a forward movement that seems to us to be peculiarly embodied in and emboldened by the great American experiment. It seems to us that America became a haven for, and stimulant of, a new way of life in the New World for waves of religious, political, and economic refugees during the 17th, 18th, 19th, and 20th centuries. It provided a fresh and seemingly inexhaustible source of individual freedom, economic and social growth, and personal development. For most immigrants, the American dream, with its promise of personal liberty, was a revolutionary concept and it has been so from its inception.

But even before then, there were democratic developments among its Native American inhabitants—demonstrating how the rich soil, variable terrain, teeming wildlife, limitless resources, yawning expanse, and temperate climate of North America provided some necessary and sufficient conditions to conceive of and gestate some strong pulsations of democracy. One brilliant American historian, Frederick Jackson Turner, saw this in terms of how democracy was the most intelligent way to handle the challenges of the bedeviling and bewildering wilderness that confronted those who lived there: "American democracy was . . . not carried in the Susan Constant to Virginia nor in the Mayflower to Plymouth. It came out of the American forest, and it gained strength each time it touched a new frontier" (Beall 1993, 13A).

What we see, then, is one continent on this globe generating a series of impulses that contain the best way for humankind to work together, live together, grow together, and govern together. Experiments in democracy have long flourished in America—in some Native American tribes, along the Oregon Trail, in small towns, in the workplace, in utopian communities, in schools, in political movements, in communications. Some succeeded. Some failed. Some became indelibly etched in our collective psyche and soul. Some mildew in damp, dank crevices of long-forgotten history.

Sure, there have been (and will be) severe antidemocratic movements and fascistic episodes in American history as well. A universal penchant for hypocrisy has accounted for much of that. Right from the start, those who sought freedom from religious persecutors became in their own right, self-righteous prosecutors. In addition, the despicable and indefensible institution of slavery was as antithetical and inimical to democracy in America as anything could be—and its bad karma continues to plague and cripple America's domestic health to this very day. What is more, in the 20th century alone, we have seen wholesale governmental and widespread private repression of women, labor, socialists, communists, civil rightists, and non-mainstream ways of life. Democracy has not, is not, and will never be the only road Americans travel.

Democratic Waves

It is our view, though, that—taken altogether—there has been a slow and steady progression, a gradual growth, a series of surges that ebb and flow, but move steadily forward in fits and starts to become—per usual—the wave of the future. There have been several famed analysts of American history who have detected and detailed this strange set of recurrent patterns.

Although each has emphasized a slightly different aspect of it, it occurs to us that all these are merely slightly different characterization of the perennial struggle we mentioned before. For example, to historian Arthur Schlesinger, Jr., there have been a series of "cycles" or "alternations" between "conservatism and liberalism, between periods of concern for the rights of the few and periods of concern for the wrongs of the many" (Schlesinger 1986, 24). Schlesinger also noted that the great American thinker Ralph Waldo Emerson saw this oscillation as vibrating between force fields of "conservatism" and "innovation," and the celebrated American historian Henry Adams likened it to a tension between "the centralization and diffusion of national energy" (Schlesinger 1986, 23).

Our own view is that analogies to cycles or spirals are too Newtonian, too geometric, too neat and tidy to describe real sociopolitical outbursts. We are more partial to metaphors of the new physics that highlight randomness, uncertainty (if not chaos), and unpredictability (Becker 1991; Slaton 1992). Thus, we view these democratic phases as highly charged, erratic, self-contradictory packets of political energy, what we like to call "democratic quanta," that appear to occur with a rough regularity, but with increasing levels of velocity and force.

We particularly appreciate the way that one "global" historian, William McNeill, interprets world history as revealing a kindred mode of political evolution (McNeill 1975). McNeill claims that institutions that allow people to develop and fulfill their potential have a high degree of survival value in the rough-and-tumble of historical change. Thus, states or polities that encouraged their people to develop such potential became strong by helping harness and channel a substantial proportion of their creative energy. The more of their population that governments can involve in this way, the stronger they become. McNeill, as sort of a democratic Darwinist, points to various events in the stream of European history that helped mobilize large numbers of democratic societies. So, we see these surges as an earthly, global pattern, with the American experience as the first and largest of a few growing and glowing stars in a rapidly expanding political cosmos, one that is mostly darkness, quasars, and black holes.

The Imminent 21st-Century Quantum Leap: Direct Teledemocracy

All this is a backdrop, though, to the current-time mélange that combines (1) space age information and communications systems (ICT) with obsolescent democratic political systems and (2) the conception, development, and promise of authentic, comprehensive Electronic Town Meetings, a modern system of teledemocracy we describe in some detail in Part II of this volume.

Electronic Town Meetings, or ETMs, are a novel blend of (1) advanced and potential Space Age communications-information hardware; (2) cutting-edge computer software; (3) leading-edge scientific deliberative polling (face-to-face and/or electronic); (4) traditional and new forms of direct democracy (DD); and (5) contemporary conflict resolution techniques. All of these, however, are set within, woven together, and informed by modern 20th-century democratic foresight, theory, history, and political aspirations of humankind. They are the key ingredients of a present and immediate future evolution of democracy in America and the world, the furthest expression and expansion of the democratic surge, the additional substance needed to reach a "critical mass." These essentials, when fused, would become a quantum leap in truly empowering all citizens of any polity up to this nanosecond in human history. They amount to what might best be called "Direct Teledemocracy."[1]

Indeed, we think these recurrent and future democratic quantum leaps are not occasional or regular phenomena, but are instead akin to an ever-expanding chain reaction. Unlike their physical counterparts in the subatomic or hypercosmic universe, however, these surges of democratic energy are generated at least in part from bursts of human brainpower. Such democratic brainstorms may appear to conventional thinking as daydreams, the musings of eccentrics, intellectual excesses, wishful thinking, or political science fiction. But to their creators, they are designed as practical potions for what even mainstream diagnosticians see as pernicious socio-economic-political conditions. In the never-ending struggle between the elites and the masses, dedicated democratic thinkers and inventors are often characterized by the conservative and condescending intelligentsia (a.k.a. mainstream experts) as being "crackpots" or rabble-rousers or patronized as dreamers and idealists.

It seems clear to us, though, that new forms of democracy (a constant in political evolution) must spring originally from the fertile minds of visionaries, trailblazers, explorers, theorists, or some combination thereof. Sometimes, they may also be doers and sometimes engineers pick up where seminal thinkers leave off. But imagination is always at least a substantial part of the equation and original thought always precedes democratic experimentation and movements. Innovations in democracy are not the product of spontaneous combustion, no more than are new schools of art or breakthroughs in technology. Vision and theory are always the spark and catalyst. So, let us see what some of these democratic visionaries of the 20th century saw for us in their distant future.

TELEDEMOCRATIC VISIONARIES AND THEIR VISIONS

As far as we know, the first person to divine the rich synergy between direct democracy and 20th century telecommunications was the celebrated Canadian scientist, poet, architect, seer, sire of the geodesic dome, and futuristic sage—R. Buckminster Fuller.

The Jules Verne of Electronic Democracy: R. Buckminster Fuller

R. Buckminster ("Bucky") Fuller, the Jules Verne of teledemocracy, was sitting in his home one night, April 9, 1940, to be exact, at the outbreak of World War II. Being somewhat despondent over immediate and imminent events, his thoughts drifted to a distant eon, a better world, one in which there was no longer a subjugation of the cumulative powers of any citizenry to the "lesser god" in the person of those who would pretend to speak and govern for them.

This was also the wee hours of 20th-century communications technologies—where the telegraph, radio, radar, and telephone were the crowning achievements. But they were enough to sow Fuller's fecund mind, to cause it to envision a future of veritable, virtual, vibrant, vivid, and vivacious electronic direct democracy where citizens would be voting on the most salient issues of the day. To Buckminster Fuller, this was the firsthand materialization of what has long been known as "democracy"—but which was up to then, and remains in the current practice of indirect democracy, in his mind, only a "second-hand god" (Fuller 1971). Keep in mind, too, that his vision preceded such present-day realities as space satellites, personal computers, and the Internet by more than a half-century.

What follows are a few choice elements of what he foresaw 60 years ago. Fuller believed that "democracy has potential within it [to fulfill] the satisfaction of every individual's need" (Fuller 1971, 9). And how could that potential be realized? His answer was that "democracy must be structurally modernized—must be mechanically implemented to give it a one-individual-to-another speed and spontaneity of reaction commensurate with the speed and scope of broadcast news [which is] now world-wide in seconds" (Fuller 1971, 9). And how would that work? By what he called "electrified voting." And what good would that do? For one thing, it would yield "an instantaneous contour map of the workable frontier of the people's wisdom, for purposes of legislation, administration, future exploration, and debate" (Fuller 1971, 11). It would also certify "spontaneous popular co-operation in the carrying out of each decision" (Fuller 1971, 11).

The beauty of such a system, in Fuller's mind, was the overwhelming power of such a collective decision-making process. In matters of foreign policy, he saw it as an irresistible force, one that "no foreign power in the world can stand up against" because of a kind of "mystical awareness of multimillions of individuals that they personally have taken responsibility for the course" (Fuller 1971, 11–12).

Fuller also believed that the United States had to take the lead in this because of its important leadership role in world democracy. Once electronic democracy was so established in America, "the credit and imagination of all outside peoples of the world will be so stimulated that nothing will stop them short of attaining a line to that voice. But so to do they must join up with Democracy" (Fuller 1971, 12).

Finally, Fuller was enough of a visionary to understand that as much as he saw a national system of electronically facilitated direct democracy in the United States as the last, best hope for the future of the teeming masses, there was no guarantee it would work. What he advocated was that it simply be given a fair chance. If it was not, then he believed that "future generations will again champion it, and there will be world civil wars until it receives adequate trial" (Fuller 1971, 13). History, since that prediction, has surely not proven him incorrect.

Teledemocratic Therapy for Political Psychoses: Erich Fromm

The next vision—in the evolution of this brave new electronic democratic worldview—that we find came in the work of another important thinker of the mid-20th century, the renowned political psychoanalyst Erich Fromm. He believed that by properly using new telecommunications equipment, the collective insanity that he saw afflicting contemporary society could be treated appropriately.

From his point of view, the vast army of common people was so regimented that they were entirely divorced from the most important decisions in their daily lives. This was, by and large, true in terms of the roles each person played in society, in economic production, and in government. All this led to a gnawing sense of anomy and frustration that affected all their human interactions. Added together, this produced endemic psychic sickness and sociopathy, or, in his opinion, a society that was insane. Political psychoses helped spread massive social and individual mental instability. Is that diagnosis off the mark today—45 years later? We think not.

Among the prescriptions he wrote to help alleviate this national suffering was a coast-to-coast network of face-to-face town meetings (each with 500 citizens, more or less) that met regularly to discuss and vote upon key national and local issues. The information and advice necessary for deliberation and debate was to be gathered and disseminated by a broad spectrum of experts in the fields of politics, business, science, the arts, and so forth. After sufficient discussion, the people within these groups and across the country would vote "with the help of the technical devices we have today" (Fromm 1955, 342).

We believe it is important to note, even at this early stage of our book, that Fromm—unlike Fuller but like most who advocate electronic direct democracy—did *not* advocate it as *a* replacement of the whole representative system of government. "Teledemocracy" and direct democracy is almost always seen as a complement to, improvement upon, and evolutionary step in representative democracy.[2] So, in Fromm's view, this electronically connected set of face-to-face town meetings was a true "House of Commons" that would have to bargain with the elected branches of government in order to hammer out policy and laws.

The Late 1960s–Early 1970s Cluster

These two isolated visions were joined in the late 1960s and early 1970s by a cluster of parallel projections. Those times were wildly colored by the so-called counterculture, a loose confederation of rebellious ways of life united in opposition to the dominant elite-controlled system and many of its domestic agendas and foreign follies. They spoke and wrote passionately about overturning "the system" and "the establishment" and returning "power to the people." Little, however, was offered as an alternative.

One of the most visible "leaders" of the obstreperous New Left was Abbie Hoffman—noted for his outrageous gab and outspoken opposition to business-and-politics-as-usual. During the riotous goings-on in

Chicago outside the Democratic National Convention in 1968, Hoffman circulated a pamphlet he wrote that made numerous demands about how the government should be changed radically in order to represent the American people more accurately and appropriately. One of the ideas in his panoply of recommendations was the following: "Be realistic, demand the impossible: A political system which is more streamlined and responsive to the needs of all the people regardless of age, sex or race. Perhaps a national referendum system conducted via television or a telephone voting system" (Hoffman, Rubin, and Sanders 1972, 105).

According to Becker and Dodson (1991), this was not an aberration in Hoffman's political thinking, but part of his general overview on how to democratize American society—a new vein in a rich motherlode of American democratic thought.

> Like Jefferson, he respected the native abilities of the ordinary working person and the collective judgment of the people. Like Dewey, he understood that the need for democracy transcends government and that every key institution of American society, including our educational system, economic system, and media is woefully deficient in democratic values or practices. (Becker and Dodson 1991, 70)

Thus, being an expert in the capture of television for the rapture of revolutionary political purposes, Hoffman's vision was consistent with his theory, his experience, and most importantly, the tenor of the times.

Almost synchronistically, Hazel Henderson, many years before gaining prominence as a premier advocate for a new system of socially and ecologically responsible economics, advocated the need for a major revamping of our political communication system. Writing in 1970, she, like Fuller, Fromm, and Hoffman before her, saw teledemocracy as a remedy to avoid "further alienation and increasing numbers of bored, apathetic, irresponsible and violent people"—new "ways of improving communications channels to inform the voter, and machinery to channel his participation and 'feedback' " (Henderson 1970, 22).

As Henderson saw it then, the "hardware" for the "instant electronic referendum" was already available and in place in just about every home in America, that is, a TV set and a telephone. Nothing more, nothing less. She noted that one major American business leader at the time, computer magnate H. Ross Perot, had already advocated national electronic referenda on major policy issues. Perot, way before his abortive bid for the U.S. presidency in 1992, endorsed the need for experimenting with televised "electronic town halls," which, coupled with newspaper ballots, would serve as a prototype of electronic referenda (voting on issues) across America.[3]

The newest device to facilitate this on a grand scale was, according to

Henderson, the computer, which could serve in several crucial capacities. Drawing on the work of Donald Michael (1968), an authority on cybernetics, she described how a computer-assisted "citizens feedback" system of planning might work at the city (or national) level. One of its cardinal features, like Fromm's, was decentralization. There would be a number of "citizen terminals" placed in each voting district, but all would feed into the planning system at city hall. Any citizen could go to a citizen terminal, staffed by an expert computer operator, and request information from the data bank and/or register his or her preferences about the master plan. This system could also be used for all sorts of policy agendas. (It could also be used for citizen input into constitutional conventions—as we will show in Chapter 6)

So, here we have an early vision of citizens with easy access to TVs and telephones in their homes, and computer centers in the nearby vicinity, with readily available facts and figures plus instant influence on the governmental planning process.

A Swedish visionary even pushed Henderson's vision a bit further along at about the same time. Tomas Ohlin, an expert in information sciences, had been working with mainframe computers in the late 1960s when he learned of an experiment in England where someone had connected a home television set to the keyboard of a computer terminal in an office. It dawned upon Ohlin that the computer and the television could also be united in the homes of citizens to provide the hardware for a true "computer-assisted democracy."

So, in 1971, he wrote an article for a major newspaper in Sweden that envisioned a future where every home in Sweden had a computer terminal hooked into huge databases, this being way before the Internet. It was his idea that this would give the citizens sufficient information at their fingertips so that they would make excellent consultants for the government on major issues confronting the country. He also conjured up a vision of a citizens' panel made up of 1,000 randomly selected people, linked into the computer system, who would stay in touch with government on a regular basis (Ohlin 1971).

What, then, do all these visions share? What are their commonalities, their connections? All of them assert or assume that (1) the present-day, Western-style representative system is insufficiently responsive to the general public and that this leads to widespread and deleterious feelings of indifference and helplessness among the populace; (2) electronic information and communications technology (ICT) exists to empower citizens to consider, deliberate, and decide on important public issues and should be used for such; (3) this will produce a more educated, active, and civic-minded citizenry, and consequently, social, economic, and foreign policies more in tune with the needs and desires of the general public, and ultimately, a better (and saner) society.

There are some other strong, but not unanimous, images in these visions, including the views that (1) any national system needs to be constructed from the grass roots up and should include face-to-face meetings; (2) in addition to connecting the citizens and governments, the new technologies need to create a lateral system of communications between the citizenry itself; (3) there must be a good deal of informed dialogue and debate prior to any voting; and (4) the process must aim toward the development of broad public consensus. Finally, it seems to us that each visionary assumed that somehow, someway, and someday this will come to pass—not that this will truly solve and resolve each and every political, economic, social, and moral problem or issue of the time, but that it is bound to happen and will be a substantial improvement over the less democratic system-in-place.

But these are simply visions—fading snapshots of distant tele-democratic tomorrows from representative democratic yesterdays. Their significance is as a part of the inspirational phase of the democracy-force, some of it coming prior to and some concurrent with the theoretical phase of this newest, most far-reaching democratic surge. *What they need is to be connected to a more rigorous thought process, a new democratic political theory set into a new democratic paradigm.* But what would that entail?

THE NEW DEMOCRATIC PARADIGM: POST-NEWTONIAN SCIENTIFIC THEORIES AND THE FUTURE OF DEMOCRACY

There are all kinds of democratic theories. All of them, though, agree more or less with Abraham Lincoln's famous definition of it being a "government of the people, by the people and for the people." However, the species of it are as diverse as elephants and insects, like what the Chinese Communist party means by a "people's democracy" and what Vermonters mean by a New England town meeting.

Aristotle, being the first empirical political scientist, induced its definition from its actual practice in comparison with other systems among the city-states of the Greeks. Karl Marx saw it as an evolutionary step in his understanding of "historical determinism." Other philosophers, during the 17th and 18th centuries, were enamored by the scientific and philosophical discoveries of their time—what is commonly called the Enlightenment—and applied those ideas to the development of an entirely new system of what we now call "representative" or "indirect" democracy. From our perspective at this point in time, that latter group of theorists is most relevant to the kind of democracy that prevails today, the one we see as in dire need of help to keep it from collapsing and taking a huge toll on all forms of life on Earth. Thus, it is our view that the "old paradigm" of democracy, the predominant one today, is closely tied to the theories and scientific worldview that 17th- and 18th-century philosophical, and political thinking were centered around.

It is also our opinion that any "new democratic paradigm" that will help evolve the "old democratic paradigm" into a new and better form of itself needs to blend several disparate, but interconnected, modern theoretical and scientific developments, including (1) post-Newtonian physics, in other words, the theory of relativity, quantum theory, and chaos theory; (2) the 20th-century evolution in participatory and direct democratic theory; and (3) the 20th-century revolution in ICT.

Certainly it is fair to say that humankind would probably be earth-bound today without some help from the 20th-century scientific discoveries in the fields of physics and communications. For example, Albert Einstein's theory of relativity demonstrated that Newton was incorrect in his view that space was a neutral background factor in the relationship between suns and planets, that it had no effect on their orbits, on the force of gravity, and so forth. Instead, space itself is curved and shaped by the movement and relationship between the planets, and that shape helps guide the movement and relative position of the planets.

In other words, space, time, and celestial bodies are not separate, isolated, or absolute. They relate to one another. They interact with each other. Einstein's correction in Newtonian thinking has boosted the human race's first penetrations into space, but it has also helped transform, in a more subtle way, humanity's contemporary view of human nature and its relationship to the rest of nature as well. Furthermore, it has tremendous potential to impact upon and alter the prevailing Western model of political thought and behavior, that is, democratic liberalism.

A good example of how Einstein's theory of relativity can inform and improve one important part of one aspect of modern democratic liberalism—American constitutional law—can be found in the thinking of one of America's premier legal philosophers and constitutional scholars, Laurence H. Tribe of the Harvard Law School. In Tribe's view, "Einstein's brilliance was to recognize that in comprehending physical reality the 'background' could not be abstracted from the 'foreground.' In the paradigm inspired by Einstein, 'space and time are now dynamic qualities: when a body moves, or a force acts, it affects the *curvature* of space and time—and in turn the structure of space-time affects the way in which bodies move and forces act' " (Hawking 1988, 33; emphasis by Tribe). Tribe contends:

A parallel conception in the legal universe would hold that just as space cannot extricate itself from the unfolding story of physical reality, so also the law cannot extract itself from social structure; it cannot "step back," establish an "Archimedean" reference point of detached neutrality, and selectively reach in, as though from the outside, to make fine-tuned adjustments to highly particularized conflicts. Each legal decision restructures the law itself, as well as the social setting in which law operates. (Tribe, in Becker 1991, 173)

Likewise, 20th-century developments in the study of the microworld (quantum theory and mechanics) that comprehend how the basic building blocks of our universe, our bodies, and our minds behave have enormous implications for the way we think about such concepts as individualism, consciousness, society, and politics. In other words, studying atoms, molecules, up-quarks, neutrons, bosons, and fermions can help us understand politics.

Furthermore, we believe that by grasping how many political theorists and designers throughout time have absorbed their epoch's beliefs about physics and nature—and how our present socio-economic-political system leans so heavily on Newton's theories—one becomes free to apply the new 20th-century physics to political phenomena, and to create new systems that comport better with the true nature of our physical reality, our consciousness, and our relationship to all of nature. In other words, we are at liberty, if not obligated, to create a new politics, new political systems based on quantum insights, that is to say, a quantum politics that in essence would be "quantum democracy" as contrasted to Newtonian democracy.

The next chapter, then, will go into some detail on how this relationship between physics and politics has been a natural and durable one in Western history and how some modern theorists and political scientists (including ourselves) have been developing a theory of "quantum democracy"—shorthand for what we consider to be the "New Democratic Paradigm." Thus, Part I will serve as an introduction to and the scientific foundation for Part II—where we set forth the chronological development of what we think are major components for at least one well-tested model of a future teledemocracy.

NOTES

1. As far as we know, Theodore Becker was the first to coin the term "teledemocracy" in print (Becker 1981, 1), and it was quite close to our definition above. Since then we have added the element of conflict resolution to the term. Many have used that term since to denote the most superficial types of voting by telephone or the Internet. Christopher Arterton, in his book *Teledemocracy*, charges us with "bandying about the term 'teledemocracy' as a catchword for the establishment of direct democracy through the use of communications media" (Arterton 1987, 14). He comes closer than most at understanding what we mean by this concept. However, at that time, as well as now, our conception of teledemocracy includes, as a vital part of it, the use of scientific deliberative polling—both face to face and electronic. The use of random samples of citizens who deliberate on an issue has been and remains key to our view of successful and efficient teledemocracy.

2. There are those who do advocate a replacement of the entire existing system. Lyn Carson and Brian Martin, in their recent book on random selection in

politics, recommend—among other ideas—randomly selected functional groups instead of elected representatives (Carson and Martin 1999). John Burnheim, also in this camp, calls this alternative system "demarchy" (Burnheim 1985).

3. According to one report, Perot tried to convince President Richard Nixon of the usefulness of this venture in 1969, but to no avail (*New York Times*, May 8, 1992, p. 1).

2

The New Physics as the Scientific Foundation for the New Democratic Paradigm

In what way or ways, then, can scientific theories of the nature of physical reality inform or guide political thinking and/or the practice of politics? Are they only, or best, by analogy? Can they not serve at least as part of the intellectual foundation for the theory and practice of government and politics? By knowing some basic ideas of physics, can each of us better know ourselves, our personal relationships, our politics, our society, our cosmic universe, our spiritual destiny?

As we have suggested in Chapter 1, the answer to all of these questions is at least a qualified "yes." This chapter will go into some depth in explaining how this works politically. It will also point out that although this critical lesson has been forgotten in recent times, it is not too late to update it and, by doing so, to help reinform our political thinking and processes in order to ameliorate some of the most debilitating and most lethal crises all modern governments face.

MODERNIZING THE MARRIAGE BETWEEN PHYSICS, POLITICS, AND THE SCIENCE OF GOVERNMENT

The use of the "hard" natural sciences as an analogy for the "soft" social sciences and humanities is well known and documented. We speak often of the "body politic"; "arms" or "branches" of government; the "balance" or "equilibria" of power; "the nerves of government"; and "the pecking order" in bureaucracy. All this is meant to liken the obtuse and legalistic apparatuses and processes of governance to obvious aspects of nature—to give us a better idea about how government evolves and works just like some other phenomena we think we understand such as the solar system, the human body, animal life, and so on.

Political analogues to physical nature are meant to be illustrative and provocative. They suggest answers to perennial conundrums, particularly ones that are difficult to grasp. Thus, they are somewhat akin to slogans in that they are catchy and an easier way to come to grips with something complex and dense. This helps explain their popularity and durability.

But there is another, even more important, use of predominant scientific theory and knowledge for politics, one that also expands its discourse; influences its political design; and justifies its past, current, or future practices. This is the impact that the prevailing idea of physical reality has—first among intellectuals and then among the general population—on how we all view and connect each and every aspect of human nature: individual, social, economic, and political.

The Enduring Relationship between Physics and Politics

Prior to the Enlightenment, in the feudal Western world (as well as elsewhere), what was then deemed to be "science" was dominated by religious dogma. The world was created as religion said it was, and the interpretation of the authoritative source(s)—the Bible in Western culture—was left to religious pundits, priests, and prelates. In the West, this was the Catholic church and its hierarchy. In its mind's eye, the Earth was created by God and was therefore the center of all Creation. Medieval "science's" exclusive mission and privilege was to prove this in infinite detail. Any deviation from this official worldview was swiftly and severely repudiated by the hierarchy. Those who dared to insist otherwise—deviants and heretics—risked thumbscrews, racks, and excommunication from the Church or life itself.

The Church and the state co-existed—each being powerful and wealthy in its own right—but each still had need for the other to protect and nurture its material interests. For example, the Church provided the acceptable physical theory that grounded and legitimized the political theory that sustained the absolute authority of monarchies throughout Europe. Accordingly, it was widely believed that God Almighty, the sublime architect of the entire physical edifice, had imbued each king with a "divine right" to rule over all within his royal domain. Just about everyone alive at that time—from the most erudite scholar to the lowliest serf or peon—believed this to be true.

With the Enlightenment and the growth of modern Western science, the facade of the "divine right" of kings was thoroughly trashed. The Earth was no longer the hub of the cosmos and many other "scientific" and religious dogmas fell into disrepute. However, none of this came about overnight. There was a lengthy time lag between the advent of the new scientific thought of Bacon and Newton and its impact on the political, economic, and social order built upon the outmoded and superceded physics and metaphysics. In other words, much time must elapse before new theories of knowledge and science are put to the use of creating and supporting drastic changes in government.

This is not to say that Newton's discoveries were an independent variable or necessary condition for new political theories to emerge. Instead, that age, like our own, was a transformational one, an age of dramatic interrelated changes in how human beings thought, worked, and related to one another and their environment. Newton's insights into the physical universe did not precede or cause the Enlightenment. They were, however, an integral part of it. Newton's experiments with the physical universe did not precede or cause the development of mercantilism, industrialization, and representative democracy. But they were a part of it. They, like everything in physical reality, interacted.

It must also be noted that Newton's unique contributions to modern science were themselves educated by and built upon the earlier and contemporary scientific discoveries of his period, in other words, those by Copernicus, Galileo, Kepler, Bacon, and Descartes. The essence of his grand and all-encompassing theory involved a precise formula that explained the motion of all bodies in the solar system under the influence of gravity. All cosmic entities, from space pebbles to asteroids to stars to galaxies, operated under exact mathematical laws. The universe was a gigantic *deus ex machina*, with varying parts that performed with great, celestial precision.

This newest and most advanced-for-its-time scientific proof of the mechanistic nature of the world-as-we-knew-it reinforced the recently emergent view in modern (Cartesian) philosophy that separated everything into distinct, component parts. Everything in nature, including the human body, the human mind, humankind, and nature was separate, albeit linked in a rational, mathematical, machinelike way. But what has all this to do with a philosophy, a worldview, that affects the way we think and behave *today* in society and politics?

According to Fritjof Capra, a noted physicist and philosopher, the physics-political philosophy part of life behaved like this:

> Descartes himself had sketched the outlines of a mechanistic approach to physics, astronomy, biology, psychology, and medicine. The thinkers of the eighteenth century carried this program further by applying the principles of Newtonian mechanics to the sciences of human nature and human society. The newly created social sciences generated great enthusiasm, and some of their proponents even claimed to have discovered a "social physics." The Newtonian

theory of the universe and the belief in the rational approach to human problems spread so rapidly among the middle classes of the eighteenth century that the whole era became the "Age of Enlightenment." The dominant figure in this development was the philosopher John Locke, whose most important writings were published late in the seventeenth century. Strongly influenced by Descartes and his personal friend Newton, Locke's work had a decisive impact on eighteenth century thought. (Capra 1982, 68)

In similar fashion, Rushworth Kidder explained this interrelationship as follows: "Down through history, every major upheaval in physics has had immense impact on mankind's worldview. When Copernicus banished man from the center of the universe, and when Newton pictured a deterministic universe ticking away like a great clock, the shock waves rumbled through philosophy, theology, and the arts—*and reverberated for centuries*" (Kidder 1988, 1; emphasis ours).

But how, specifically, can theories in physics impact on political thought? One way is as we have said before: by analogy. Here is an example that Northwestern University historian Steven Toulmin used: Newton's theory about atoms being active, individual units was picked up by the newly emergent intelligentsia who were hostile toward the traditional theories used to support the hierarchical monarchical systems throughout the world. Since all matter, including human beings, was recently discovered to be composed of independent, active building blocks, this was used as a simile to bolster the growing youthful ideology that emphasized that people, individually and collectively, could "be politically active instead of doing what they were told" (Toulmin, as quoted in Kidder 1988, 6). A new physical science reinforced a new political science by making a friendly comparison.

This was done by such people as Locke, Adam Smith, and James Madison via numerous comparisons between government, political economics, and the new mechanistic physics—definitions, concepts, and analogies that we continue to employ today. Indeed, isn't our entire system of government and political economy firmly planted in these early Newtonian physical definitions, concepts, and analogues?

After all, the social, economic, and political theorists of the day, the intellectual cream of the crop, were dazzled and swayed by such a powerful new explanation of physical reality. How could they not be? It made so much more sense than ancient and medieval physics and metaphysics, which were awash in mind-stretching myths and orthodox superstition. Furthermore, the new scientific paradigm had begun to produce technological wonders the likes of which had never even been dreamed of before.

This helps explain why brilliant minds of that era were convinced that political and economic institutions also combined in like manner, being merely the sum total of their constituent parts (human beings) who acted in highly predictable ways, that is, to maximize their material ends and selfish purposes. Institutions like social contracts, divided government, and laissez-faire capitalism were thus conceived and put into effect.

In other words, by separating the political factions (powerful cliques) within any government, by enumerating the respective functions of the government and the free market, there will be a balance of power, a political equilibrium, an "invisible hand" to channel such individualistic human behavior for the good of the whole, to maximize the "wealth of nations," and to achieve the maximum "public interest." So, the political/economic institutions in the United States that operate to this very day are based largely on the very same assumptions about human nature, government, economics, and the world at large.

But physical analogy is only the most obvious way that the "hard sciences," like physics, biology, and so forth, impact the "soft" social sciences. There is another crucial relationship, one that is actually more significant, though less visible and less well understood. This is Kidder's point on the *changing worldview*, that is, how a wholly revolutionary upheaval in the way humankind understands the physical universe will slowly but surely infiltrate humankind's views on social/economic/political reality as well.

Ben Barber's critique of such classic "liberalism" in his acclaimed book *Strong Democracy* (1984) maintains that such a "Newtonian worldview" amounts to no more than a "thin democracy." How could such a polity be otherwise, embracing as it does such a Newtonian worldview that contains a plethora of interrelated axioms, like atomism, indivisibility, commensurability, mutual exclusivity, and sensationalism? In applying these axioms to humans, the political theoretical worldview that emerges emphasizes the related concepts of individualism, hedonism, equality, power and conflict, utilitarianism, and interest group theory (Barber 1984, 34–35).

By way of example, James Madison's classic defense of indirect democracy and elite rule found in "Federalist Paper #10" explains the necessity to create a political system based on a worldview that emphasizes that humans act *purely* out of self-interest. Moreover, cliques or "factions" are the core of politics. Individuals in competition with each other to advance their own personal objectives are the political behavior that follows from the self-centered nature of men and the fact that men are born with different faculties that result in the unequal distribution of property. Whereas it is the government's first task to protect each citizen equally, it is also the government's role to protect the property holdings of citizens, which are inherently unequal.

Although recognizing that all men are susceptible to being ruled by their passions and selfish motives, Madison believed the greatest way to preserve freedom was to place power in the hands of an enlightened elite who would "refine and enlarge the public views" (Madison 1961, 82). And to guard against elite abuse of power, government would be divided into three branches with defined and divided powers and checks and balances that would be placed on each branch by the two other branches.

In creating American representative democracy, the Federalists created a hierarchical system that assigned greater powers to those branches of government furthest removed from the citizens. Indeed, ordinary citizens acting primarily on their passions were—in Madison's view—inclined to mob rule and oppression of minorities. The minorities that needed greatest protection in a "democracy" were the large property owners because the masses would continually want to advance their selfish ends and redistribute and equalize property.

Thus, it should be perfectly clear that the Founding Fathers were entrenched in the Newtonian worldview of their time. They thought in mechanistic terms, saw individuals as independent units, were guided by cause-and-effect determinism, and accepted the supremacy of reason over emotion. They hoped to create stability, strive for certainty, and move closer to a model of mechanistic perfection.

In administering government, the same Newtonian worldview rules today. Representative democracies have attempted to shield administrators from politics, to create a barrier between administrators and citizens, and to develop uniformity and consistency in applications of law. Legislators make policy. Administrators are said to simply implement the policy. Each part of the (mechanical) system has its functions, its clearly defined role. If the system is not functioning properly, find the malfunctioning piece, repair or reform it, and the system will run smoothly again.

"It's the Theory, Stupid!": The Estrangement of the New Physics from Today's Politics

In the 1992 presidential election, Bill Clinton's campaign managers and handlers kept him hitting at the underlying theme of his campaign with the now famous phrase—"It's the economy, stupid!" We revise that phrase to emphasize the point that our outdated politics and practice are linked to our outdated theory. In order to discuss the future of teledemocracy, we must enter a new democratic paradigm that rests on a transformed democratic theory.

Look at us today! Do not the ideas, if not ideals, of unabashed, unashamed individualism still flourish, particularly in America and among its recent converts and legions of emulators? Do such people not see life as unending and ferocious competition among all persons to achieve wealth and position? Is it not, in their view, a "dog eat dog world out there"?

American politics and political science continue to exalt the idea of well-organized "special interest groups" who are in perpetual combat to "maximize" their goals and who use government as an "impartial referee" in the struggle. (Modern American political scientists award this the euphemism of "pluralism.") The legal system is seen as the epitome of an "adversarial" process and "zero-sum game" extraordinaire where combatants vie for victory over their opponents and where triumph is tantamount to justice. Indeed, "rugged individualism," "free market economics," "rational man models," "the litigation explosion," and "interest group politics" are ample proof of the continued sway of Enlightenment philosophies over contemporary American (and more and more global) thought and life.

Yes, Newtonian analogies and their comprehensive worldview are alive and well and thrive in modern industrialized America and the global village. However, very few people in modern-day society—even the top intellectual stratum and loftiest power brokers in Western industrial nations—have more than the fuzziest glimmer of what the new 20th-century scientific corrections of Newton are about. Additionally, there is precious little appreciation of how these new discoveries about fundamental physical reality—our quintessence—can help *explain*, by analogy and by changing the way we perceive reality, why many Western social, economic, and political institutions are faltering, whether they are "socialist" or "democratic" or "capitalist."

And they will continue to sputter and dysfunction, because in large part they are *all* based on decisive errors in modern-day thought about physical realities and their actual and analogous relationship to human nature. These are cardinal mistakes derived from misassumptions in Newtonian physical thinking and procreated through its influence on the underlying Western worldview and its multiplier effect on our social, economic, and political philosophies. Once this set of gross misconceptions is more widely understood and the nature and importance of quantum theory are integrated into a new popular worldview, we will finally be ready to make systematic, theoretical corrections in our operating philosophies and more freely experiment with alternatives to our present institutional structures, including political ones.

The necessity for this should be quite apparent as the year 2000 has begun. We find that as the new millennium starts, representative democracies throughout the world are undergoing major transformations. As leaders of these nations seek to build a New World Order and establish a global economy, they are facing legitimacy crises at home from a widely educated citizenry who are employing new communications technologies to challenge quivering elite rule and quavering commands. Media and government elites in the United States in particular are distressed at the diminution of their "gatekeeper" and agenda-setting roles. Communications technology, which is so often used to manipulate the citizenry, is also the mechanism by which citizens have become more aware and capable of refocusing the agenda.

In the United States (and elsewhere) voting rates have been on a steady decline since the 1960s, while other forms of political participation of citizens have been increasing. Powerful nongovernmental organizations (NGOs) are springing up around the United States and the rest of the world. A serious "anti-politics" (Sartori 1994) is underfoot here, there, and everywhere. How did politics get so complicated? How did hierarchical structures get so disarrayed? What part of the system needs fixing? What is the real problem here?

To paraphrase Bill Clinton's successful 1992 campaign slogan, "It's the theory, stupid!" Einstein's theory of relativity and the essence of quantum theory and mechanics have proved beyond the shadow of a doubt that there were some glaring, critical errors of omission and commission in Newton's ideas. Indeed, the new physics of the 20th century has been likened to *a "revolution" in physics*, or what Thomas Kuhn has called a "paradigm shift" (Kuhn 1970).

Yet, despite the fact that many of its core concepts have been disproved and corrected by the new physics of the 20th century, Newtonianism still reigns supreme in the late-20th-century social and political sciences and in the rhetoric and value systems of the Western political, social, and economic elites. What is sorely missing is the corresponding social-scientific, and in particular, the political-scientific quantum correction.

This is not just a simple matter of straightening out semantics and imagining clever analogies to add some scientific richness to a poor political theory. Instead, what is needed is a broad-based and serious effort to alter dramatically the dominant, but erroneous or incomplete, *Weltanschauung*—the comprehensive worldview—that continues to impede and hinder our ability to think clearly and anew. Such a lack of clarity and freedom of thought retards our capacity to invent and substitute novel social, economic, and political systems that comport better with the more incisive 20th-century grasp of all physical reality, both micro and macro.

Transformational Politics: Reconciling the New Physics with Modern Political Thought

There are many scholars, theorists, political activists, and leaders who are well aware that we live in an era of extraordinary, rapid, drastic, and dangerous change in all Western thought and institutions, an epoch that might be called a period of social, economic, and political "transformation." Some call it a new "age" (Satin 1979; Ferguson 1980). Others see it as a new "wave" of developments (Toffler 1980). However one defines it, though, there is no doubt that it is simply the contemporary version of a recurrent, if not regular, historical phenomenon, that is, an extended age of major alteration in all important areas of human existence. But whatever the nomenclature, it is widely believed that we are presently dealing with a grand transformation or, in "hard" scientific terms, an emerging, new paradigm.

Newtonian physics, though, is neither the best nor an adequate way to think about irregular and grandiose systemic change because Newtonian physics is about fixed systems. Of course, it addresses some kinds of change because it has a well-defined notion of cause and effect. But Newton's laws (involving the mass and velocity of bodies) are highly deterministic and predictable. Is that consistent with what we know about ancient or current social, economic, and political upheavals on this planet?

For example, who in the 1950s could have had the prescience to foresee, and the audacity to foretell of, the confluence of the civil rights movement, the women's liberation movement, the environmental movement, and the counterculture in the 1960s that presaged the present transformational period? Who, as well, predicted that a frail woman who had never run for or sought political office or power would overthrow the regime of Filipino "strongman" Ferdinand Marcos with the help of unarmed citizens swarming over and suffocating tanks on the streets of Manila? Which experts foresaw that an army of self-flagellators, thrashing themselves with chains on the boulevards of Tehran, would force the armor and air force of the Shah of Iran to beat a hasty and almost bloodless retreat, sending the Peacock Throne into exile? Who among the battalions of Kremlinologists and the data-rich CIA dared forecast that a secretary-general of the USSR's Communist party would destroy that party—the vaunted "vanguard of the proletariat"—and put Russia on a rocky road to free enterprise and representative democracy? And who among the most perspicacious of futurists and Wall Street geniuses predicted the quadrupling of the U.S. stock market in the mid-to-late 1990s? No one could and no one did.

Such major divergences in trends and course are utterly unforeseeable or unexpected in positivistic terms, under the Newtonian paradigm. They are, however, *de rigeur* and routine in the world of quantum physics. Imagine if Venus suddenly jumped out of its orbit around the sun and settled somewhere in an orbit beyond that of Neptune. That kind of behavior happens all the time in the micro-cosmos—and the very cells of which we are made act just like that. Planets do not act like that (as far as we know now), but people we know, surely including ourselves, do it all too often.

In fact, the essence of quantum physics includes, *inter alia*, such concepts as uncertainty, probability, randomness, and unpredictability—as well as some incredibly mysterious facts like non-local causation that totally defy our slippery hold on reality under the dominance of Newtonian thinking. Nonlocal causation means that certain events simultaneously occur, or are inextricably linked, at incomprehensible distances and without any observable exchange of energy. Could it be ESP? Could it be the Hand of God? Maybe it is "synchronicity." Perhaps all three. It is reality, though, quantum reality. And in combination with the realities of chance and paradox that also characterize quantum theory, it is a much better thought-paradigm to address the vagaries and amazing turns of political events than the warmed-over Newtonian-inspired positivism that pompously pretends to understand and guide our politics and science of governance.

So, in order to better comprehend and participate intelligently in the process of political change, which is *the* permanent condition of politics in all its forms, we find it instructive and helpful to come to grips with the philosophy, theory, and experiments of quantum physics and to include them in our writing, teaching, and political life. Analogies to the physical world and physics have proven important in the development of the predominant socioeconomic-political worldview of the Western world. Therefore, we believe it useful to acknowledge the improvements made by quantum theory on Newtonian theory and to integrate this new knowledge into the data bases and memory banks of the intelligentsia and to make it comprehensible to the general population as well.

Those who study and practice what has come to be called "transformational politics"—and who think seriously about a new democratic paradigm for the 21st century—realize, in true quantum terms, that there can be no neat separation between scholarly work, politics, and personal values (Woolpert, Slaton, and Schwerin 1998). They are interested in studying modern political transformation and are equally interested and comfortable in facilitating it. Thus, to ignore the key role that the theory of physics plays in shoring up the presently disintegrating system is to help obstruct a more enlightened and, hopefully, more peaceful expedition of change.

By way of example, a number of modern transformational theorists point out the role of the "spiritual," "sacred," and religious in this current phase of political transformation (Halpern 1998; Abalos 1993; McLaughlin 1993). Most contemporary political analysts and "establishment" political scientists will probably blanch, bluster, and buck at this kind of thinking and dismiss it curtly. "Surely," they will say, "this is not something that can be studied scientifically." In fact, they are convinced that Newtonian physics has given us the sole correct path to understanding, one that was an alternative to the perilous trail of religion and mysticism that prevailed prior to the Enlightenment. Some transformational political theorists, however, view quantum theory as one way to help expand our understanding and to create a useful collaboration, if not synthesis, between Newtonian and spiritual ways of thinking about material and materialistic reality.

Another area of political life that seems stuck in past times and thinking is that enormous and vast world of applied government and politics: bureaucracies. As we noted above, government departments and agencies around the world are stubborn bastions of Newtonian thought and action, being, by and large, top-down rigid organizations that cling devoutly to the illusion of tightly controlled cause-and-effect relationships. Although there has been some actual change in the thinking of a few more progressive politicians, organizational gurus, and business leaders who use quantum-like concepts such as "Total Quality Management" or "Reinventing Government" (Osborne and Gaebler 1992), these are still mainly effervescent "buzzwords" that are poorly understood and that fizzle out over time.

What could prove valuable is for those government and bureaucratic leaders who understand some need for less hierarchical, centralized, and remote systems to truly grasp the basic concepts of quantum theory and how it differs so radically from classic Western ways of thought and understanding of fundamental physical reality. By coming to grips with this modern way of thought, they can more creatively invent and institutionalize fresh ways of organizing and implementing policies efficiently and effectively. By appreciating the unfathomable mysteries and exquisite beauty of quantum theory, they can confidently construct and maintain truly participatory environments and systems of administration.

In this way, quantum theory becomes the potential physical basis for an inevitable new transformational politics, government, and political science:

- one that emphasizes processes and waves, not structure and matter;
- one that emphasizes permeable and overlapping interaction, not separation and isolation;
- one that emphasizes the inevitability and positive aspects of change, not stasis and order;
- one that emphasizes randomness and change, not logic and law;
- one that emphasizes the interdependence of everything, not the independence of individuals and component parts;

- one that grapples with the true complexity, mystique, and wonder of our world;

- one that does not pride itself on inaccurate and vainglorious traditions, long dysfunctional and obsolete.

For these reasons (and more), quantum physics can serve as the hard scientific base for a theory of a transformational, more democratic politics—from its spiritual underpinning (Halpern and Abalos, *supra*), through its psychological foundation (Zohar 1990), to its views on new ways of governing one's own life and health (Chopra 1993); one's family, one's community, one's society (Capra 1982); and one's nation, one's world (Becker 1991; Slaton 1992; Uphoff 1992; McLaughlin 1993). Any fully integrated theory of transformational politics can utilize its integrative power as a new and persuasive source of analogy; as the quintessence of a new intellectual paradigm about social, economic, and political relations; and as the building block of its newest models of political consciousness and continuing political change. Let's go into some more depth on how some of these may work.

QUANTUM THEORY AND SOME NONGOVERNMENTAL APPLICATIONS IN PHILOSOPHY AND LIFE

Quantum Medicine

Modern Western medicine has long been a prisoner of the Cartesian/Newtonian paradigm. From this limited viewpoint, the human body is conceived of, diagnosed as, and treated like a broken machine. It has distinct parts that are, of course, connected to one another in multiple subsystems.

The emphasis in modern Western medicine, thus, requires the use of and reliance upon a wide variety of specialists—each having unusual expertise in different parts or subsystems of the body and the variety of malfunctions and diseases that hamper its effectiveness or even survival. Cardiologists, gynecologists, and oncologists flourish in modern times. The old-time GP, or general practitioner, still can be found but does not command the respect and remuneration enjoyed by the specialists and super-specialists.

Within this prevailing medical paradigm, the brain and the automatic motor response system are important parts—since they influence so much of the entire system's workings. But the "mind" is quite another story.

Until comparatively recently, if the mind was at all involved in the health of a person, a vast majority of modern Western medical practitioners considered it to be abnormal. After all, in good Newtonian/Cartesian thinking, the mind and the body are separate. Dr. Deepak Chopra—a most unusual physician—sums up the present situation like this: "The image of the human body as a mindless machine continues to dominate mainstream Western medicine" (Chopra 1993, 20).

If the mind of a person actually "caused" some physical reaction in the body, the best Western medicine could say about it was that the relationship was "psychosomatic." Translated from medical lingo into English, this meant that the symptom or illness caused by that person's mind was not "real." It was just "imagined." If someone did that kind of thing on a regular basis, then he or she would be labeled as a "hypochondriac," that is, someone to be ridiculed or to become grist for another kind of medical mill: psychiatry.

Some Newtonian-style medical experts, though, conceded this mind-body relationship actually existed and were pragmatic about it. In fact, they even put it to scientific use. For example, they built it into a wide range of medical experiments as "the placebo effect." Thus, if medical scientists wanted to measure the effect of some new wonder drug on some malaise or condition, they would set up a true experiment and administer (or not administer) the drug to three similar groups of patients who had the disease: Group 1 gets the drug; Group 2 does not get the drug; Group 3 gets a sugar pill and is told that it is the drug. Group 3, then, gets the placebo and is studied to see its effect as compared with groups who did or did not receive the actual drug. What usually happens, if the drug is effective, is that the biggest difference is seen in Group 1, no effect is seen in Group 2, and a slight effect is seen in Group 3. In other words, some of the patients who *thought* they were getting the drug actually got better because of the working of their minds. The human mind by itself caused a positive change in the condition of the patient.

In recent years, however, a larger number of medical researchers and theorists have come to see this effect in a more positive and proactive way. They have come to understand, for instance, that the amount of psychic stress a person is under has numerous physical effects on various and sundry parts and systems of the body. Thus, they have been undertaking numerous methods of "stress reduction" (for example, biofeedback, meditation, and support groups) as part of the treatment for heart disease, cancer, autoimmune diseases, and so forth.

However, very few among even this growing number of doctors and medical researchers use quantum theory to either explain just why and how this might work or to help them consider other innovative approaches to stimulating this mind-body interdependence. A glaring exception to this is the aforementioned Deepak Chopra, the preeminent theorist and practitioner of a quantum-based Western-style medicine. In true quantum fashion, Chopra understands and teaches that one's health is a product of one's own "worldview." Alter it from the Newtonian/Cartesian mode of materialism and one's mind, body, and well-being can improve immeasurably. Why is this possible?

This is so because once the mind has become *aware* of, and accepts and reinforces, the quantum worldview, then that person can begin to *control* the mind-body relationship more directly and efficiently than just by learning and repeating some mechanical, robotic techniques. According to Chopra, it works something along the following lines where one's quantum mindset advances past the Newtonian one:

"Flowing"	instead of	"Solid"
"Flexible"	instead of	"Rigid"
"Quantum"	instead of	"Material"
"Dynamic"	instead of	"Static"

As Chopra puts it, the human mind is "a network of intelligence instead of a mindless machine" (Chopra 1993, 47).

Chopra's theory and mental prescriptions have been accepted and used by many doctors and by many individual citizens with some astounding results. There are other ways and ideas of "holistic," "Eastern," or "New Age" medicine that tap a related kind of thinking, but Chopra explicitly draws from the quantum worldview.

The Quantum Society

Another thinker and writer who has tried to stimulate and "popularize" the importance of understanding and acceptance of quantum theory in modern thought and life is Danah Zohar. In her first book along these lines, *The Quantum Self* (1990), Zohar advanced no less than a general theory of human consciousness based on and defined by quantum theoretical reality. In it she demonstrated how a knowledge of quantum theory—and an application of it—could revise how we think about our "self" and even how we relate to the "inanimate" world. She wrote: "The mechanical worldview . . . owes most to the dualist philosophy of Descartes and the mechanistic physics of Newton. In recent years, many people have begun to sense that the new physics, primarily quantum physics, holds out the promise of a new worldview, one that would give some physical basis to a more holistic, less fragmented way of looking at ourselves within the world" (Zohar 1990, 236).

What this inexorably leads to is a completely different perception of human beings in time and space. This new quantum-based philosophy is 100% in contradistinction to social and political philosophies based on the Cartesian/Newtonian philosophy/physics—such as Thomas Hobbes's "war of all men against all" and the egomaniacal individualism of Ayn Rand's "objectivism," where the individual person is the exalted and solitary center of the universe.

Instead, Zohar's quantum worldview

transcends the dichotomy between the individual and relationship by showing us that people can only be the individual they are within a context. I am my relationships—my relationships to the subselves within my own self (my past and my future), my relationships to others, and my relationships to the world at large . . . the quantum self thus mediates between the extreme isolation of Western individualism and the extreme collectivism of Marxism or Eastern mysticism. (Zohar 1990, 237)

Zohar continues to elaborate on the social implications of this new quantum theory of consciousness in her book *The Quantum Society* (1994), which was co-written with her husband, Ian Marshall, himself a well-known psychiatrist. One of the most useful and intriguing advances that Zohar and Marshall make is showing *how a quantum worldview's explanation of social coherence differs from the Newtonian one.*

According to Newton, all the various components and parts of the world—whether persons, planets, or worlds—are kept from flying apart by "force" and/or "forces" such as gravitational pull. Without the force of gravity, for instance, we would all be sucked right into space, along with just about everything else on the face of the Earth. It is gravitational pull that explains the orbits of the planets around the sun and it is the orbit of the moon around the Earth that explains the rise and fall of tides on Earth.

The social, economic, and political equivalent of this, by analogy of course, is how political philosophers who are in debt to Newton explain society and government. People being individual and separate units or entities see one another as potential threats to their own personal orbits and space and they need government's force to protect one against the other. After all, it is government, and its legal monopoly of force, that gives us "property rights" and that enforces the criminal laws against trespass, assault, robbery, rape, and murder. In other words, it is the force of government that keeps people in their place much as the force of gravity keeps all celestial bodies in their place. "In an atomistic picture of our personal and social lives, this same concept of force takes the form of power relations that supposedly bind us together" (Zohar and Marshall 1994, 96).

The quantum model, however, does not believe in the existence of individual, independent atoms, but it is equally antiethical to collectivist thinking, that is, "the oneness of a 'higher reality' that transcends or subsumes all individual differences" (Zohar and Marshall 1994, 100). Rather, quantum theory is, in their view, the foundation for a social and political entity that is "a true community of individuals." For example, it is the "shared repository of skills, knowledge and potential" that Zohar and Marshall see at the heart of David Osborne and Ted Gaebler's concept of "participatory organization" (Osborne and Gaebler 1992). In this kind of quantum-based community, individualism exists and is important, but it is "enriched by participation."

APPLYING A POST-NEWTONIAN WORLDVIEW TO GOVERNANCE AND THE SCIENCE OF POLITICS

Quantum Politics

Given the support Newtonian thinking lends to hierarchies of individuals—and how quantum theory is more consistent with networks—it is not surprising that one major political application of quantum theory is to decentralize government and diffuse political power. Thus, in government, a quantum approach emphasizes reallocating powers back to communities, local polities, and individuals wherever feasible.

Fritjof Capra, in broaching the idea of a quantum politics approach, advocates a strategic plan of political decentralization aimed at solving all kinds of human difficulties at various levels of governance:

> During the second half of our century, it has become increasingly apparent that the nation-state is no longer workable as an effective unit of governance. It is too big for the problems of its local population and, at the same time, confined by concepts too narrow for the problems of global interdependence. Today's highly centralized national governments are able neither to act locally nor to think globally. Thus political decentralization and regional development have become urgent needs of all large countries. (Capra 1982, 398)

It also follows from Zohar and Marshall's thinking about the potential effect of a quantum worldview on the organization of society that their theory of politics embraces the idea of smaller, less centralized government because it is easier to develop communities and dialogues when fewer people are involved. Their version of quantum politics emphasizes "conciliation" rather than conflict over scarce resources. From a quantum worldview perspective, government should not be playing the role of a "referee" at a boxing match—or as any other type of "arbiter" or "judge" in such situations. Neither should it provide any other kind of "top-down solutions." Solutions to conflict must, in their opinion, come from the grass roots, a grass roots that "celebrates" diversity.

However, the essence of government's role—according to Zohar and Marshall—is to promote and facilitate an "inner dialogue" among the many "independent" and interdependent participants in the dispute or problem, one that seeks and results in some "shared public meaning" (Zohar and Marshall 1994, 269–276). We emphasize this here because we will be referring back to it from time to time in later chapters. Only in this manner, say Zohar and Marshall, can society move beyond what Jane Mansbridge calls "adversarial democracy" to a new quantum-based consensual democracy (Mansbridge 1983).

What kinds of actual, concrete structures and institutions and processes will this new kind of democracy, a quantum-based paradigm of democracy, produce? How will this new dialogue be facilitated in heavily populated mega-cities, states, provinces, regions, nations—and even transnationally? Zohar and Marshall, like Capra, scatter a few ambiguous clues. They set some vague parameters, like governments of the future should be "more flexible," "more responsive," and "more dialogue oriented." They also tell us that such new paradigm institutions and processes must "emerge" and "evolve" over time. But what will this look like in reality? Precisely what kind of processes are needed to compose this New Democratic Paradigm?

Quantum Political Science

American political science is often (and justifiably) critiqued as being "irrelevant," "impractical," and "too theoretical"—just to mention a few of the snide epithets hurled in its direction. The problem with this is that the practice of political science that is the object of this abuse is usually that which is mainstream, conventional, and closely identified with and beholden to "the old paradigm" of political science. After all, the practitioners of this brand of political science are most visible to those outside the discipline or profession. Why is that? It is because those in political and economic power, and in charge of the mass media, celebrate the expertise and wisdom of political scientists who fail to challenge old paradigm power, status, and agendas. After all, as in almost all fields of endeavor, most of the financial and material support for research originates with those who have money to spend on such work. This means that there is an intimate association between those who are prominent leaders in the "old paradigm" political and communication systems and those who study them or do research for them.

Still, as in any field, there are a few who do not play that game and who are themselves trenchant critics of the system. Some among them even dedicate their analysis and creative work to developing radically different ways to restructure government. In fact, there has been a small group of American political scientists who have been engaging in precisely the same kind of thinking as Capra and Zohar and Marshall, in other words, exploring the relationship between quantum theory and political systems and, believe it or not, they have been doing so since 1927! Not surprisingly, though, precious few know of this "new paradigm" political science either inside or outside the discipline, even though this theoretical approach has helped generate a number of real-life experiments that have successfully tested hypotheses consistent with the New Democratic Paradigm. We will trace this development in one tiny faction of American political science that has been trekking a parallel path with Capra and Zohar and Marshall and agrees with them; has added important pieces to a steadily emerging quantum political puzzle; and, best of all, has amassed a body of experimental proof as to how well some "new paradigm" processes work in reality.

Quantum Political Science's First Voyager: William Bennett Munro

The first person we know who thoroughly grasped the significance of the new physics on political thought, concepts, and processes was a highly regarded and prominent professor of government at Harvard early in the 20th century—William Bennett Munro. He must have truly startled his colleagues when he gave what must have been a shocking "Presidential Address" to the American Political Science Association on December 28, 1927.

Munro did not mince words or veil his feelings about how American political scientists should forthwith totally abandon their old-fashioned Newtonian thinking, ditch its old-fangled political theory, and start to wrestle with a new, quantumized political science. In trying to awaken this cloistered segment of America's political elite to the significance and importance of the new physics to politics and political science, he first advanced the issue we are discussing here—the impact of physics on fundamental political thought and discourse.

According to Munro:

It has been said that no metaphysical implications are necessarily involved in the quantum theory or in the doctrine of relativity, but it is difficult to believe that this can be the case. A revolution so amazing in our ideas concerning the physical world must inevitably carry its echoes onto other fields of human knowledge. New truths cannot be quarantined. No branch of knowledge advances by itself. In its progress it draws others along. By no jugglery or words can we keep Mind and Matter and Motion in watertight compartments; hence it is inconceivable that a greatly changed point of view, or a series of far-reaching discoveries, in any one science can be wholly without influence upon the others, even upon those which are not closely allied. (Munro as quoted in Becker 1991, 4)

Specifically, Munro chided American political scientists, political commentators, leaders, and gurus for continuing to be "in bondage to eighteenth-century deification of the abstract individual man" (Becker 1991, 5). In Munro's view, "Both the science and art of government still rest on what may be called the atomic theory of politics—upon the postulate that all able-bodied citizens are of equal weight, volume and value, endowed with various absolute and unalienable rights; vested with equally absolute duties; and clothed with the attribute of an individual sovereignty" (Becker 1991, 5). What this led to, from his perspective, was a body of writing and a lode of speeches that "are still heavily saturated with the idea that there are metaphysical principles of human liberty to which all governmental practice must conform. And these principles are "embodied in a series of imposter pietisms which stultify the thought of the people" (Becker 1991, 5).

According to Munro, what existed in 1927 was a gaping lag in applying new scientific thought to help repair the obvious failures in weather-beaten processes, breakdowns that rose as pressures from an increasingly changing environment continued to mount. The way Munro stated this in terms of political science was as follows:

So long as the social order was simple, without the unending complexities that have been infused into it during the past half-century, these older formulas were not beyond the power of rational minds to accept—just as the old concepts of natural science were able to pass muster in the days when laboratory experiments were simple and few. But we have now passed into an age when the vast laboratory of world politics is conducting experiments of every kind with unmeasurable rapidity, and we continue to explain our election dynamics in terms of mechanics, an attempt which the physicists abandoned a generation ago! (Becker 1991, 5)

Keep in mind that Munro was writing about the rapidly accelerating pace of political change in an 1880–1930 time frame and that the rate of technological, scientific, and political change since then has been much greater. Also, it is critical to note that Professor Munro was not simply worried about political theory and political science as a profession. He was concerned with how those involved in politics applied their theories (as the Founding Fathers of the U.S. Constitution had done) in the real world. He believed that the hiatus between a modernized theory of government and politics and the ancient theories and withered institutions was creating an impediment, if not a dangerous threat, to "the orderly progress of social control" (Becker 1991, 5). Indeed, at one point in his speech he mused that if the framers of the U.S. Constitution had time-traveled up to his thoroughly modern America of 1927, they would have been astounded by the technological achievements, but flabbergasted at the relative lack of progress in governance. The answer to the increasing malfunctions of government in the modern age was to turn to quantum physics in order to reconstruct "our postulates and methods" (Becker 1991, 10). This would help establish "concepts that will stand the test of actual operations" (Becker 1991, 10).

Recent Explorers of the Quantum Political Science Terrain

If Munro was that upset about the state of the union then, about the theories and practices that were so out of synch with reality in 1927, imagine his state of mind if he time-traveled to America at the outset of the third millennium. He would find an even more unbalanced relationship between the same old concepts, the same flaccid and floundering institutions, the same porous and prideful rhetoric, and a nation at war with itself economically, politically, and socially. As for his profession, at least he would see some buds of a quantum-based American political science appearing during the winter of that discipline's subservience to Sir Isaac Newton.

But those first signs of intellectual life did not sprout during Munro's lifetime. In fact, it took several decades before some of the more "scientific" among his colleagues began to realize that a truly new political and political-scientific paradigm had to draw upon quantum theory's insights. What they divined was quite distinct from the ideas and insights of the likes of Capra and Zohar and Marshall, but they are just as consistent and add to the body of thinking about a quantum-based politics and political science.

R. J. Rummel—a political scientist with formal training in physics—developed a *field theory of international relations* based on quantum theory (Rummel 1977). A bit later, Glendon Schubert wrote, after bowing in the direction of quantum theory, that we "ought to be constructing models of politics and political behavior in which *chance* plays a major part" (Schubert 1983, 109).

These first attempts were consistent with Munro's desire to reconstruct and improve on the scientific aspect of American political science, but they did not at first address his concerns about employing them in a way that would challenge and reconstitute the wobbly structures of world and national politics. Later on, though, Schubert appears to have been the first to take a big step in that direction by advocating nothing less than *quantized constitutional thinking* that would take a "quantum leap" in transforming the U.S. Constitution. Now that is the kind of thinking that Dr. Munro would have relished in the 1920s—but it took nearly a half-century after his beck and call to forge the linkage of quantum theory to new constitutional thought. The importance of this is that nonpolitical scientists, as we mentioned earlier, do not think in terms of having to change the U.S. Constitution in order to transform the American political structure—but quantum political scientists correctly do.

Schubert's transformational thinking along these lines influenced another American political scientist (and political futurist) to utilize quantum theory as the foundation for his work in designing more practical, efficient, and modernized political systems. Professor James Dator, a founder of the World Futures Studies Federation, picked up on Schubert's ideas and managed to "invent" a solution to a major problem plaguing all Western republics: the glaring unrepresentativeness of legislatures and how they are subject to the numerous genetic and generic corrupting influences on all electoral processes. His idea was to *randomly select legislators.*

Dator's invention was not entirely novel, since a variation on that theme had been tried a mere 2,400 years before him in Athens. In fact, Athenian democracy not only selected its lawmakers and courts via a lottery among its citizens, but it also used this method to choose the Council, which prepared the agenda for the Assembly. In addition, the decisions of the Assembly were subject to review by the people's courts. Much later in history, the famous political philosopher Thomas Hobbes noted that the only fair way to distribute things in society that could not be divided up was by lot (Hobbes 1985, 212–213). Like Pericles, Hobbes, and Schubert before him, Dator was impressed by the consequences of randomness and he consequently devised the modern variation on this idea whereby "each eligible citizen would be assigned a different number, and representation (would) be chosen by reference to a table of random numbers." Only by this method could "true representation" be achieved in a huge modern nation-state, and be totally free from the inevitable defiling effects of electoral campaigning (Dator 1987).

There were other recent promoters of random legislatures who preceded Dator (Becker 1976; Callenbach and Phillips 1985) and there have been modern proponents of the use of lotteries to achieve an equitable distribution of wealth, goods, and services by lottery (Goodwin 1992). Dator, though, was the first political theorist and institutional designer to propose the application of random selection and chance in political design on the basis of quantum theory.

As Dator was directly influenced by Schubert, so was Slaton's thinking seeded by Dator's. Slaton had been working for years on several innovative projects that were successful in generating enthusiastic random citizen participation via electronic media (telephone, television), which we will describe in Chapters 3, 4, and 5. When she learned of quantum theory's focus on randomness and interactivity, she saw a close connection between these experimental democratic subsystems and quantum theory. Further examination into the nature of the microworld revealed a number of other tie-ins. Quantum theory, then, helped her germinate new insights into her experiments and into her analysis of the results. Thus, the subtitle to her book *Televote* was *Expanding Citizen Participation in the Quantum Age* (1992), and in it she discusses "how theories and research of citizen participation are approached differently if one is guided by a belief in objectivity and predictability (Newtonianism) or guided by a belief in randomness and no objective reality (quantum)" (Slaton 1992, 25–26).

At roughly the same time that Schubert, Dator, and Slaton at the University of Hawaii were developing their thinking and research on the connection between quantum theory and political science, a group at Cornell University in Ithaca, New York, began to examine the broader implications of quantum theory. Led by Professor Norman Uphoff, this group had as its goal the development of an irrigation rehabilitation project in Sri Lanka. Are we actually saying there is some kind of connection between quantum theory, democracy, and irrigation?

Chaos Theory, Quantum Theory, and Social Energy

Before we supply an answer to that question, though, we need to address the subtle but important difference between quantum theory and its more modern offshoot, chaos theory. What is most important to us in the context of this book is that they are both post-Newtonian worldviews that share a great deal in their perception of all physical reality from supernovas to molecules.

Whereas quantum theory has its roots in the early part of the 20th century, chaos theory traces its inception to the 1960s when an MIT meteorologist named Edward Lorenz became convinced that complex, dynamic systems like weather were beyond certainty. The multiple interconnected factors (like wind, heat, barometric pressure, etc.) were supersensitive to extremely small variations within the system. Thus, although the weather was still theoretically a Newtonian-like cause-effect system, there was no way that anyone could measure all the variables at any one time to predict exactly what was going to occur. This, like quantum theory, pricked the balloon of natural order and began to produce a new study of uncertainty—or chaos.

Chaos theory, as it has since evolved, is the study of open, complex, nonlinear dynamic systems and how they are constantly in a process of transformation. Its key elements are uncertainty, unpredictability, nonlinearity, and interactivity. Quantum and chaos theories thus share miles of common ground about how to approach the phenomena of politics as complex, dynamic, nonlinear systems. After all, we know that it is virtually impossible to predict earthquakes or the paths of hurricanes with any certitude (and it is equally difficult to predict, much less understand, major upheavals in, or the future paths of, political systems).

Neither quantum nor chaos theory, however, abandons the scientific enterprise at this point. They both continue to pursue something else: fact-based patterns of behavior, particularly in the transition zones between order and disorder. Although these regularities-within-irregularities are incapable of pinpointing particular events at certain times, they can guide scientists into predicting specific ranges of behavior with some exactitude.

According to one chaologist,

> Scientists learned that there are certain repeatable, rough patterns that systems seem attracted to as they break down into or emerge from chaos. This discovery delighted scientists because it meant they could still hold on to their scientific reverence for predictability—though now it was a strange and unpredictable kind of predictability.
>
> But how do we account for this strange aesthetics of chaos? One rather unexpected answer is "holism." Dynamical systems are sensitive and nonlinear and unpredictable in detail because they are open, either to "outside" influences or to their own subtle internal fluctuations. With the advent of chaos theory, it became impossible to ignore the simple fact that dynamical systems—which, after all, include the most significant processes in our world—don't operate in isolation . . . at any moment, the feedback in a dynamical system may amplify some unsuspected "external" or "internal" influence, displaying this holistic interconnection. So paradoxically, the study of chaos is also the study of wholeness. (Briggs 1992, 21)

Thus, as John Briggs notes, chaos theory "echoes" the findings of quantum theory that the universe is chaotic, unpredictable, paradoxical, and holistic. The difference is mostly philosophical, where chaologists believe more in some kind of ultimate or underlying order to the universe, an idea that is irrelevant to applied quantum theory. For our purposes, though, it is the huge overlap between quantum and chaos theories that is most salient and relevant. What is important is that they are both post-Newtonian and both utilize extremely similar concepts and worldviews.

Still, what possible connection can there be between post-Newtonian theory, chaos/quantum political theory, and irrigation in Sri Lanka? The answer, in the argot of the Cornell associates, lies in the concept of *social energy*—a socio-physical aspect of our world that helps us develop a contemporary social science that is a counterpart of the new physics (Uphoff 1992). This idea of "social energy," it should be added, is consistent with the theory of Zohar and Marshall. However, it must be noted that Uphoff is not applying a quantum correction to Newton because he believes, like Einstein, that the universe is not *totally* random. Instead, he holds, along with other chaos theorists, that despite the uncertainty and unpredictability of events, patterns can be found and order and disorder co-exist (Uphoff 1992).

On the other hand, he is equally critical (as quantum political science would be) of the social-Newtonian way of thought that ignores the importance of the process of *human energization* in organization and politics. Uphoff turns to this concept when the Newtonian ideas and theories that rely on "materialistic interests and individualistic incentives" do not adequately explain real human behavior in many situations, but social energy and energization do.

The basic sources of this important motivational aspect of human behavior are (1) ideas, (2) ideals, and (3) friendship. Thus, the Cornell group's experimentation to improve the quality of a particular irrigation system in Sri Lanka relied not on the Newtonian political ideas of maximizing individual material interests, but on the post-Newtonian, nonmaterial view that people could produce better if the organizing principle were based on maximizing social energy by utilizing such non-Newtonian concepts as ideas, ideals, and friendship. The results were sobering. A new sense of collective action among the previously warring, competitive farmers transformed this water project from one of the most conflictual and least productive in the nation to the most productive and collaborative.

Although not using quantum theory as the underlying theoretical foundation, it is hard to ignore how well it fits Uphoff's explanation of the success of the entire experimental project. The project designers saw a collective phenomenon of *mutual energization*, where their organizers energized the farmers, who, in turn, energized each other. Although the organizers were originally intended to serve as the catalysts, they unexpectedly found themselves energized each time they visited Gal Oya and interacted with the farmers. They described the project as developing a process in which people were "bringing out the best" in each other (Uphoff 1992, 359). Uphoff found that this network of social energization was far-flung and transcended real time and space.

Uphoff continues by developing a quantum-like counter-idea to the Newtonian-like thinking that underlies so much of our contemporary thinking in politics and economics, in other words, that life is a zero-sum game. By reorganizing human organization in order to maximize social energies, using the concepts of quantum/chaos-theory to guide his research and analysis, he derives a new concept that he calls a *positive sum relationship*.

Becker tries to synthesize this new type of post-Newtonian thinking and research (including action and thought experimentation) into a catch-all rubric that he called *quantum politics* (Becker 1991). He (like Dator, Slaton, and Uphoff) believes that this new natural scientific paradigm closely parallels the increased emphasis in late 20th-century thinking on increasing participatory democracy through interactive information and communications technologies (ICT); a move from confrontational politics to consensual politics; from adversarial politics to collaborative politics; from individualistic property rights to "relational property rights"; and toward a user-friendly environmental politics of eco-feminism and deep ecology (see DiZerega 1991, 91–94). Not only that, but properly understood, the laws of physical nature—according to the new 20th-century physics—have an integrating, holistic capacity and provide a hard scientific foundation for all these socioeconomic, political, theoretical, and activist movements.

What follows in Part II are Slaton and Becker's real-life experiments and experiences guided by these visions and theories and how they seem to us to become—one after the other—a sharper and clearer pathway into the New Democratic Paradigm.

PART II

Synergizing Teledemocracy: Scientific Deliberative Polling + Comprehensive Electronic Town Meetings + the Internet = Critical Mass

Vision and theory, no matter how insightful, are never enough to execute radical change in anything. But they are big steps in the right direction. The next step in the development of any science, commercial enterprise, political, social, or economic movement, or transformation is *action*.

One way of doing that is by thoroughly *testing the vision and theory in reality*. In exploration, it might be a mission, expedition, or voyage. In politics, it would be by organizing some kind of movement. In scientific terms, one conducts an experiment. In the social sciences, an excellent way of testing is that invented by social psychologist Kurt Lewin. He called his method "action experimentation" or, as others have described it, practical theory (Marrow 1969).

His modus operandi was the laboratory experiment—usually in a university setting with students and/or community volunteers as subjects. In one type of his "action experiments," small groups of subjects were organized into units that were either run in a democratic fashion or under dictatorial rule. Next, all were asked to perform similar tasks and the object was to measure how the students worked under these two different systems of political organization. The goal and his findings refuted the "common wisdom" of established elites that totalitarian systems are more "efficient."

Another kind of pro-democratic action experimentation uses the real world as its setting. The idea here is to create an original, novel type of electronic democratic process in everyday life—one that is more consistent with quantum theory and the New Democratic Paradigm. The object is to see and measure whether this new participatory system works at all, and if so, in what ways.

We chose the real world option because, despite the greater obstacles, the results—if positive—would be a far more valid test of the new technique. What works in a clean, orderly social science laboratory may not work when exposed to the harsh realities of the disorderly political world. Besides, if we wanted to test future elements of teledemocracy, many of the critical tools were already in place in modern society—as Fuller, Fromm, and Henderson realized. Television sets, telephones, and radios are ubiquitous in American society. So, why not see how the theories and visions of the New Democratic Paradigm, in other words, electronic democracy and teledemocracy, work with random samples of real people in ordinary homes? After all, this was the very kind of political reality the visionaries imagined would succeed admirably.

We wanted to see how the full range of any citizenry would respond to something completely different, something like what the Fullers, Fromms, and Hendersons of the world were forecasting as being desirable and inevitable. Was their (and our) "faith" in the Information Society's common person really justified or just impractical utopianism?

Or, to the contrary, was Walter Lippman, in his famed book *Public Opinion* (1921), correct? Was the public really incapable of forming a valid direction for society? Could everyday citizens not work together to develop a sense of the common public interest because they were so fundamentally bound to their private interests and personal values (the Newtonian view)? Or was Aristotle right over 2,300 years ago when he stated that the general public should formulate the general direction and interests of society and then let the natural aristocracy implement their wishes? This is what the great American political theorist George Sabin calls "the best practicable state" (Sabin 1961, 157).

One major hurdle we had to overcome was how to work within a Newtonian system of political communications, one tightly and hierarchically structured in accordance with the demands of an obsolescent representative democratic system. Its properties are characterized by a one-way, downstream flow of information with heavy bias toward the Newtonian worldview where knowledge experts are paramount. Under this communications regime, there are very sparse, weak public-feedback mechanisms. They are used occasionally, but even the best of results, what is called "scientific public opinion," is often disparaged. Noam Chomsky calls this the "propaganda model" of democracy (Chomsky and Herman 1988).

In addition, there was the problem of the "commercial imperative" in American mass media. In America, so little time, energy, creativity, and production skills and equipment are ever put to the use of "public programming." In the late 1970s and early 1980s when we did the bulk of our "action experiments" on electronic democracy, the idea of interactive TV was more "blue sky" than actual—an idea whose time had definitely not come.

Another problem was how to handle a political establishment that was not particularly fond of the idea of "electronic direct democracy," if not downright hostile to actually experimenting with some exotic democratic political communications system. Would anyone with political muscle really encourage or participate in such a scheme? If so, in what way? Would any of the substantive results of such experiments actually be used by those in politics? If so, how? If it worked, would they use it or bury it?

So, with these theories, visions, goals, and questions in mind, we embarked on a series of experiments in teledemocracy for the next 20 years. With quantum theory as our underlying theory and guide, we had a treasury of hypotheses to test, new paths to construct, many steep mountains to climb.

Over the years, though, we also have been keenly aware that we are not alone in this quest to develop a new form of teledemocracy. As in any transformational time—in any field of endeavor—there are always many people blazing parallel trails, locating different pathways through the wilderness. Some are faster than others. Some are better at navigation. Some have greater resources. Some have a genius for organizing. All are determined to save the world on their terms. Sometimes there is collaboration between these people at the edge of the new paradigm. More often, there is not. But the work goes on—and more and more proof is accumulated, slowly but surely.

Some of these fellow explorers have become close friends, even allies over time. Others continue on their own separate journeys. Although this volume is mainly a collection and recollection of our own applied theory and experimentation with three major components of a future teledemocracy—scientific deliberative polling, electronic town meetings (ETMs), and new democratic uses of the Internet—our independent paths have been converging more often and more collaboratively as the years have gone by. This has been accelerated and intensified in the past few years by the developments in interactive technology and the Internet.

What follows, then, is the chronological development of our thinking and work on realizing some of the possibilities inherent in a quantum-driven, new teledemocratic theory through a series of innovative action experiments in the real political world near the end of the 20th century. The way we see it, these are our contributions to the next major democratic surge in human history. They are the products of our personal teledemocratic energy that are combining with others with greater frequency over time to become what we are convinced will be a critical mass that leads to a transformation in democracy in the 21st century.

3

Empowering Citizens by Televoting: An Experiment in Scientific Deliberative Polling

What the public-in-general thinks about the way its government is being run—its integrity, priorities, agenda, and policies—is a very important factor in democracy, whether it be in a representative or direct democratic form. The classic theory of representative democracy maintains that public opinion is channeled through the electoral process and helps decide who attains office and/or whether those in power are doing a good enough job to be reelected. If not, public opinion—as manifested through the behavior of a majority of the voters—will result in their recall from office. It is a check on political power and political leaders ignore it at their peril.

Indeed, in modern republics (the usual term for representative democracies or, as they are also called, indirect democracies), those who run for office use public opinion polling in a wide variety of forms to see what is in the minds and hearts of those most likely to show up at the ballot box. They hire expensive political consultants to analyze scientific "snapshots" of public opinion most relevant to their election so as to determine how to shape and style their campaign.

Once in office, public opinion polls, particularly those conducted by the mass media, continue to inform them of shifts in public opinion so that they may respond in some fashion to them. According to Dick Morris, a political consultant and a very close advisor to President Clinton before and after he entered the White House, the president conducted such polls routinely to gauge whether or not to use certain catch-words and catch-phrases in his speeches and in his policy recommendations. Thus, public opinion polls are a technological re-creation of the key philosophical foundation of the republican form of government, for example, they reveal and calibrate the "consent of the governed" and/or the lack thereof.

Public opinion has an equally, if not more, significant role to play in direct democracy. In direct democratic forms like initiative, referendum, and New England town meetings, public opinion (that segment of it that turns out to vote) is what becomes active policy. In other words, public opinion gets directly transformed into law by the voters. Legislation, in this case, is no longer left to the representatives of the people. It becomes the handiwork of the people themselves.

PROBLEMS WITH THE THEORY

Of course, as with all theories, reality does not fit so neatly. In fact, the gap between the theory of how public opinion is supposed to work in representative democracies and how it actually works is so great that the theory is often referred to these days as "mythology." Shelves full of books over the past decades have demonstrated that public opinion (whether it is determined by scientific samples or by self-selected samples of voters) has little relationship to keeping representatives accountable to the people. Indeed, it is now clear that a huge industry has been constructed to "manufacture" the consent of the governed so that it is consistent with the values system, and for the benefit, of ruling political, economic, and social elites (Lippman 1921; Chomsky and Herman 1988; Bennett 1996).

Ironically, though, these very same elites—along with those in the mass media—are quick to disparage such "public opinion" and discredit any politician who admits to deferring to it in order to make public policy. There are a number of justifications given as to why those in power should pay scant attention—if any—to "public opinion," particularly that part of it measured by modern opinion survey companies.

The first justification is to rely on an ancient view that asserts that once the voters have elected their "representative," such a person only owes the public a duty to make decisions based upon his or her own "wisdom." Those few who concede that legislators should at least check out the views of those who put them office usually turn a jaundiced eye toward that modern voice of public opinion, the results of the scientific public opinion poll. They hiss that what passes for public opinion is really nothing more than off-the-top-of-the-head reactions to simpleminded questions posed by the pollsters.

Actually, they are correct. Many studies have revealed that such public opinion is spontaneous and often is based on little information and/or a lot of misinformation. So, legislators and other political leaders who discount it as being either (1) an inaccurate reading of what public opinion is or (2) an accurate measure of the poor quality of the opinion of scientific samples of the citizenry are on the right track. Another reason used to dismiss the value of public opinion is to note that legislators have lots of information at their disposal and time to give some thought to the issue, that is, to deliberate on it. The public, in the conventional polling process, does not.

All modern issue polling, no matter how scientific the sample and how careful and unbiased the design of the questions, fails to provide the respondents with much (if any) relevant information and/or expert opinion. Moreover, the reply sought is immediate, no matter what the person might be doing or thinking at the moment. Political and professional critics of such public opinion are right: adequate information about the subject and time to think about it are the essence of coming to a sound judgment on a policy. We expect our elected officials to take at least some time to grasp an issue and consider its implications and consequences. We want them to marshal at least some data while considering various sides of an issue. Small wonder that elected officials are quick to disparage the opinion of citizens who have had no opportunity to do the same.

Of course, pollsters using such faulty instruments are not the only source of shoddily informed public opinion. There are many manufacturers and disseminators of public mis- and dis-information on issues, including the electronic media, the newspapers, and even elected officials themselves. Study after study indicates that over 70% of the American people now get all or most of their news and information on politics from television—a medium notorious for its shabby memory and minuscule attention span. Furthermore, today's issues seem ever more complex, requiring even more information and more time for reflection. Thus, public opinion is probably in a more precarious situation today in America than ever before. The public wants and needs to be included in the policy-making process, but public opinion pollsters continue to utilize the outdated and worn-out methods that produce an abysmally low quality of public opinion based mostly on superficial and sensationalistic TV reportage.

SCIENTIFIC DELIBERATIVE POLLING AS A SOLUTION TO THE PROBLEM

In the 1970s, there were several completely unrelated, uncoordinated, and unorthodox efforts to remedy all these flaws in ascertaining a scientifically derived, high quality of public opinion. They were the first experiments in what we categorize as *deliberative polling*.

Citizen Juries and Planning Cells

Two of these innovative projects, one in the United States and one in what was then called West Germany, used small, "stratified" samples of citizens. This means that the inventors of these new systems (Dr. Ned Crosby in Minnesota and Dr. Peter Dienel in Wuppertal, Germany) selected between 12 and 25 citizens in such a way as to constitute a demographic approximation of the population in terms of sex, age, ethnicity, income, and educational level. Crosby set up an independent nonprofit organization in Minneapolis called the Jefferson Center (www.jefferson~center.org) and called his model "Citizens Juries." Dienel, who operated out of Wuppertal University, called his *"Planungszelle"* (Planning Cells).

The rationale behind the "jury" design is explained by Crosby: "In the broadest sense, the purpose of the Citizens Jury is to build a trustworthy way of eliciting an authentic voice of the people. We believe the best way to create an authentic voice is by starting with a microcosm of the community, presenting them with witnesses and giving them enough time to carry out a respectful dialogue over solutions" (Crosby 1996, 1).

In both experimental processes, the citizens were asked to come to a central meeting place. (Actually Dienel used several simultaneously at different locales in the same community.) Once there, they were given a certain amount of information and were exposed to a variety of viewpoints expressed by various and sundry experts. Then, they were afforded ample time to discuss the matter(s) with their fellow "jury" or "cell" members. The result was *scientific, informed, and deliberated public opinion* on agendas, plans, issues, and so forth.

Since 1973 Crosby has conducted more than 20 projects under the names "Citizen Juries," "Policy Juries," and "Citizen Panels." He has demonstrated consistently the capacity of citizens to develop thoughtful policies on issues such as national health care, peace making in Central America, and low-income housing. The work of Crosby and Dienel has yielded and stored a substantial body of data to show how well this kind of scientific deliberated polling works: (1) that citizens respond positively to these face-to-face deliberative processes and (2) the quality and depth of the resulting "public opinion" is well worth taking seriously.

The Original Televote Experiment

Over the past 20 years, there has been another series of experiments in California, Hawaii, and New Zealand that we dub the "Televote experiments." Televote, as a generic term, simply means voting by telecommunications (telephone, computer, etc.). However, as a method of public opinion polling, it is highly innovative and responsive to many of the aforementioned criticisms.

Televote differs from conventional polling in that it provides scientifically selected pools of about 400 respondents with a dollop of undisputed information about an issue, several balanced arguments for and against various aspects of proposed solutions, and a wide range of options. As one of several new methods of *interactive polling*, it encourages the respondents to discuss the issues with as many friends, family members, co-workers, or experts that he or she desires—at the respondents' own convenience. The Televote method thus differs from the Crosby-Dienel method of scientific deliberative polling in that it measures citizen deliberation at home instead of at public meetings.

Dr. Vincent Campbell invented the first phase of Televote polling under a National Science Foundation grant in 1974. In cooperation with the San Jose, California, Board of Education, the local Parent-Teachers Association, and some concerned citizens, Campbell set up an agenda of what were the most pressing educational issues facing the city of San Jose. He then invited all citizens in the San Jose area to participate in the project by registering to vote using a form in local newspapers. Upon registration, all new "Televoters" were given personal identification numbers that they had to dial before their vote would be counted. Prior to the balloting on each issue, the Televoters received a packet of information in the mail about the issue under consideration. An automated computer program tallied the votes of those Televoters who telephoned in their responses. Within a few days, the results of each of the nine Televotes were mailed by the Televote staff to the Board of Education, to the PTA, and to the media.

How successful was this initial Televote experiment? Campbell put it like this: "If citizen opinions are to have beneficial effect on government decisions, they should be well-informed and thoughtful. The Televote system informs people by giving them summaries of information relevant to the issues, easy access to more detailed information, and time to think the whole matter over before deciding" (Campbell 1974, 5). It might not be too amazing, then, to report that the San Jose Board of Education actually utilized some of the results to help it formulate policies for the school system.

Perhaps the major drawback in Campbell's process was that it produced a highly biased sample of Televoters. As in most real referenda, those who participate do not represent the values and thinking of the entire spectrum of the population. It is "public opinion" all right, even informed and deliberated public opinion, but it is also an awkwardly skewed mutation of the public-at-large. This was to be expected given his system of self-recruitment. In addition, the first Televote system was quite expensive, costing $30,000 in 1974 (what would translate to six figures in 2000). If we wanted to improve on conventional polling, some drastic changes had to be made in the Televote method devised by Campbell.

IMPROVING THE TELEVOTE METHOD OF SCIENTIFIC DELIBERATIVE POLLING

A team of political scientists—including ourselves—at the University of Hawaii read about the Televote experiment in 1977 and was impressed by its design, execution, and its impact on policy making. The state of Hawaii was just about ready to embark on a Constitutional Convention (ConCon), scheduled for the summer of 1978, and there were some extremely important, relatively esoteric issues that were going to be on the agenda: initiative and referendum, the method of appointing judges, nuclear power, protection of the environment, and so forth.

We saw how this new method of polling developed by Campbell could be ideal for such complicated issues as those that a constitutional convention might generate. The citizenry needed some basic information and some time to think and talk about it. What other method of polling could provide those essential elements? On the one hand, we had not yet learned about Citizen Juries or the *Planungszelle*. On the other hand, Televote had such glaring problems. How could we eliminate the huge bias in the sample? Then there was the matter of money. Who would pay for the most expensive parts of such a polling system, in other words, the Televote staff and the interactive communication system? Maybe there was some way to cut back on expenses. After thinking the problems through, we came up with some answers.

First, the method of recruiting the Televoters had to be changed. Instead of letting the Televoters choose themselves, our revamped Televote method would employ the conventional scientific polling method of telephone random-digit dialing. Upon reaching a citizen, we would ask if he or she would be willing to (1) receive a Televote information brochure in the mail; (2) read it; (3) take time to discuss it with friends, family, co-workers, and so forth; and (4) answer the questions on the brochure by phoning in his or her opinions to the Televote staff. If a citizen agreed to all this, we would sign her or him up and then mail the Televote brochure—with facts, opinions, questions, and instructions.

The next problem area was how to get enough Televoters to follow through with their commitment so we would not still end up with a highly biased sample. We realized from Campbell's original Televote experiments as well as from data on return rates for mail surveys that only a small percentage were likely to take the initiative to call in their votes. We also recognized that citizens' lives are very busy with many pressing demands for their time and that Televote brochures were likely to get misplaced, lost in the mail, and unread in many cases. So, we decided that we needed to build in a call-back system to serve as a reminder and reinforcer to the Televoters and to maintain telephone contact with Televoters to help stimulate discussion.

The final problem was money. How could we hire a full-scale Televote staff without any money? How were we going to pay for mailing out the brochures? How were we going to pay the telephone bills? Where would we get money to rent an office? The only answer possible finally occurred to us; it was staring us in the face as we pondered these questions in the offices of the Department of Political Science. The key was to come up with the right question: *Why not make Televote into a university-based course and internship?* If we could prove that such a scientific deliberative survey could work using undergraduate students as part of a college course, it obviously could be converted into successful uses by paid government staffs, and highly motivated, altruistic volunteers in a nonprofit agency or organization—and certainly by a commercial polling company with plenty of resources.

HOW THE TELEVOTE METHOD OF SCIENTIFIC POLLING WORKS

The next section of this chapter, then, will be devoted to the particular experiences we had in using the university as our base of operations. We learned a great deal about teaching and about the learning process—but most of all we learned some unbelievable lessons about what citizens are willing and able to do and how the new Democratic Paradigm functions in the Age of Information. Although this new democratic structure and process was developed in a university context, we will also point out how well it can be applied in governmenal, nonprofit, or even commercial organizations as well. The remainder of the chapter will discuss several nonuniversity-based Televotes that we executed as well—and we will particularly focus on the impact of those Televotes on government itself.

Fitting Televote into a University Curriculum

Once the idea of a university as the major source of funding and staffing hit the Televote team, everything began falling into place. We would add a "practicum" or "internship" course into our curriculum that specified "Televote" as the practical experience. What is the difference if the experience takes place inside the university, particularly if the relationship is with the outside community? In terms of program, it could fit within the broad spectrum allowed under the rubric "American Government," and if it would be utilized by a particular agency of government, like the Department of Health, it could readily be an internship within a Public Administration program.

For starters, the course would touch on classic modern democratic theory and the fundamentals of American government, the legislative process, and public administration. Some of the readings would focus on the plethora of modern criticism of all this theory and institutional analysis, particularly that emphasizing the difficulties and lack of citizen participation and the problems of public opinion mentioned above.

After a short course in the history and procedures of modern public opinion polling in America, the students would be introduced to the Televote process developed by Campbell and the shortcomings thereof. At that point, the Televote team would introduce its innovations and the class would be ready to "morph" itself into the Televote staff.

With agreement from the department chair, the Televote office was ready for action. We needed a telephone bank and mailing privileges. The main office telephone system was used as the telephone bank, particularly since all the Televoter recruiting and interaction with the Televoters could be limited to evening hours and weekends. These are the best times to reach a representaive sample of the population anyway, since these are the best times to reach the bulk of any workforce. The office phones of one or two faculty were utilized to recruit and interact with other citizens during ordinary working hours, in other words, to enlist those citizens who work evenings and weekends. Random-digit-dialing lists can be purchased from regular polling companies for a modest sum and the mailing privileges of the university were used for such public educational purposes. Designing and printing the Televote brochure, while somewhat costly in the late 1970s, is relatively easy these days with the advent of personal computer desktop publishing or the downloading of an Internet document.

Organizing and Supervising Any Televote Staff

Organizing and running a Televote out of the curriculum, employing students who have had no experience at conducting even an ordinary public opinion poll, is not easily done. However, if there are an adequate number of students (12–15) and they are organized into functional departments, the entire operation can be run smoothly and professionally. Actually, this can be done with any similar-sized group—community volunteers, a political office staff, and so forth. Here is what must be done.

Agenda Setting

If the agenda is not mandated from outside or above, the initial function of the Televote staff is to determine what issue(s) will serve as the focus of the Televote. This is an important matter and staffers must understand that setting the agenda for the process is not something to be taken lightly. In fact, it is something for which they may take a lot of flak subsequently. The reason for this is that some critics are likely to claim that the Televote staff—if it acts capriciously in selecting the subject of the Televote—is merely showing its elitist bias, one and the same as those of elite-controlled or elite-influenced survey companies and/or legislators.

One method of determining what are the important or the most important issues on the public's mind is to do a content analysis of recent newspapers—the articles, the editorials, and of course, the letters to the editors. If there was a recent political campaign, the literature of the candidates could be examined as well. The staff could be "scientific" about it (do a "content analysis") or, if it is pretty obvious from the written materials, come to some kind of agreement on what are clearly major problems or issues on the public's mind.

The latter methodology was used mostly in determining what issues should be the subject of our first two Televotes. However, we later tried another approach that proved to be quite successful. What was done was to gather a long list of issues from the newspapers and electoral campaign flyers and classify them into clusters, like education, crime, public transportation, and so forth. Then we put them all into a Televote brochure and used the Televote random-digit dialing method to recruit a random sample of citizens. These Televoters were requested to check off those issues they thought were "important" (one check) and to double check the five most important issues to them. Those issues that were at the top of the numerical rankings were then called the *Public Agenda* and it dictated the subject matter of the next two substantive Televotes we conducted.

A number of positive democratic lessons were learned in the Public Agenda Televote. First, we got an excellent response from the public, in other words, it was easy to sign up Televoters for this process. This indicated that citizens were equally, if not more, willing to think about and give their opinions on agenda setting as they had been on making policy decisions or deciding constitutional issues. Second, much as the critics had warned, the Televote staff view on what was foremost in the public mind was wrong. The random sample of Televoters came up with a much different ranking than what the Televote staff expected. Third, despite our care in the entire process and the fact that the Televoters' demographics were as good or better than our previous Televotes, the mass media was highly skeptical of the results. They thought they had a better idea of what was important to the public than did 400+ demographically correct Televoters. Fourth, despite the previous finding, one of the major network stations used the Televote results as the basis for a five-day series of issue-oriented news shows the following week. The agenda-setting process, then, was excellent experiential learning in how the public and elites think differently about what are the most pressing issues of the day, as well as how to handle them.

Research

Once the Televote staff or the public has selected the Televote topic, the next major step is to do the research. This is an intensive process and a great deal must be done in a short time. So, the entire staff becomes the Televote research department. In the early 1980s, most of the research needed to be done in libraries or newspapers. Today it can all be done online, with an Internet search. Next, the staff must understand that the Televote brochure is not going to be book length, so they must choose only some basic facts that are completely undisputed. For example, when the topic was whether or not to add the initiative and referendum process to the state's constitution, they needed to find out how many states or nations had such procedures in their constitutions; when they began doing them; what percentage of them are passed; what are the different types of initiative processes; and so forth. The general rule is not to overwhelm the Televoters with data but to give them enough knowledge to educate them in the fundamentals, stimulate their thinking and talking about the issue, and encourage more attentiveness on the issue from other sources. With online computer researching being so available today, modern Televote staffs can become "search engines" for the Televoters during later stages in the Televote process.

Another major function of the Televote research staff is to obtain and write up the pro and con arguments of advocates of two or more positions on the issue under consideration. It is vitally important that experts or proponents of various viewpoints personally agree with the verbiage describing their positions in the Televote brochure. Thus, once the major opposing arguments are written down and agreed to by the staff, they must be taken to prominent proponents on both or multiple sides for their editing. This will help minimize any bias in the Televote and make it as impartial as it can be.

There are a multitude of important lessons in this part of the Televote course/process. First, students/staffers learn to do basic research on public issues via the library or Internet sites. Second, they learn to work together—to collaborate and cooperate—with one another as researchers and analysts. Third, they meet with political and community leaders in the role of facilitator in order to work out the best wording in the pro-and-con-argument section of the Televote—and play an important public relations role for the Televote process while doing that.

The final stage of the research process comes when professional pollsters are invited to attend the Televote research staff meeting that must sign off on the finished product. The pollsters are provided copies of the draft prior to their arrival. Thus prepared, they can then pepper the staff with questions about the data; the wording; or any factual, value, or structural biases they detect in the final draft of the Televote brochure.

This gives the staff an opportunity to be criticized by experts and, once they have made necessary changes satisfactory to the professionals, it gives them a good deal of confidence in the final version.

Meanwhile, other members of the research team have been working with illustrators or Web designers to come up with the final design of the brochure and to procure the random-digit dialing lists. Televote brochures must not be like so many issue pamphlets sent to voters by states preceding initiatives and referenda, in other words, drab, dull, and dreary. They must be colorful and utilize graphics, photographs, cartoons, and color and be attractive to the eye. Once this is accomplished, the Televote survey process is ready to begin.

Deliberative Polling Process

The Televote polling process, in contradistinction to all other conventional public opinion survey processes, is *highly interactive* with the respondents over a long period of time (one to four weeks). This puts a great deal of work and pressure on the Televote staff as telemarketers, public relations personnel, interviewers, and educators. In addition, because of the persistent load of work required, the Televote staff must learn to work together very closely in a high pressure situation.

Right from the start, the Televote staff is well aware that the key to success is to get a high percentage of citizens who are reached by phone to sign up for the process. At least 50% of those contacted need to be recruited in order to get within or very close to the $+/- 5\%$ on each demographic variable. So learning how to be a good telemarketer is a quintessential aspect of the program.

Once again, everyone in the class or on the staff, including professors or supervisors, is part of the Televote interview team, and remains in that position until the required number of Televoters complete the survey. We do this to ensure that the Televote process itself is as democratic as we can make it. The professors and/or supervisors need to be in direct contact with the citizenry so that if problems arise, they will have first-hand knowledge of them and not learn about them too late or indirectly through the staff interviewers. The minimum quota of completed interviews is that number theoretically required for a $+/- 5\%$ margin of error, or approximately 400 Televoters.

This call-out (recruitment) and call-back (encouraging the Televoters to read the Televote, discuss it, and vote on it) period takes between two and three weeks. Because of all the call-backs that are usually necessary, an elaborate system of record keeping is needed, and in order to maintain some quality control, supervision is also required. Once again, the democratic lessons that are learned in this stage of the Televote are numerous and impressive.

First, the staff learns the importance of everyone working together as a team, a team that is dedicated to improving the quality of public participation in the political process. Second, they come to see that there really can be an independent, impartial, neutral agency to facilitate a fair and informed deliberative process—with no hidden policy agendas. Third, they discern that citizens in all walks of life are not only willing, but eager, to take some time out of their busy and troubled lives to participate in a purely civic enterprise for no material reward. Fourth, they discover that only a very few of those who must be recalled numerous times get angry and/or drop out. Fifth, they find out by asking all those who completed the Televote whether they would like to participate in the project again in the future that fully 90% of them (even those who have been recalled a dozen times) say they would.

Being a Televote staff member, then, is a superb lesson in participatory democracy through one's own personal experience. It is a clear rebuke to those in power who repeat their tired refrain that the public is apathetic and disinterested in politics and would never take the time and trouble necessary to study the complicated issues and trade-offs that "real" legislators must resolve. Televote interviewers learn firsthand just how wrong this argument is and understand from an intense personal experience how grateful many citizens are to be asked to be Televoters— even though most of them are highly skeptical that anyone in government will care anything about what the results of the Televote will be. They are satisfied enough when they are told that the results will be broadcast on radio and TV and will appear in one of the major newspapers in their town, state, or nation. In other words, it is just as, or more, important for citizens to know what a random sample of the citizenry has to say about agendas and issues after informed deliberation as it is for them to believe that those in power care about and/or would act on it. Once the Televote staff responds in this fashion to skeptical queries from prospective Televoters, it usually sets their minds at rest and they agree to participate.

Yes, this experience runs contrary to modern public opinion polling's "dirty little secret" about a huge drop-off in the response rate in the past 10 years, to as low as 20% in some surveys—due in large part to citizens' fatigue over ever more commercial telemarketing at all hours of the day in America. However, when non-commercial sponsors like government, non-profits, or universities are involved, "people are more willing to respond," particularly "with polls that adhere to rigorous standards and controls" (Van Natta, Jr. 1999, Wk1).

Public Relations

As the Televote call-back process is winding down, some of the interview staff is relieved of their duties as such and form the Public Relations Committee. The duties of this committee are many.

First, they take the substantive and demographic information from the records—which can be constantly updated on the computer system—and analyze the results. Meeting as a staff, they decide how to organize this information into a short "news release." After they have come up with the draft of that, they present it at a full Televote staff meeting for criticism, additions, and editing. Then, the final version of the news release is written.

Second, the Public Relations (PR) committee then sends a copy of the news release to all media outlets in the city, state, or country by snail mail, fax, and/or e-mail. At the same time, they will be telephoning key people in the major newspapers, TV stations, and radio stations and telling them that they will have a press conference in the next day or so to discuss the news release. Finally, the PR committee will mail a copy of the press release to all the important people in the community who have an interest in this particular issue, including legislators, administrators, community leaders, and the like.

That evening, the PR committee is grilled by the rest of the Televote staff on various questions concerning the theory and methodology of the Televote process, the results, and what they think the government will do with the results. This is a sort of "dress rehearsal" for the main event, which, from our experience, is usually attended by a fair representation of the press.

The lessons learned from this experience are also dramatic and rewarding. For example, the members of the PR committee learn the rudiments of the public relations game—in terms of how to set up a news release and a press conference and how to deal with various members of the mass media. The way modern mass media relate to surveys and to citizens is an important part of contemporary democracy and this gives students/staffers an inside view of their attitudes and modus operandi.

Next, in a very real sense, those on the PR committee learn to play a novel and difficult role as advocates of this innovative method of polling and citizen engagement. At the same time, they are reporters of the state of informed and deliberated public opinion on important topics. As such, they also gain valuable insights into the range of attitudes and opinion in the media on these subjects. Finally, once again, staff members are thrust into a collaborative, teamlike relationship—this time under the glare of the white-hot television lights.

Establishing a Televote Network at a State or National Level

One aspect of our experience, using Televote as a college course, was also replicated at a national level during the New Zealand Televote in 1981. This was done by weaving together a *Televote Network* that connected three universities at different parts of the country (Christchurch

College, Victoria University of Wellington, and Auckland University). Each professor used a similar syllabus and mode of operation and corresponded and communicated via the mail and telephone. The country was divided into regions (south, central, and north), which were serviced by the Televote staff (students) in each part of the country. (E-mail makes this much easier and more efficient today.)

The organizing of the data and preparing for the press release and conference were all done at the central location. Thus, the students at Victoria University of Wellington were the only ones to be on the Public Relations committee. But the students at the other universities participated in all the other aspects, for example, learning the theoretical material and applying it through all the other experiences in the Televoting process. Finally, after discussing the entire project with the professors at the other universities, they agreed that the students were completely engaged by the process and that they all gave it high evaluations as experiential learning.

THE IMPACT OF TELEVOTE

This brings us to evaluating Televote—not only as an exercise in experiential learning at the college level but also as a new method of scientific deliberative polling that can be used by any association of citizens, by governments (at any level) that are truly interested in learning what citizens deeply want, or even by commercial polling companies that wish to improve the quality of their product by a quantum leap.

Impact on the Quality of Public Opinion

So, how effective, and in what way, does this new method of polling have on the substance of public opinion? What kind of evidence, if any, supports the view that it improves, enhances, or enriches the quality of public opinion?

There are two distinctive types of evidence obtained from all these experiments over the years—each demonstrating convincingly that information plus deliberation equal a different breed of public opinion with much different qualitative and quantitative results. The first is common-sense and impressionistic evidence. The second is hard, empirical, experimental proof. Each, in itself, would be proof positive of how well scientific deliberation works in reality. Together they make an airtight case.

Common-Sense Proof

Isn't it patently manifest to everyone, except those who are mentally shackled to the old paradigm and its old-fashioned methods, that if you give random samples some minimal basic information about an issue and time to think about and discuss it, that you will get rather different results from the conventional polling methods, which assume that the respondent is knowledgeable about complicated matters and insist on an immediate response? We rarely ran any true experiments during our 12 Televotes to prove the obvious, but we found an abundance of non-experimental indicators to support our view that the new process made a world of difference in what the Televoters had to say.

Right from the start, it was crystal clear. In our first Televote on initiative and referendum, we found that fully 56% of our sample favored either "indirect initiative" by itself, or in combination with direct citizens initiatives. How many workaday citizens know what a citizens initiative is, much less what an "indirect initiative" might be? Our estimate is maybe one out of 500, give or take a hundred. Yet, over half our sample included it as their choice. We might add that not one single person running for ConCon, and not a single, solitary newspaper article or TV show (of which we were aware at the time) even dropped a hint about "indirect initiative." *It was only mentioned in Televote-1.* Thus, we would have to say that the intellectual level of our sample in the only scientific deliberative poll during that time was miles higher than the general level of public opinion as measured by conventional scientific polling.

Not only was the Televoter opinion more sophisticated, but it was also surprisingly fair-minded—in part because of the wide menu of options we included in the Televote information and alternatives. Slaton describes this in her book *Televote*:

> 74% felt that getting initiatives on the ballot for the vote of all the citizens "should not be made too easy," that is, they preferred a large number of citizens' names on the petition. (The Televote brochure told them that the usual number of registered voters necessary to get an issue on the ballot was 5% to 15%, with the higher percentage being more difficult to obtain.)
>
> In addition, 74% of the Televoters felt that a certain percentage of the citizens' names on the petition should come from *all* the islands—so that the largest or larger islands could not force legislation on the smaller islands. This is significant because approximately 80% of the Televoters were from Oahu, the most densely inhabited isle in Hawaii (with approximately 80% of the people of the state being located thereon). If they wanted to give all the power to set up initiatives to themselves, they had the clear majority to do that. But they did not. Therefore, given the choice . . . most Hawaii Televoters chose a higher threshold for initiatives and . . . safeguards for minorities. (Slaton 1992, 136)

Another example of how the Televote system can strengthen the fiber of public opinion, particularly where the subject matter is extraordinarily complex, was the New Zealand Televote—where about 1,000 randomly selected Televoters had to choose between four alternative futures for their country. Each of these futures was related to the platform of one of the four major parties at that time. Each potential future was comprised of building blocks in the areas of government, philosophy, the economy, and the environment and each of the building blocks had several components as well. Making such a difficult choice would have been virtually impossible in a conventional phone survey. However, not only did these Televoters perform this arduous task with glee, but almost 30% of the sample opted to "create your own future" by taking pieces from two or more of the already-structured futures and constructing their own highly individualistic ones. There is no way this could have been achieved with Newtonian-style "scientific" polls. One might as well try flying a pick-up truck to the moon.

Experimental Proof: Televote and Fishkin's Deliberative Poll

We did one true experiment in our series of Televotes where we set up two random samples of 400 respondents at the same time and asked the same questions of the Televote sample and the non-Televote sample. It did not come out as hypothesized. What we found was that both samples were about the same on the substantive issue (what was the best way to solve Honolulu's traffic congestion). There was only one big difference between the two samples: the 20% who said "don't know" in the non-Televote sample nearly disappeared in the Televote sample. This is one major advantage that scientific deliberative polls have over their conventional competition: there are almost no respondents who remain indecisive.

So what explanation could we have for there being no substantive differences between the two sets of respondents in this experiment? The issue of transportation options (more buses vs. a light rail system vs. building new roads) had been debated for years and years and years in Honolulu and no clear consensus had been reached among the proposed options. Several mayoral and gubernatorial elections had featured this as a major difference between candidates who were entrenched in their positions and unlikely to compromise. Thus, the information and opinion we presented in the Televote were already widely accessible to the general population and the Televote did not present any new or mediating alternatives. So, it did not make much of a difference. In a sense, we picked the wrong issue with a limited set of alternatives to do our experiment. However, there have been other methods of scientific deliberative polls that have set up true experiments to see what, if any, differences are caused by the introduction of information plus time plus deliberation.

The best of this comes from James Fishkin's series of "deliberative polls," developed and tested since the early 1990s. This variant in sci-entific deliberative polling is similar to the Citizen Jury and *Planungszelle* models because it is a face-to-face process. In Fishkin's brand, the ran-dom group meeting consists of approximately 200 to 300 citizens and thus is organized more like a legislature than a jury or a planning board. Like its cousins, it too has been extremely successful through a number of real-life experiments in the United Kingdom, Australia, and the United States. Here is the way it works.

When the randomly selected citizens convene, the first thing they must do is fill out a survey, with their name on it, pertaining to the issue under consideration. It is an objective-style questionnaire—agree or dis-agree. They check off their opinions and these are stored for later use. Then comes the intensive two-to-three-day process of information dis-semination, hearings, discussion, and deliberation. After all of this, the citizens come together again and are given the exact same poll. Then Fishkin checks to see what differences, if any, the information-hearings-discussion-deliberation made.

In every one of them, there were substantial changes in the opinions of many of the citizens who participated. In his first poll, done in Eng-land, on the issue of crime in the United Kingdom, there were several 10% to 20% swings in opinion on many of the items, like capital pun-ishment, long sentences, harsh imprisonment, and so forth. However, startling discrepancies were measured in one of his deliberative polls conducted in Texas for the Central Power and Light Company. This power company wanted "to have a clear picture of what our customers really want us to do, what direction our customers really want us take." So, they used Fishkin's method.

As usual, the respondents (265 of them) were, as the first order of business, given a questionnaire asking their opinion as to which of sev-eral future directions the company should follow. The results were as follows: (1) 67% favored building renewable energy plants; (2) 11% favored increasing efficiency; (3) 11% favored building a fossil fuel plant; (4) 11% favored buying power from outside the service area and trans-porting it in. Then they experienced a two-day schedule chock full of videos, expert panels, and discussion sessions—all moderated by expe-rienced facilitators—and after all that they took the same survey once again.

Here were the final results: (1) 46% favored increasing efficiency; (2) 29% favored building a fossil fuel plant; (3) 16% favored building renew-able energy plants; (4) 8% favored buying power and transporting it in. The degree of change here is eye-popping. According to Fishkin, "the changes were large and statistically significant because the participants had not thought about these issues much before the process had begun" (Jones 1997, 16). This underscores the point we made above about our using "transportation in Honolulu" as the subject of our true experiment. Also, Fishkin has continued to conduct these experiments up to the present, the most recent up to this writing being a national one in Australia in October 1999 on the issue of whether to jettison the British monarchy in favor of a type of republic. The reader can check out the most recent news on the Web site of the Center for Deliberative Polling (www. la.utex.edu/research/delpol/news.html).

Thus, we think it is accurate to say that all of us who have been experimenting with scientific deliberative polling over many years have been favorably impressed by the results of our studies, not only by how diligently citizens carry out their perceived civic responsibilities in these exercises, but also by how tremendously effective these processes are in improving the thoughtfulness of public opinion. Fishkin probably summed it up best when he said that the deliberated opinion of the people is "a voice worth listening to" (Fishkin 1991, 104).

Impact on Governments and the Media

Cynics would say that it defies belief that an experimental poll like Televote, particularly one designed and staffed by undergraduate students, could ever penetrate the noisy halls of government. Skeptics would say that the likelihood of such was minimal, at best. But idealists would see government welcoming Televote results as a guide toward promulgating widely acceptable legislation. The truth lies somewhere between the views of the doubters and the altruists.

The Televote Experience: Mixed Results

From our experiences, we found mixed results in whether or not Televote had an impact on government and the media. One of our most successful Televotes in terms of impact was sponsored by the Hawaii State Department of Health and staffed by public health nurses. Another was sponsored by the Southern California Association of Governments and staffed by a professional polling company. In each of these, the results of the Televote were plugged immediately into decision-making processes and were directly related to policy changes that met with substantial public approval.

Televotes that were based in the college curriculum were noticeably less impactful. But that does not mean they came to naught. For example, in the very first experiment emanating from the Department of Political Science at the University of Hawaii, the effect was actually quite dramatic.

Whether or not to have initiative and referendum at the state level was far and away the hottest topic that the 1978 State Constitutional Convention (ConCon) was about to handle. It was the major issue in the campaigns for the 102 seats at ConCon. It was the fault-line that divided the delegates. So, even though it became the subject of the very first Televote, which was a decision made by the Televote staff along with the group of professors who organized it, there was no doubt of its political importance and salience in the public mind.

There had been two major conventional polls run prior to the ConCon that had surveyed the people of the state on the issue of initiative and referendum. The first, about six months prior to the convention, found about half of the voters were undecided on the issue. The second, a few months before the event, found that nearly one-third of the respondents were still unsure. Both of these surveys were revealing the hidden secret, in other words, that very few citizens knew much, if anything, about initiative and referendum—a subject rarely covered in the 1970s and earlier in high school civics, college courses, or the ordinary run of political campaigns.

The opponents of initiative and referendum warned of many dire consequences should the state of Hawaii write such a provision into its new constitution. But the blackest smear was that initiative and referendum was the darling of white, mainland intellectuals and that the "local" folks of Hawaii—the Hawaiians, the Japanese, the Chinese, and the Filipinos—were opposed to such alien notions of self-governance.

Meanwhile, the Televote team was busily at work researching and printing up the Televote and recruiting a random sample of the people of Hawaii to read it, think about it, and talk to their circle of friends and relatives about it. The process—being spanking new—was not easy and there was a lot of anxiety as to whether we would really get good demographics. Ultimately, what we—the students and the professors—had hoped for and worked so hard to accomplish came to pass. We got about 400 completed Televotes, the demographics were similar to those of any conventional telephone or interview poll in Hawaii, and the substantive results were mind-bending.

What we found was that fully *86%* of the Televoters—an excellent, representative sample of the people of the state—favored some form of initiative and referendum. Better yet, as we noted earlier, they were particularly smitten with indirect initiative (which had been ignored in the press, in the campaigns, and during the early stages of debate at the ConCon). But we had described it as part of our undisputed facts section of the Televote, and this showed us that most of the Televoters were actually reading and thinking about the material. What was particularly interesting was that the "local" demographic groups—the Japanese-Americans, the Hawaiian-Americans, and the Filipino-Americans—*were all heavily in favor of initiative and referendum by 75% or more.*

So, the Public Relations Committee prepared its news release and delivered the results to the press—as well as to the delegates of the ConCon, via a Televote Room that we had been allotted in the building in which the ConCon was being held. As luck would have it, the CBS-TV affiliate in Hawaii led off its news broadcast that night with an exposé on the power clique that was controlling the ConCon. They were strongly opposed to initiative and referendum, but had claimed that they never held any secret meetings about it (since that was in violation of the Sunshine Laws of the state). But the CBS camera had caught them coming out of a downtown restaurant together and highlighted that on its 6 o'clock news.

Right after this investigative revelation, they broke the news about the Televote. They described the process in some detail and then presented the results. They played up the huge consensus in favor of initiative and referendum and then mentioned that the consensus held throughout all ethnic and economic groups. The clear thrust of both stories was that a small power elite in the ConCon was violating the law in order to oppose what the people of Hawaii overwhelmingly wanted.

So what effect did this Televote have, other than to support some vigorous TV reporting? Most importantly, initiative and referendum was defeated at the ConCon. This hardly meant that Televote had no influence. For one thing, the vote in 1978 was extremely close whereas in 1968—on the same issue—initiative and referendum was resoundingly defeated. Also, a number of delegates in favor of these forms of direct democracy employed the results during the debate. In a follow-up survey after ConCon, many delegates said that they were aware of the Televote and its results and thought it was a good idea for the state legislature to use it in the future.

However, sometimes the impact of Televote is not readily seen and does not instantly transform into votes or law. In the case of the Televote on initiative and referendum, Becker was called on the telephone the day after the TV broadcast by the president of the ConCon—the man who was the leader of the opposition. He asked Becker to come to a well-known Waikiki restaurant the next morning for breakfast. At that time, the president conceded that the Televote had "backed us into a corner." Clearly, then, those in power had felt the heat and seen the light of informed and deliberated public opinion facilitated by undergraduate students in an experiential learning course at the state university. The public had formed a deliberated judgment that they wanted to be empowered and these students had delivered the message to the media, which responded quickly and effectively.

No, the Televote did not make the big difference. Hawaii in the year 2000 still does not have initiative and referendum at the state level. Yet it remains heatedly debated in legislative sessions and two legislative committee chairs suffered electoral defeat in the 1980s immediately following their refusal to hold public hearings on legislation to establish initiative and referendum at the state level. Also, the day after the breakfast meeting with the president of ConCon, Becker was notified by the academic vice president of the University of Hawaii that he could not continue to provide extra funding for the project (for computers, long-distance telephone calls, brochures, etc.). "The people downtown" (as he put it) had pressured him, but he said he still would give the Televote project his "moral support." Sometimes the impact is painfully clear.

The New Zealand Televote offered another version of the same scenario. It was sponsored by a quasi-governmental organization known as the New Zealand Commission for the Future and was endorsed by its director, Dick Ryan. Funded by the New Zealand Parliament, it conducted studies and projects that helped New Zealanders think about alternatives for the future of their nation. One of its major projects was a 100-page report that presented four widely differing alternative futures for New Zealand. It received a lot of media publicity and angered the prime minister.

The New Zealand Televote project capsulized these four scenarios into Televote form, as we described earlier in this chapter. Over 1,000 New Zealanders, recruited through the three-university nationwide Televote Network, participated. Another 4,000 New Zealanders participated directly by filling out Televote brochures printed in our 12 newspaper national network. The New Zealand radio network ran a series of talk shows on the Televote. Indeed, the New Zealand Commission for the Future's Report had become very accessible and discussable and the Televote process permitted the New Zealand public to have an informed and deliberated vote on it as well.

So what was the impact of the New Zealand Televote, aside from some consciousness raising and increased debate over the four scenarios for the future of New Zealand? Perhaps the most immediate consequence was that it was the last straw for the prime minister. He had become a foe of the Commission for the Future, and this project rankled him greatly because the scenario most closely associated with his own party's platform had received a low grade from the Televoters. That was not the future they wanted for New Zealand. Shortly afterward, the Parliament voted the Commission into oblivion. Once again, there was a direct but negative impact.

A few years later, though, the man who ran the Auckland University center for the New Zealand Televote (Brian Murphy) came to the East-West Center in Hawaii for a conference. We met with him to review the Televote process and its consequences. At that time, he was the dean of the School of Commerce at Auckland University and was the research director of the leading national public opinion survey company in New Zealand.

Murphy stated that the New Zealand Televote actually had been the harbinger of dreadful news to the prime minister and his party and that subsequent elections in New Zealand bore that out. From his vantage point, he was surprised as to how accurately the Televote had predicted a general shift in public opinion toward a completely different set of preferences about how the country should move into the future. He also believed that the widespread publicity about this strong sentiment had encouraged those who held this view to push it in the subsequent elections. Indeed, three years after the demise of the Commission for the Future, the prime minister and his party were removed from power by a political party espousing views much more consistent with those revealed in the New Zealand Televote. Furthermore, in November 1999, an emerging party in New Zealand (the Super Democratic Party) contacted us and told us that after just reading the official New Zealand Televote Report they were astounded at how accurately it reflected public opinion even now.

However, the results on politics, on government, and on government policy were not always so indirect and, from the viewpoint of some, negative. *In two Televotes, the results were clearly direct and positive.*

In the 1982 Los Angeles Televote, the sponsor was the Southern California Association of Governments (SCAG)—a loose confederation of local and county governments from Los Angeles to San Diego. They were all facing a number of serious problems in the near future, not the least of which was how to deal with the potential horrors of handling the 1984 Olympics in Los Angeles. There were many ideas floating around about how to handle security, traffic, pollution, and so forth. SCAG wanted some public discussion and input on a range of alternatives, so they decided to try the Televote process.

The Los Angeles Televote utilized much the same formula as the New Zealand Televote, but had the active participation of a major Los Angeles television station as well (KTLA). The process was widely publicized and the results were a clear indication as to how the member governments in SCAG should proceed. Most of the alternatives strongly supported by the Televoters were adopted and the Los Angeles Olympics were a big success. Televote played a part in that.

It played a far bigger role in an experiment backed and funded by the Hawaii Department of Health (DOH) in 1985. DOH was considering a proposal to change the way it did business in a health clinic in a heavily Hawaiian community on Oahu called Waimanalo. The people at DOH had made a unilateral decision to make some drastic changes in another of their Hawaiian community programs a year or so earlier and had run into a storm of protest and a swarm of political repercussions. They felt that using the Televote process in a small community might just help them avoid the same difficulties. The idea was to use the Televote to involve the people of Waimanalo in the decision-making process.

One of the biggest obstacles facing the Waimanalo Televote was that this process had never been used on a population that had such demographic characteristics as low income, low educational level, high unemployment, and the like. Would such a "ghetto-like" community participate in a project that relied so much on a lot of reading material? Also, being sponsored by a government agency in such a community was not necessarily a plus.

What happened was nothing short of astonishing. Our recruitment rate was higher than in any previous Televote. The percentage of those recruited who completed the Televote was higher than in any prior Televotes. Why was that? Why would such a low-educational-level community want to read a long brochure about a political issue? The reason, we believe, is because this issue was of primary importance to them personally and to their close-knit community. It was not some abstract political issue that polling companies usually ask about over a phone. It was about the future of their health clinic. And the very government agency that had the power to make changes was asking them and their neighbors for their opinion about it.

This Televote provided us with an important serendipitous finding. Because we recruited about 400 households in a community of about 2,500 households, our interviewers were told about a good deal of the networking going on. Well beyond our expectations, the Waimanalo Televote had become an instrument of increased face-to-face community deliberation. This was not something we predicted, but it was startling to behold. Person after person told us, "Yeah, send me a Televote. My neighbor got one and we've been talking about it in our backyard." So, this method of electronic scientific polling can be used—if the penetration rate is high enough—to stimulate a community dialogue on an issue and then facilitate an electronic vote by a random sample. We never hypothesized such a scenario, but there it was.

Finally, the results provided a clear direction for the DOH and ultimately it followed the lead of the community and made some of the changes that were indicated by the Televote without suffering the consequences of negative political feedback.

The European Experience: Impact by "Contract"

The most immediate, direct, and *nearly binding* impacts of scientific deliberative polls on government, however, have come in Germany and the United Kingdom. Peter Dienel is quite blunt about it:

> Public trust in the reliability of our state seems to wane. Today even formally legitimized measures sometimes occur as not feasible. Solutions are blocked by vested interests. The foggy reasoning of permanent campaigning keeps the real issues invisible. . . . In that

respect people selected at random behave uninhibited[ly] and impartial[ly]. They immediately will ask you what will happen to the results at the end of their 4 days' work. To stand the strenuous situation of learning and acting in a Planning Cell and to develop an appropriate identity people have to be convinced of the seriousness of their new position. Among other things this means to have a good reason for expecting a true political effect. (Dienel 1998, 7)

Thus, according to him, Planning Cells "do not start without administrative orders." In other words, before this kind of citizen deliberative panel even begins, there must be an official connection made and there must be at least an implied guarantee that their panel's recommendations will be adopted. This is reinforced by the procedure of having an important government official "open" the proceeding and then by having a formal ceremony at the end when the Planning Cell's report is "handed over" to the government official(s) responsible for implementation. Also, extra pressure is put on the government to follow through since Dienel's model usually has a multitude of these panels going on simultaneously around the community, thereby transforming it into more of a public event.

However, the main factor that makes the results so binding is that Planning Cells are frequently called upon when the usual political processes are in gridlock. When that occurs, the government body involved finds itself "forced to hand over its problem . . . to the citizenry." They then seek out the organizing body for them, which for a long time was Dienel's institute at Wuppertal University, but which is now a private institute called CitCon (Citizen-Consult) located in Bonn, but with branches in Spain and Japan.

In Great Britain, the main organization that contracts with governmental agencies to put on Citizen Juries is the Institute for Public Policy Research (IPPR) in London. Originally a "leftist" think tank associated with the Labour party, it is now more of a mainstream institute. One of its main priorities is experimenting with a wide variety of citizen empowerment tools—but in particular, it is a cross-breed between Crosby's and Dienel's models. Conceptually, they are a descendant of Crosby's brainchild; practically, they borrow from Dienel.

To cut to the chase, the United Kingdom model is quite like Dienel's in that the citizen jurors have every right to believe that their efforts will have a direct influence on government. Although the governments that sponsor and sign an agreement to put on a Citizen Jury do not 100% obligate themselves to do exactly what the jury recommends, it can come pretty close to that.

According to the IPPR, it works something like this: The jury's conclusions are not mandatory on the commissioning body. However, the government agency is expected to: (1) publicize the fact that the jury has been convened; (2) announce the questions it has been asked to consider; and (3) respond publicly to the jury's report within a set period of time. Where the jury made recommendations that were clear, the commissioning body is expected either to abide by them or to make a public statement why it did not intend to do so. At the very least, the government contractor agrees to "feed the findings of the jury into their long term . . . strategy, alongside other consultation processes" (Coote and Lenaghan 1997, 16).

Follow-ups to a number of experiments along these lines seem to indicate that the commissioning bodies (usually local health agencies) have done everything asked of them, except bind themselves to follow the recommendations. They have, however, implied publicly that they would do so. The IPPR, however, in summing up its initial "pilot" studies along these lines prefers that an actual "contract" be made, including the binding of the agency to follow the jury's clear recommendations. This is crucial, for as the IPPR notes in a book summing up its experiments: "Many jurors expressed cyncism about the outcome. Positive remarks were often qualified to the effect that their final judgment (on the citizen jury process) would depend on whether or not the authorities listened and took note of their recommendations" (Coote and Lenagham 1997, 59).

Thus, all the scientific deliberative polling experiments end up with a similar set of findings. How much do they impact on governmental decision making? It depends on some combination of factors, including how much pressure the government is under to consult with the public; whether the government sponsors the process or not; how much the government appears to bind itself to the result beforehand; the degree of media involvement; and the clarity of the results of the process itself.

SCIENTIFIC DELIBERATIVE POLLING AND THE FUTURE OF TELEDEMOCRACY

We believe that the Televote experiments conclusively demonstrate that it is a method of scientific public opinion polling that delivers what it promises: informed, deliberated public opinion in a natural political environment—the home. It also, along with a number of other highly successful experiments in scientific deliberative polling, demonstrates conclusively that (1) *random* groups of citizens (2) who are encouraged to *interact* with one another (speak, listen, and discuss issues) (3) generate a dynamic of *social energy* that (4) produces a high quality, richly textured, in-depth publicly spirited type of public opinion. All of this demonstrates vividly how this new form of polling—where the polling agency interacts closely and interpersonally with the respondents and the respondents interact with expert opinion and other people of their choosing at their convenience—is much more consistent with quantum theory than a Newtonian worldview.

The scientific deliberative poll, then, is an important component for the New Democratic Paradigm and the future of teledemocracy. Its differences from conventional scientific public opinion polling are consistent with the theoretical variations in quantum and Newtonian theories. As we have seen, the qualitative difference in the process and results is enormous. Since the measurement of public opinion is essential to any form of modern democracy, then any evolutionary form of democracy, like teledemocracy, must have an evolutionary form of public opinion polling driving it. The advances made in scientific deliberative polling— whether they be Televote, Citizen Juries, Planning Cells, or The Deliberative Poll—would seem to fill that bill for the future. And we can expect many new variations on this theme to be invented and tested in the coming years.

The biggest unanswered question about scientific deliberative polling concerns what kinds of applications it can have in relationship to other potential new citizen empowerment innovations consistent with the New Democratic Paradigm. In order to answer that, we need consider some other critical components. In the next chapter, we will take a look at another essential feature in the emerging teledemocratic mix, in particular the untapped potential of *televised* town meetings and public hearings.

4

The Untapped Potential of Interactive TV Town Meetings and Public Hearings

An essential tool of the New Democratic Paradigm's system of political communication is television. In all modern representative democracies, TV is ubiquitous. It is found everywhere, saturating over 95% of all homes in the United States and in percentages close to that in almost all industrialized nations. That is one reason it is so crucial. Another is its use as a, if not *the*, chief source of information in the lives of most citizens. The key, however, is how it is structured into the extant and predominant system of political communication in the United States and the rest of the industrialized world. Under the present paradigm, it is used by the powers-that-be to serve the primary function of maintaining the hierarchical status quo—political, economic, social, and cultural.

THE PREDOMINANT, NEWTONIAN SYSTEM OF TV POLITICAL COMMUNICATION

In other words, television in America and worldwide is a top-down flow of information and values from those who own and/or control all television channels—whether they be over-the-air, cable, or satellite TV. This is true whether the ownership and control is in the hands of a large corporate commercial enterprise, is the exclusive prerogative of government, or is some hybrid of each (PBS in the United States). Thus, whether capitalist, dynastic, communist, socialist, or social democratic, TV works to preserve the pyramidical nature of the society and its power elites by transmitting its electronic river of data and prejudices.

This may be done, as C. Wright Mills has noted, as a tool to divert people's attention from important matters or as a device to stimulate the appetite to consume, consume, consume, in other words, to promote mindless economic growth—jobs, jobs, jobs (Mills 1956). This is done by favoring the value system of the ruling elites—whether that be "the commercial imperative" or "the socialist imperative." In both extremes, and in mixed systems as well, those who own and control the system (or "mode of production") set the agendas, decide what is important "news," choose which "experts" are "credible" enough to "educate" the public, determine the ratio of entertainment/public affairs programs, and so forth. It is all about limiting the parameters of public discourse, and keeping the general public as isolated spectators of civic matters and insatiable as customers.

From the vantage point of those in the control rooms of this Newtonian-style political communications system, it helps to camouflage its infrastructure. Thus, it is strategically important to construct the *appearance* that TV is not entirely a unidirectional system of communication. Several "feedback" mechanisms are used to create the "necessary illusion" that those in power truly care about and are responsive to what the general public wants, says, and thinks. One way is to televise forums where political leaders preside over question-and-answer sessions with citizens and call these Electronic Town Meetings to inflate their importance. Another is to report the results of the heavily managed, conventional scientific polls—which we have seen concoct a rather weak species of public opinion at best, one heavily dependent upon what the "news" staffs of television stations and network anchors have decided is useful information for public consumption and digestion.

In recent years, though, other electronic feedback fads have been popularized. For example, the "call-in" show has been widely used in the United States. In this format, citizens can phone into a televised discussion between handpicked "talking heads" and voice their viewpoints or tender a question to one of these middle-of-the-road politicians, experts, or hosts. Another ploy is to encourage viewers to "vote" impulsively on some question quickly posed, with results subsequently flashed on the screen to show what the viewing "public" says about it. A more recent innovation along these lines is to ask viewers to send e-mail messages to a TV show's Web site, and these might be posted on the TV screen for one and all to read or read out loud by the moderator. All this is touted to assure the viewing public that the government, or the party, or the TV station "listens."

The variations of this "democratic facade" are endless. In most cases, citizen input is relatively meaningless because (1) it is an acutely self-selected sample and (2) nary a thing comes of the input received. It is just a way to claim how "connected" the show is with its audience and to amuse them. It allows the viewing audience to feel as though its voice has some significance when, actually, it has virtually zero. One might say that this kind of feedback allows a segment of the population to "ventilate" its frustration over being alienated from important decision making without really empowering them.

All this fits well into old paradigm thinking and values. It is the reason why, in a number of recent so-called people's revolutions—like those in Iran, the Philippines, and Rumania—the "revolutionaries" made their primary target the government-controlled TV station(s). Once occupied, they began to broadcast their own one-way, downstream messages of the new order, which, in point of fact, proved with electronic irony that the new order was going to be a replica of the old. Only the slogans have changed. Power hungry elites—whether capitalistic instead of socialistic, monarchistic instead of republican, Islamic instead of Western, "democratic" instead of democratic—keep an iron grip on the TV cameras and towers and use the medium, as usual, to propagandize citizens instead of introducing them to self-governance. Elites do not share effective TV power with the people in any contemporary system.

INTERACTIVE TV AND THE NEW DEMOCRATIC PARADIGM

On the other hand, as the teledemocratic visionaries saw many years ago, TV can be used as an interactive, upstream, and lateral communications tool where educated and thoughtful public opinion can be used effectively for positive economic, political, and social purposes—particularly when coupled with electronic communications devices like the telephone and, now, the Internet.

"Genuine" Interactive TV Town Meetings and Public Hearings

The key to "genuine" interactive TV town meetings and public hearings is a combination of an effective presentation of information and discussion (including involving the viewing public in the process), voting from the home, and plugging this public into some decision-making processes. These latter two elements, electronic voting and popular pressure to use this data, are most impalatable to those in power. But there is no technical or theoretical reason why such a system cannot be constructed for regular public use, and such a system is a critical part of the New Democratic Paradigm. But what would it look like? How would it work? What could be done with it? How would citizens respond? Will officials actually use the results?

Fortunately, there have been a number of "authentic" experiments along these lines to give us a fair idea of some components, combinations, deployments, and reactions from the public. The first part of this chapter will discuss a few important pioneering ventures along these lines. The second part will discuss the Honolulu Electronic Town Meeting Project: its design and findings that—combined with the earlier experiments—yielded compelling information about the utility of the untapped potential of genuine TV town meetings and interactive public hearings on TV.

A Few Pioneering "Authentic" Electronic Town Meetings (ETMs)

The New York Regional Plan (1973)

A group called the Regional Plan Association (New York) was perhaps the first to envision, design, and execute a multimedia citizen-involvement process that emphasized the use of interactive TV in what group members called "mass media town meetings." The idea was to engage as many citizens as possible in planning for the future of the New York urban region.

Their design utilized a number of tools to dispense information and options, including books, a documentary film shown on many TV channels, newspaper articles and questionnaires, and a wide assortment of face-to-face meetings in towns, schools, and communities. According to their research, over 600,000 people in the area tuned in to the TV programming. The two ways people "voted" from their homes was (1) by filling out paper ballots they received from a wide variety of sources (newspapers) and (2) by scientific telephone polls conducted by the George Gallup Organization.

Its most significant findings compare well with what we found in our own research on Televote and Electronic Town Meetings (discussed later in this book). For example, they found that those who watched the TV programming and read informative materials had substantially different opinions from those who did not. In other words, informed opinion differed greatly from uninformed opinion. They also found that deliberation, added to the information, had a moderating effect on extreme positions as well.

The main "flaws" in this far-sighted effort were that there was no TV-voting system and no electronic lateral interaction between citizens via the television-telephone system that was in place at that time.

Berks County Community TV (1976)

One of the first truly interactive TV (two-way and lateral) political experiments was co-sponsored by the National Science Foundation (NSF), New York University's Alternative Media Center, and the city of Reading, Pennsylvania. This system, called Berks (County) Community

Television (BCTV), started in 1976 and was intended to allow elderly citizens (who found it difficult to travel) to connect themselves electronically to the local city council. It worked so well that it was extended to all citizens.

The design included a weekly dialogue using two-way television set-ups in the City Council room and in remote centers around the community. However, whenever any local "crisis" occurred, special TV town meetings were scheduled. These TV interactions between citizens at the remote locations—among themselves and between them and the City Council—were also available on local TV for all citizens to view. Citizens could also give input into the discussion from their home by telephone.

The Alaska TV Town Meeting (1980)

Alaska, having its population scattered throughout a multitude of small population centers that are separated by vast distances, has led in the use of interactive TV politics. In 1977, the Alaska legislature held an "interactive committee hearing" over public television. The legislators set up a toll-free telephone system so citizens watching them on TV could provide opinions and alternatives from around the state.

This led to the Alaska TV Town Meeting (ATTM), co-sponsored by the Governor's Office and the Department of Transportation. The goal was to get informed input from Alaska's citizenry on long-range planning and spending, particularly on matters of public transportation.

The heart of the design was as follows: (1) a series of seven TV programs over a 10-day period in which the viewing audience interacted directly with state government decision makers; (2) viewers communicated individually by telephone from their homes or in randomly selected groups gathered in Electronic Town Meetings around the state. The ETMs were face-to-face meetings facilitated by electronic handsets and the results were transmitted by computer to the central studio; (3) individual citizens could call in opinions and views from around the state and these were put live on the air; and (4) a number of random sample polls were co-ordinated with the interactive TV program and there was a heavy newspaper, TV, and radio advertising blitz.

Since the goal was to expand the opinion-gathering capacity of the traditional public hearing, it was achieved with ease. Where the traditional public hearings on such issues may have attracted a few hundred people at best, this method involved over 4,000 directly with over 90,000 viewing the TV interaction. In addition, the random selection methods obtained excellent representation in terms of geographic location and gender.

Their conclusion on the effect of the TV Town Meeting project seems reasonable: "The main discovery of the Television Town Meeting project was that the new form of public participation could be produced. New technological tools were combined with television to enable more people to take part in a town meeting. . . . The project resulted in a design for low-cost, high efficiency public participation" (Alaska 1980).

THE HONOLULU ELECTRONIC TOWN MEETING (ETM) PROJECT

The New England Town Meeting has long been revered in American history. It encourages and permits citizens to come together, share information on important issues, and have an equal say on what they think, and it then gives them an equal vote on what they want. It is an authentic face-to-face, two-way, lateral communication and people-based decision-making system. In other words, it is a primary way to stimulate and gauge public opinion and then transform it directly into law. The town meeting has been around almost since America was first settled and continues to play an important political role wherever it survives.

On the other hand, it is in trouble in many places where it exists in New England. Attendance is way down. Small groups organize to control the vote before the actual meeting. Certain powerful interests dominate the discussion. Frank Bryan of the University of Vermont, a leading advocate, analyst, and critic of New England Town Meetings (Bryan 1989), believes that the use of TV and electronic voting may well be the best way to rejuvenate them.

A major obstacle to expanding the basic town meeting assembly has been its inappropriateness where populations are large (cities, states, nations). How could one hold a Chicago Town Meeting or a Texas Town Meeting? Neither Soldiers Field nor the Cotton Bowl is large enough to accommodate the citizens of either polity, particularly on a hot issue.

As we have seen from our discussion of a number of real-life experiments from 1973 to 1980, the electronics revolution of the 20th century has provided the wherewithal to remove the space-distance barrier. Anyone with a TV and a telephone in the home has access to almost everyone else and to instantaneous two-way "interactive" channels of information. Virtually 95% of the American population can participate in various kinds of Electronic Town Meetings while sitting at home, with their TV turned on and their telephone at hand.

The Honolulu Electronic Town Meeting (ETM) project worked out of the Department of Political Science, University of Hawaii, from 1981 to 1988 and experimented with *how to construct authentic, genuine citizen-empowering ETMs* in Hawaii, New Zealand, and Los Angeles. Its goal was to imagine, consult on, develop, organize, coordinate, and research true ETM designs and projects, from the most basic forms to the most complex. Its long-range objective was to help implement ETM systems that strengthen and improve both representative (indirect) and pure (direct) democratic institutions, and help those with power consult with—if not defer to—the rank and file through more advanced interactive technologies and techniques.

The Honolulu Electronic Town Meeting (1981) and the Los Angeles Televote (1982)

The Honolulu Electronic Town Meeting (1981) and its cousin, the Los Angeles Televote (1982), utilized interactive television as an integral part of their design. These projects combined over-the-air TV (with call-ins), cable TV (with call-ins), radio programming (with call-ins), Televote random sample polling, computer conferencing, school programs, and newspaper coverage to entice citizen input on major policy issues (Becker 1981; Becker and Scarce 1986). Two of the major features of the Honolulu ETM were that it was spread out over a one-month period and that it concluded with an interactive TV call-in show on PBS, hosted by the lieutenant governor of the state, asking citizens to vote on whether ETMs should be used by the state government. The overwhelming response (over 80%) was "yes."

The Honolulu Electronic Town Meeting organizers also experimented with "situation comedy" shows and found that citizens liked to vote on serious issues when the information was dispensed through satire (Dator 1983b). The Los Angeles Televote ended its two-week series with a half-hour television news feature that summarized the voting on 12 issues (Southern California Association of Governments 1983). This program was so successful that it received a local Emmy nomination for public affairs. It also, according to its sponsor—the Southern California Association of Governments—was used to help develop an integrated plan on how the region would deal with the huge crowds in the area coming to see the Los Angeles Olympics in 1984.

The KITV Mini-ETM Series: The Value in Enhanced Mini-ETMs

The simplest type of the ETM is the Mini-TV Town Meeting. The Mini-TV Town Meeting uses one TV station and concludes the meeting within one day. In this simplified, expedient variety, the citizen gets some information and contrasting opinion over the tube and then has a certain period of time to offer her or his vote by telephone or electronic handset attached to the TV. Electronic counters can tally enormous numbers of votes quickly and flash the results instantly on the screen.

Consequently, some American television stations now use them regularly—"polling" their audience after providing a modicum of balanced information and snippets of expert and public opinion on an issue of local or national interest. Usually this is done during the early evening news. Rarely, if ever, is the information funneled to decision makers or is any pressure put on officials to adhere to the results of this "public opinion." Moreover, very little information is gained about this process because rarely, if ever, do these stations commission any research on the process itself. We decided to do something about that.

During February–May 1984, the Honolulu Electronic Town Meeting project cooperated with KITV, Channel 4 (a progressive ABC affiliate in Honolulu at the time), and helped produce, coordinate, and study the KITV Electronic Town Meeting (KITV-ETM) process. Although this was a relatively simple Mini-ETM, it ran 14 consecutive weeks and tested several innovations. Thus, we call this variation "the enhanced Mini-ETM."

Every Monday evening, we presented information and opinions on a major issue in the community for three to four minutes during the 6 o'clock nightly news. The audience was given a telephone number to call to cast their votes with members of our staff, who answered the phones. However, instead of asking for an instantaneous vote, we gave the audience three and a half hours to vote by phone. They were encouraged to discuss the matter with everyone in their home before voting and were informed that the ETM results would be announced during the 10 o'clock evening news and the early news the following morning. Finally, the audience was assured that KITV would hand-deliver the results to those public officials most interested or involved in the issue of the week. (This promise was faithfully executed.)

All of these features—(1) the 14-week series; (2) the extra time to vote; (3) encouraging discussion at home; (4) staff to answer the phones to collect votes, demographics, and additional comments from voters; (5) conveying public opinion to officials; and (6) studying the process and demographics—were innovations on the standard "one-shot" American TV-voting format. All of them were intentionally designed to improve the quality of the one-shot immediate-result process and to study its effects.

We added one other novelty: When the electronic voters telephoned, they were asked whether anyone else in the house wanted to come to the phone and vote as well. We found that many families (or groups of friends) would become involved in the voting when given this opportunity. This method generated (sometimes heated) discussion on issues in the home and increased the number of people who voted in each ETM.

During half of these ETMs, operators asked a random sample of the electronic voters questions about their age; their level of education; whether they were registered voters; where they were born; and what their ethnicity was. The operators also noted the sex of each electronic voter in the sample. The total number of electronic voters surveyed in this way over 14 weeks was 1,432.

We discovered that electronic voting in major network Mini-TV Town Meetings embedded within a nightly newscast is extremely popular among almost all segments of the population. We were a bit surprised by this finding since data we had collected in Televote experiments found that the demographics of self-selected respondents varied dramatically compared to those of randomly selected respondents. Further, the self-selected respondents in Televote experiments conducted in Honolulu, Los Angeles, and New Zealand were remarkably similar on a number of variables. Those taking the initiative to mail in the ballots that were printed in newspapers tended to be male, Caucasian, and conservative.

In the KITV Mini-ETM series, we very consciously featured issues that would attract diverse groups and that had already generated a good deal of interest and discussion. Examining the demographics of those who called in during the 14-week series led to some discoveries we did not anticipate. As we analyzed the demographics on a week-by-week basis, we found that the demographics were often skewed. The unexpected result was that the skew did not always overrepresent white, conservative males as we had found in self-selected responses to mail-in ballots. Instead, the skewed results revealed different segments of the population were more or less interested in different issues.

Another revelation came when we assessed the demographics from the entire 14-week project. When we combined the demographics of the more than 1,400 voters in the series, we found an amazingly close resemblance to the population at large in Hawaii on a number of demographic variables. A detailed analysis of the electronic voters follows.

Youth Participation

Voting in regular elections is not a big thing among young Americans—compared with other age groups in the population. (We understand that this is also true in many European countries.) In fact, during the 1998 U.S. congressional election cycle, only 36% of eligible voters bothered to go to the polls, an all-time low. However, the news was even worse where young people were concerned: less than 20% of those between the ages of 18–24 voted in that election.

But young people voted in the KITV Electronic Town Meetings in close proportion to their true numbers in Hawaii. Furthermore, when the issue really concerned them (for example, the idea of lowering the minimum wage during the summer for teenagers), they became the *major* interest group in that ETM (and were overwhelmingly opposed!). *There is a great deal of talk about how to involve the youth in politics.* Based on this and many other of our experiments in teledemocracy, our recommendation to those in power—if they are true to their word on wanting to engage young people of the Information Age in politics—is to *let them vote electronically*. This will be a big attraction for them to join in the political process.

Educational Level of Participants

Another fascinating discovery concerned the impact of educational level on KITV-ETM voter participation. Frankly, we expected to find a pattern similar to the voting at the ballot box on Election Day, in other words, people with higher formal education are more likely to vote than are less educated citizens. This, too, is true in almost all industrial nations.

However, when we compared the educational demographics of our 1,432 electronic voters with the 1980 census figures for Hawaii, we were a bit taken aback to find that people with lower levels of education were equally likely to vote (proportional to their true numbers) as were people with more schooling. In other words, *high school dropouts and high school graduates showed up in our ETM series in their real proportion, just as people with professional degrees did.*

This is particularly intriguing since even traditional, random sample, telephone polling frequently ends up with an "upscale" group in terms of education. This makes sense since professionals and managers are used to expressing their opinion and appreciate the value of "scientific" survey work. But ordinary citizens do not seem the least bit reluctant to speak their minds in TV Town Meetings.

Participation by Gender and Registered Voters

There was more good news about electronic voting behavior concerning two other major background factors. First, we found a close 55%–45% split on gender (with females slightly more likely to vote). Second, we learned that the percentage of registered voters who voted in our ETM series (79%) was almost the exact percentage of registered voters voting in the 1982 elections in Hawaii (82%).

Therefore, on four major variables—age, level of education, sex, and registered voters who vote—the sample of electronic voters in our network station series of Mini-Electronic Town Meetings was nearly a mirror image of the Hawaii citizenry. In fact, these figures were about what one could expect to get in a top-ranked random sample poll, yet we achieved them via a series of self-selected samples.

How could this be? How can such a "self-selected" group be so close to the actual population? We think it is because when an ETM is run regularly in prime time during and after a major network news program, all classes and types of Americans are in the audience. Apparently, they are equally attracted to participate in the voting-from-the-home-by-phone process itself. Voting on issues, expressing anonymous opinions by telephone, seems to fit well into today's electronically oriented American (and European) political culture.

Furthermore, there may be some kind of randomizing effect inherent in the present state of the technology, in other words, only a small percentage of those who try to vote by telephone actually get through. In the Los Angeles Televote on the "nuclear freeze" issue, Pacific Telephone (which donated its 900 "Dial-It" system) monitored the call-ins. The company reported that although some 8,000 voters were received, approximately 50,000 people tried to call. This inadvertent bottleneck might produce a systematic random filtration process resulting in a precise electronic composite of the entire voting audience/public.

Cultural Background of Participants

There was one major factor that was way off the census figures: the cultural background of our ETM voters.

We found several cultural groups that either voted substantially more or substantially less in the ETM series than their proportional number in the actual population. For example, American citizens from the U.S. mainland were much more likely to vote. Japanese-Americans were much less likely to vote in our ETM than their actual numbers. Finally, people who identified themselves as "Caucasians" (white Americans) were much more likely to vote than their actual numbers.

These data indicate that people with roots in cultures that do not promote open expression of opinions on public or political matters may not participate in such a novel experiment at their full strength. Japanese-Americans are an excellent example. By way of illustration, even in present-day, urbanized Japan, Japanese citizens do not like to express their political views over the telephone. Because of this, Tokyo's Public Opinion Research Institute, a subsidiary of the Japanese national television network (NHK), resists telephone polling and favors in-person interviews.

Hawaiians and part-Hawaiians, whose culture has a strong oral tradition, adapted readily to voting by telephone. And white Americans took to the TV Town Meeting like bird dogs to water. Our thinking at this point is that two major factors that may impede participation in the early rounds of national network ETMs are (1) coming from a culture that is not particularly favorable to expressing one's political opinions openly, and (2) not being able to understand or speak the dominant language well.

As noted in the earlier discussion of Televote, the Hawaiian power elite used cultural norms as a way to attack those proposing initiative and referendum in the 1978 ConCon in Hawaii. This evidence on ETMs might seem to contradict what we said in Chapter 3, but actually, it does not. For example, Japanese-Americans in Hawaii happen to vote far beyond their true proportion in regular elections because they are mobilized to do so by the political machine that runs the state (right up to the present time). Thus, whether or not cultures vote in elections for representatives or on issues is not purely cultural and can be modified by whether that culture is motivated to vote in an election by the nature of the issue, by interest groups, or by a culturally attractive format.

Participation of Interest Groups

Naturally, on many single issues during our KITV-ETM series, there were substantial shifts among our electronic voters according to their own priorities. In other words, even though nearly all segments of the citizenry are willing, if not eager, to participate in ETMs, whether they will or not depends on their degree of personal involvement in the issues or problem itself.

Thus, in the ETM on whether convicted sex offenders should be "chemically castrated," women turned out in force (they were 62% of the electronic voters in that ETM). In our ETM on whether Hawaiians should be given reparations for the overthrow of their monarchy (with U.S. government complicity), Hawaiians comprised fully 50% of the voters. Black Americans made their presence felt on the issue of lowering the minimum wage for teenagers. And when the issue involved the raising of property taxes, older citizens became a major part of the electronic vote.

We do not interpret this as a weakness of the TV Town Meeting process—whether one-shot or of the highly sophisticated variety. As in any genuine New England Town Meeting, citizens initiative, or referendum, only those citizens interested enough in the issue or issues on the agenda that day will be there to vote. If the issue is a heated one for the community, the turnout will be relatively heavy. If the issue is lukewarm, the turnout will be relatively light. Depending on the issue, certain groups of citizens will be more or less attracted to any particular town meeting—whether electronic or face-to-face.

Multiple Voting

Of course, there were "multiple voters," those who voted more than once. Actually, there were two kinds: Type A—those who cast ballots several times on one issue; and Type B—those who voted in two or more ETMs in the series.

As to Type A, we recognize that this may be a serious problem when ETMs become "electronic initiatives" or "electronic referenda." In other words, one of the biggest fears about electronic voting in the future (where citizens directly elect officials or make laws from their homes via electronic means) concerns the potential corruptibility of the democratic process, that, one person, one vote.

While this is a genuine problem to handle for the future, we felt it was not, and is not, a problem for ETMs at this time or in the near future. At this stage of development, we advocate the use of ETMs or electronic voting merely to help inform the public, stimulate debate on problems, and as another useful measure of public opinion on major issues to be considered by public officials and the public itself. From this point of view, Type A multiple voting on issues is no problem. In fact, since it sometimes takes so much time and effort to get through on the telephone lines, the amount of multiple voting on an issue is an extra indicator of emotional intensity.

Then there is Type B, the ETM "regular customer." It became apparent, after a few KITV-ETMs, that some people liked electronic voting so much that they participated frequently in the series. Many of these people told the operators how important it was to them to vote electronically and how much they reveled in it. Some even considered it part of their patriotic duty. Our research indicated that 35% to 40% of our electronic voters on any issue had voted in other ETMs. We feel this form of multiple voting is most welcome.

The Interactive TV City Council Hearing

In December 1987, the Honolulu Electronic Town Meeting Project was hired as a consultant to help design and co-ordinate another innovative interactive TV project. The local cable TV company (Oceanic) was telecasting Honolulu City Council meetings and hearings over one of its channels on a regular basis. There was one major problem though. Almost no one was watching. Such telecasts are inherently boring.

So, the director of this program agreed to try something new. Suppose we added two interactive features to the broadcast of a real public hearing: (1) live testimony from the homes of viewers by telephone and (2) voting by phone on the issues after several hours of testimony and discussion? The general idea was agreed upon by the chair of the City Council.

The day of the program, the plan was announced to the public—and a small article appeared in the morning newspaper. When the hearing began, we ran "crawls" across the bottom of the TV screen telling viewers they could call a certain telephone number and they would be given the opportunity to express their views in the hearing room and on TV.

That telephone line was clogged for hours. We permitted approximately 35 people to wait in the "electronic line" to testify. When the chair told us to allow the first three to testify, each was given one minute. Then, when they were done, three witnesses present in the hearing room were given their chance to speak their minds—although no time limit was placed on them. After that, three more TV witnesses were called to testify, and so on.

Many people watching on their TV sets, who were standing in the "electronic queue," waited for hours. Hundreds more never got through the busy signals. Almost all of the testimony given in person at the hearing room was in favor of the project. But the testimony from the homes around the city and county was almost unanimously opposed. This took both the City Council and the people in the hearing room by surprise.

We also ran another "crawl" across the bottom of the screen with two other telephone numbers that told the viewers that they could start voting at a certain time. One number was for "yes" and the other for "no." When that time came, all those lines were jammed for hours. Still, in about two-hours time, we tallied over 7,000 votes, which were 3 to 1 against the project. The results were announced in the next morning's newspaper.

The results of this experiment are obvious. Once again, the citizens showed how much they appreciated teledemocracy—as a way to participate in usually obscure public hearings and as a way to voice their opinions. The number of telephone witnesses doubled the amount of people who were allowed to testify at this dramatic hearing. The number of people in the hearing room was 75. We estimate by the call-ins and jammed lines, that well over 20,000 people viewed at least some of the hearing. It was also clear that those who called in to testify had prepared their remarks while waiting and that many of the comments they made referred both to what was said in the hearing room and by other electronic witnesses. This indicates, again, how genuine teledemocratic systems, as a tool within the New Democratic Paradigm, increase the interactivity between participants in a representative democratic system.

What was also manifest was that the Council heard the public point of view—which was diametrically opposite from their own. Three weeks later, the Council voted 6 to 2 to kill this project (by that same 3 to 1 margin).

But to show their full appreciation of the demonstrable impact of this experiment in genuine interactive TV and electronic democracy, they also killed the ETM project. Never again was there an interactive city council meeting in the City Council of Honolulu. The voice of the people was gagged by an old-system power elite who had made—from the point of view of the old way of thinking—a cardinal blunder: creating a two-way, lateral, New Democratic Paradigm political communications system that genuinely empowered citizens deliberating and voting from the home. They were not going to repeat—to their outdated way of thinking—another error. Of course, by doing this, they and their compatriots at the state level—without benefiting from the accumulated experience and knowledge of the populace—have managed to develop a political economy in Hawaii that has been frozen in a near-permanent state of economic and social recession since that time.

OTHER INNOVATIONS IN INTERACTIVE DELIBERATIVE TV

There are two other innovative experiments that wed interactive TV, deliberation, and voting-from-the-home that we would like to describe. One, in California, ran near the end of our work on the Honolulu ETM Project and the other was conducted several years afterward. The first was called Choosing Our Future and Bay Voice. The second was a collaborative effort by the Markle Foundation and the Public Agenda Foundation in San Antonio, Texas.

Choosing Our Future and Bay Voice

We developed a close relationship with two kindred souls in the emerging field of teledemocracy in the early and mid-1980s: Duane Elgin and Anne Niehaus. They had started a nonprofit organization in Menlo Park, California, called "Choosing Our Future." Like most similar operations, it was motivated by a strong belief in the value of teledemocracy for the future and had to scramble and scratch for meager funding.

Their objective was to serve as a permanent agency for conducting ETMs in the San Francisco Bay area. In conjunction with corporations (e.g., AT&T), media companies (e.g., KGO-TV), and nonpartisan organizations (e.g., League of Women Voters), they hoped to put on several of their model ETMs regularly—most of them dealing with deteriorating conditions that needed to be fixed before they got worse (overdevelopment, inadequate transportation, increasing pollution, etc.).

The specific model they crafted had several parts to it: (1) They recruited a random sample of 1,000 households in the Bay Area by telephone. (2) This group agreed to watch a TV program aired by one of the major TV stations in San Francisco. The program included a television documentary concerning an issue, which was followed by a moderated discussion among some experts and the studio audience. (3) The home viewing audience received information by mail telling them how to vote by telephone on the questions that were flashed on their TV screen. A computer quickly tallied the votes of the scientific sample who had watched the information, discussion, and deliberation. This information was immediately televised so that the people in the studio could see it as well as all viewers of the program.

The most intriguing results were that (1) 68% of the entire random sample watched the TV program and voted; (2) 84% said that they voted over the automatic telephone voting system with little to no difficulty; and (3) the ETM got an eight rating and 12 share in its time slot (approximately 300,000 viewers in the Bay Area)—which was about equal to that of the nightly news on that network.

In other words, Elgin and Niehaus had created a new type of scientific deliberative poll, one that utilized interactive TV as its medium, one that could make a profit for the TV company while also serving the public interest. We will elaborate on an excellent application of this in real political life in Chapter 6.

The San Antonio Interactive TV Experiment

The Markle Foundation and the Public Agenda Foundation are two New York City institutions that have been determined and resilient innovators and experimenters in the field of multimedia citizen empowerment and/or teledemocracy. In 1994, they collaborated on an entirely different type of deliberative poll via interactive TV.

The subject matter of this exercise was the widely perceived crisis in American national health care at that time. The TV program starred several experts, who explained the process and moderated a discussion among eight citizens who had been selected as a "focus group" that was somewhat representative of the San Antonio, Texas, community.

There were seven major subissues on the agenda—with several alternative solutions for each. A mini-documentary film was shown on each of the seven issues and the focus group discussed them. The viewing audience was in possession of electronic voting handsets by which they could vote on the various questions posed on the TV screen.

The key to this experiment was to ask the same questions of the viewing audience three times during the show: at the beginning of the discussion on that issue; somewhere in the middle of the discussion; and at the end of the discussion. Not to anyone's surprise, what was discovered was that the voting changed on each issue over time with "undecideds" disappearing (much like in the Televote experiments) and with a good deal of rethinking of positions occurring on all issues. The home-voters began to understand that gaining something by one position meant losing something else of value in another. Even though the home-viewing audience was not a scientific sample, as in the Bay Voice experiment, this proved again how valuable interactive TV can be in getting people at home to deliberate in depth on complex issues via TV and in quickly tallying the results.

THE FUTURE OF AUTHENTIC INTERACTIVE TV AND ELECTRONIC VOTING

The fact that we feel the need to use words like "real," "authentic," and "genuine" as a prefix to "ETMs" illustrates one of the major problems we face in trying to break out of the old paradigm attitudes and value structures that permeate the political and media institutions in modern industrial societies. It is almost habitual for those in control of present-day government and electronic and print media to designate highly manipulative and spurious forms of polling and face-to-face forums as "new" forms of true citizen participation in representative democracies.

After all, who in the general citizenry, or even who in government or in the mass media, actually knows about these new concepts of "ETMs," "scientific deliberative polling," "electronic voting behavior," and the like? It is hardly common knowledge and even the few "experts" who have heard about them seem content to ignore or find some ways to discount or dismiss their value. Thus, nothing much is said in public or professionally about it.

For example, we examined the indexes of dozens of up-to-date (1998–99) American government textbooks and books on media and politics to see what was listed under the concepts of "scientific deliberative polling," "electronic town meetings," "interactive TV," "teledemocracy," and so forth. We found not one single listing for any of the above.

This fits together nicely with what we discussed in Chapter 1 about the difficulties Kuhn mentions in getting those stuck in old paradigm thought to engage the new paradigmers in debate. However, as in the hard sciences, this does not keep those who understand the New Democratic Paradigm from conducting more and more experimentation consistent with the new knowledge. And that is what the last two chapters have shown—a growing number of highly successful experiments proves how well new paradigm thinking works in real-life experiments with the public via the electronic media.

Realizing that Kuhn is correct, and that we cannot really expect those who benefit so much from the present system to even try to understand its theoretical and systemic errors, it occurred to us that there was little we could do about them. But there was another important group who was also part of the problem—all the new paradigm experimenters themselves.

The reason for this was that each of us, in our own way, had built a wall around our own research. Most of us were largely unaware of the work of others in this same field. Hardly anyone built upon the work of others, or even referred to it. The new paradigm experimenters, the very same people who were talking about new paradigm concepts like "interdependence" and "collaboration vs. competition" were acting in old paradigm, competitive, isolated ways.

So, here was a problem we felt we could do something about. After all, the truth of the matter is that we are actually collaborating, but on separate pathways to the same future. It finally dawned upon us that if the future of teledemocracy was to expedited, then what needed to be done was to begin to spend some of our time and energy in getting this army of different drummers to begin to march in some unison.

5

The First Step Toward Synergy: Collaborative Designs for Advanced, Genuine Electronic Town Meetings (ETMs)

As we have shown, for nearly two decades, small groups of academics, government officials, community organizers, democratic activists, and media professionals have been experimenting at different times and sites with electronic media and modern communications technology. Their common goal has been to see how ICT and new paradigm–style democratic processes can entice citizen participation; diffuse and accentuate public education; encourage citizen dialogue and deliberation; and make the results of these valuable exercises count in official decision making (Becker 1981; Becker and Scarce 1986; Arterton 1987; Abramson, Arterton, and Orren 1988; Slaton 1992).

Projects across the nation, including the New York Regional Plan (1973), Berks County Community Television (1976), Alaska Television Town Meeting (1980), Hawaii Televote and Honolulu Electronic Town Meeting (1978–88), Bay Voice (1984–88), Community Design Exchange ETMs in Roanoke, Savannah, Houston, and Racine, Wisconsin (1988–99), and Americans Discuss Social Security (1997–99)—to name some prominent American ones—have all found receptive, if not thankful, audiences of citizens. The universal findings of these projects profoundly contradict the portrayal of the American "couch potato," a nation full of potbellied male dolts who would never swap their six-packs of beer and recliners in front of the television set for styrofoam cups and plastic chairs at a public policy forum. Actually, almost all the designers of these projects have been amazed at the *gratitude* of ordinary citizens for being asked and included.

When government officials have had a stake in funding, planning, supporting, and/or participating in these experiments, they have been

favorably impressed and at least somewhat influenced by the results—
at least at that time or subsequently. For the most part, though, the general notion of teledemocracy and ETMs is met with obstinance and sometimes open enmity from elected representatives who are prone to scoff
at and scold public opinion as the babble of rabble—myopic citizens who
fail to see beyond the ends of their noses. Dire warnings of rule by the
unkempt and unruly, rampant anarchy, counterelite Pollyanna-ism, ir-
rational choices, and the trampling of minority rights accompany the
official dismissal of even the mildest proposal to institutionalize teledemocratic processes designed to truly increase citizen participation in
government.

With sporadic exceptions like the projects already discussed, the electronic media, supposedly hungry to exploit each and every opportunity
to swell audiences and market share, still balk at actually turning over
power to citizens via two-way interaction and lateral communication—
even when there is compelling hard evidence that it can increase ratings.
They, too, lay claim to some invisible, innate expertise plus an inspired
vision of what is in the public interest—genetically transmitted qualities
that ordinary citizens lack. When challenged that this is not very democratic, they then recite as gospel truth some heavily biased data and
"expert" analysis to "prove" that their programming decisions also reflect what the public "really" wants.

Worse than these old paradigm attacks upon the proponents of electronically enhanced, quality citizen participation is the practice of refus-
ing to deal with consistently positive results. This is an excellent example
of that old saying: "Please don't confuse my unassailable theory with
contradictory facts." Those who hold power, whether political or economic or both, correctly understand their material self-interests and how
to fortify them. For instance, it is frequently better to silence your critics
by ignoring them—particularly if the challengers have few resources to
get their message out without your high-priced equipment. Indeed, to
answer critics crowns them with legitimacy, not thorns. It also calls attention to their position, which may, in turn, lend them credibility
(power). When one thinks he or she holds all the cards, why should one
acknowledge those who want a new deal? Or, in Kuhnian terms, those
whose life's work—and a high rung on the social ladder—depends on
the Newtonian paradigm cannot be expected to even consider merit in
arguments based on the New Democratic Paradigm. It is just impossible
for them to believe anything that questions their worldview.

However, not responding to new paradigm thought only increases the
tension and conflict between the two. The "powerless"—under old paradigm systems—often have another kind of power, the power to undermine, stall, or even stymie the goals of the "powerful." Thus, if legitimate

avenues to power (which can produce constructive results) are closed to the "powerless" or marginalized segments of a populace, it is not uncommon to find that they will eventually resort to illegitimate or illegal means (often leading to destructive results). Ignoring a burning dissatisfaction with the "way things are" does not douse the flame, it only makes it simmer longer. This makes it easier for a sudden addition of fuel or fresh air to bring the situation to its boiling point and create the conditions for a "critical mass" of opposition to coalesce and catalyze a quantum leap of change. That is why social movements suddenly emerge.

As we observed in Part I, no teledemocratic, quantum-based transformation will occur without a surface political eruption caused by deeper philosophical and scientific rifts yet unreconciled. Recent American political history shows how the preconditions for this emerging "crisis point" are cohering as the 21st century begins.

A TURNING POINT: THE 1992 U.S. PRESIDENTIAL ELECTIONS

Events preceding the U.S. presidential election of 1992 served to cool temporarily the growing anger American citizens have with their political institutions, processes, and leaders. While the people of the United States reveled in the implosion of the Soviet Union, the collapse of the Berlin Wall, and the "coalition's victory" over Iraq in the Persian Gulf, many American political leaders and commentators continued to eschew, at their peril, the deeper and broader and dissatisfaction brewing at home.

In early 1991, President George Bush seemed unbeatable with 90% "approval" ratings from the American public, still in a euphoria over the aforementioned triumphal world events. Thus, national American politics reflected "business as usual" strategies. Suddenly, seemingly from nowhere, a few politicians appeared on the scene who offered anti-establishment alternatives to the public just as the 1992 presidential election was gearing up. They tapped into the long-festering American public sentiment that "politicians don't care what we think" and "government is controlled by special interests." These broadly held and deeply embedded attitudes are clearly not consistent with what representative democratic government is supposed to be about and what the people in such systems are supposed to be thinking about their governments. So, this new breed of anti-system politicians began to pound away at the failings of a system and political process that gave Americans a $5 trillion national debt; $200+ billion annual trade balance deficits; "the best Congress money could buy"; decaying inner cities and a rusting national infrastructure; a stagnant standard of living for the working and middle classes; and a strong sense that global forces in tandem with the "special interests" controlling government were working mischief on the American economy, community structure, and way of life.

Unconventional Candidates: The Rise of the Anti-Establishment Politicians

The 1992 presidential election produced a gaggle of radical change-oriented candidates including: mainstreamer Bill Clinton (with social democratic mantras about universal health care); citizen and consumer advocate Ralph Nader; former counterculture icon, ex-California Governor Jerry Brown; and "billionaire populist" Ross Perot, a living oxymoron.

This was the start of a trend that continues in the United States and that is manifesting itself today in a number of ways. This trend might be called "get the established politicians out of power," because it is part of a growing "anti-politics" (Sartori 1994) that includes the "term limits movement" (where many states limited the number of times anyone could be elected to office); the growth in citizens initiatives at the state and local level throughout the United States; and the election of "anti-politicians" like former professional wrestler Jesse Ventura as governor of Minnesota in 1998. More and more, then, we are seeing Americans voting for "none of the above major candidates" and endorsing anti-establishment laws through citizens initiatives. The election of Ventura probably augurs the beginning of a whole new breed of anti-mainstream electoral politics driven by Internet fund raising and organizing. After all, Ventura's campaign slogan was "Retaliate in '98."

Back in 1992, though, when the strength of anti-establishment political sentiment was just beginning to jell on the national scene, the only two of these nontraditional candidates to garner any national media coverage were Brown and Perot. Brown pledged to accept no more than $20 per person in order to develop a genuine grass-roots campaign that would preclude big corporations and wealthy donors from calling the shots in his campaign. He never missed an opportunity to disseminate his 800 toll-free number to encourage small-scale supporters and contributors to donate 20 bucks to his campaign—by using their credit cards! Perot, on the other hand, volunteered to spend up to $100 million of his own money to run for office—but only if voters demonstrated enough interest in him and dedication to his anti-politics to organize and place his name on the ballot in all 50 states.

Those candidates who utilized unconventional campaign tactics and remained independent of established powerful interests, however, were often ridiculed by the news reporters and analysts. They were painted as irrelevant, irreverent, nonsensical, egomaniacal, megalomaniacal, or just plain "whacko."

Yet the American public would not allow them to be so easily "bumped" from the campaign trail. Jerry Brown kept demonstrating significant support across the country throughout the entire 1992 primary season. He received four million votes in the Democratic primaries, racking up victories in Colorado and Connecticut, and finishing a close runner-up in Minnesota, Utah, Wisconsin, and California (Baker 1993, 49). Ross Perot, running an explicit change-the-system campaign, in a few short months had over 30% of American citizens—in random sample polls from coast to coast—saying they were going to vote for him in November.

Interactive Media: The Politics of Pseudo-Connectedness

Prior to the 1992 election, most major candidates avoided direct communication with average citizens via the electronic media. Instead citizens were treated as infantile customers of political pablum. What was considered an "important issue" and who were considered "viable candidates" were all handpicked by the master media moguls and their hirelings. When candidates appeared on TV, the questions were asked only by these self-appointed and annointed political wizards—with the public dutifully playing its lonely role as bemused spectator. With the singular exception of President Jimmy Carter, who deigned to travel about the country and go one-on-one with citizens in forums that he mislabeled "town meetings," it was considered demeaning for a "leading candidate," particularly a sitting president, to stoop to engage in a give-and-take with improperly schooled citizens asking banal, silly, or personal questions.

In 1992, though, citizens were finally ready to decline their traditional role and reject the elite's insistence that they were unwilling and/or incompetent to be more fully engaged. The new era of interactive electronic campaigning thus began with Jerry Brown's success at mass political telemarketing and Ross Perot's brilliance at interactive TV campaigning.

While some candidates remained "media aloof" as long as possible, all candidates eventually accepted—and even solicited—invitations to radio call-in shows and televised "town meetings" to respond directly to questions posed by the electorate. Whenever TV programs built in viewer call-ins and/or voting, the demand greatly exceeded capacity. Voter interest in issues was so high that for the first time in American political history, an establishment-sponsored and -mediated televised debate among the two major-party presidential candidates featured rank-and-file citizens, rather than celebrity reporters, aiming pointed questions at them. And most viewers, and many media experts, believed that was the best of the debates, bar none.

One of the biggest and most obvious differences totally reversed what the media and political elites had harped on forever. For the first time it became painfully clear in 1992 that it was the "professional," "objective," and "expert" media who were locked into personalities and scandals—such as the youthful pot smoking and extramarital affairs of Bill Clinton. When the working and middle classes came to bat, their queries about the then-current recession that plagued the American economy were the order of the day. In fact, audiences often showed impatience and irritation when reporters asked one more time whether Bill Clinton had really committed adultery.

In point of fact, "hard news" reporters, "talking heads," and anchor people right up to the present have an increased flirtation with the salacious and prurient stories that they zealously pursue as "character" issues. This surely was the case in 1998–1999, when the self-styled "hard nosed" news media continued to force the President Clinton–Monica Lewinsky White House sex scandal down the throats of the citizenry, while over two-thirds of America gagged. Repeatedly, polls showed that the average citizen was desperate for the mass media to stop sniggering and turn its cameras on issues of substantive policy, like the trouble with the Social Security, health, and educational systems. This resulted in the November 1998 backlash against the Republican party, which—in cahoots with its close allies in the conservative Christian right wing—had fueled this "investigation" of Clinton's sexual appetite for years.

This turnabout—the public interested in issues and the establishment and media portrayed as backyard gossips—became initially manifest in the 1992 presidential cycle, when voters were much more concerned about whether American politicians had betrayed the public trust than whether one candidate had betrayed a spouse. Moreover, ordinary citizens were curious to learn the degree to which the candidates (two of whom were enormously wealthy) were in touch with the daily drudgery and monetary crunch of the American working class. While several of the media elite belittled questions citizens posed about whether the candidates knew the cost of a loaf of bread or a pair of jeans, Americans across the country understood this as a "reality check." They knew that a correct answer to such an earthy question spoke volumes about a candidate's awareness of the impact of "abstract" national economic policies on the struggles of the middle and lower classes.

But it was Bill Clinton, a skilled and astute politician with impressive academic credentials, who fared best on national TV in interactive settings where he met face-to-face with voters. His greatest media strength was how he meshed the dull details of policy issues with a "real-world" understanding of policy implications. When he demonstrated a sponta-neous knowledge of supermarket prices in one of these interactive TV forums, many voters were instantly persuaded that he was one high echelon political leader who was still grounded in the daily grind. Through this medium, one and all could see how "warm" he was and how he was still comfortable in the presence of the average laborer, woman, and teenager.

John F. Kennedy was the first master of political TV, projecting the image of a leader in control (while Nixon sweated) in the early stages of top-down TV. William Jefferson Clinton was the first master of political TV to project the image of political connectedness—in reality a pseudo-connectedness—to the public in the early stages of interactive TV. Clin-ton knew how to be a "reflective listener" to citizens' concerns. George Bush knew only how to connect to his watch. The contrast in style sent a wake-up call to millions of Americans observing this kind of "debate" between the son of the working class and the son of the patrician class.

Despite a hail of insults from the District of Columbia set (including the 'Washington press corps'), Perot cleverly played to the broad public dissatisfaction and lingering desire for change far better than most other candidates. Were he not in the campaign as an unquestioned American patriot with pots full of money, many issues of concern to most Amer-ican voters would have probably been swept under the rug by the other "major" candidates and the "Inside-the Beltway" media experts. His fo-rum of choice was the TV call-in-show.

While most TV news shows and talk show hosts showed more interest in Clinton's unsavory personal life, Jerry Brown's past peccadilloes, and Perot's eccentricities than in their public track records, Perot had suffi-cient funding to raise questions about the Iran-Contra fiasco, the $150 billion savings and loan bail-out by the taxpayers, the domination of Congress by domestic and foreign lobbyists, and the enormous national debt and deficit. Perot refused to let major public issues be lost in neg-ative personal attacks on candidates. The public responded with interest and enthusiasm. And this came across particularly well when Perot had the opportunity to address them directly and interactively via the media.

Much to the puzzlement of powerful nay-sayers and pontificators, Perot drew large (record) audiences for his paid electronic infomercials that featured him as the leading man, holding a low-tech wooden pointer to help him explain his third-grade pie charts. There was nothing glam-orous or dramatic about the straightforward Perot data-heavy presen-tations. Instead, Perot had a Huckleberry Finn aura about him, which he reinforced by sprinkling his critiques and remedies with folksy homilies that produced catchy sound bites for TV.

Sad to say, though, Perot's TV teleconferences, call-in show votes, and lectures, combined with the media's ignorance and/or disdain of important research in the field, produced little more citizen empowerment than run-of-the-mill American campaign trickery.

CITIZEN PEROT'S ERSATZ ETM AND THE MASS MEDIA'S COMPLICITY

Ross Perot was also the first presidential candidate to promise a quantum leap of change in how presidential candidates and government leaders communicated with or represented the citizenry. As we noted in an earlier chapter, Perot had long been an advocate of ETMs. Now was the right time to test them out as a plank in his political platform. Citizen Perot appeared on TV talk show after TV talk show championing national public dialogue by way of television, telephone call-ins, and polling. He said he wanted to use these interactive TV town halls not only to calibrate the public mood, but also to defer to it as well once he was living and working in the White House.

Citizens responded with strongly positive vibrations to this idea, but media and political elites—clinging to their Newtonian axioms about human nature—denounced it in the most sonorous of tones and a fusillade of epithets. From the Far Right, the conservative political columnist George Will called it a "crackpot" idea. From the slightly Left, the dean of American TV anchors Walter Cronkite denigrated the idea of Electronic Town Meetings as downright "dangerous."

Ross Perot, himself, did little to endear himself to academics through his promotion of simplistic measures to decide complex issues. Even the most senior researchers in this field, many of whom—like ourselves—had actually designed, tested, and analyzed Electronic Town Meetings, after a favorable initial reaction, became highly dubious about Perot's brand. Unfortunately, reporters and editors of major newspapers and news magazines (the self-congratulatory reporters who allegedly "do their homework" and ask "the tough" questions) conveniently overlooked two decades of systematic and rigorous research on authentic teledemocracy and rarely acknowledged or cited any scholar who had actually participated in constructing, conducting, and/or evaluating such processes.

Instead, the billionaire businessman, spending a fortune of his own cache, was allowed to define ETMs for the country and the world. The mass media happily and uncritically accepted and publicized his version, one that was highly partisan and shabbily fabricated. In other words, the media helped build an ETM snowman—one that would quickly melt under the scorching, white lights of TV. Perot's shabby masquerade of an ETM also fit the mass media's own dominant Newtonian paradigmatic thinking—that is, it was, in truth, a top-down manufacturing of consent disguised as something it was not: a new way to empower citizens. Perhaps that was the only kind of 'Electronic Town Meeting' they could fathom given their outmoded worldview.

Perot's model of an ETM was, at best, Icarus's wax wings in the age of the space shuttle. It consisted of information being collected, distilled, and disseminated by one source (Perot), a man with a personal political program. The entire Perot-ETM process was lopsided and distorted. It allowed no time for extensive lateral discussion among citizens or any face-to-face deliberation. There was no hint of scientific random sample polling to determine in-depth, informed views of representative samples of the populace. It included no political views or options other than his own.

Thus, the public's warm embrace of Perot's attractive but false Electronic Town Meeting proposition was the idealistic yearning of an uninformed citizenry. But the proximate cause of that was the media's feeble attack on the process with little knowledge of and/or great antipathy toward sophisticated, true experiments in ETMs. How else was the public to find out about real ETMs? Wasn't it the responsibility of the free, professional, neutral press to at least present the findings of the scientific enterprise that had tested them out and could offer professional criticisms of them and let the public decide? The truth, however, is even worse than that.

Actually, very early in the 1992 campaign, after Perot's movement was gaining tremendous momentum, several advocates and experimenters with ETMs had sought to counsel Perot and the media on the ETM experiments conducted at the state and local level across the country. Hazel Henderson (one of the early visionaries we discussed in Chapter 2), Alan Kay (developer of "Americans Talk Issues," a major scientific polling device to measure deliberated opinion), Duane Elgin (co-organizer of the San Francisco Bay Voice project), and Ted Becker and Christa Slaton (experimenters with statewide ETMs and Televote public opinion polling) all made repeated attempts to update Perot and the media on the extensive research in the field.

Neither the Perot camp nor any in the inner-circle media showed the slightest inclination to let these people infiltrate their iron-clad minds. Instead, both proceeded, for the most part, to keep the American public misinformed or disinformed about genuine ETM processes. Perot, paying for what he alone wanted, dictated the priorities and format of his bogus ETM. The media, in collaboration with some well-placed mainstream academics, responded as though Perot was conducting a genuine ETM instead of a pathetic charade of it. Rather than criticize Perot's subversion of the process, they treated his imitation as the "real thing," giving themselves an easy target to lambast.

But much good came from this. What had occurred, the mountain of misrepresentation of the term "Electronic Town Meeting" by both Perot and the mass media, led several of us, from different parts of the country, to commiserate about the dilemma in which we now realized we were in—together. How could we ever make ourselves heard and understood individually—as we had been doing for what seemed like forever? There was a united front of imperviousness to our individual work. *Within this present system of governance and political communications, it seemed that nothing failed like genuine teledemocratic success!* Those of us working within the New Democratic Paradigm, no matter how clearly we proved that our systems worked as hypothesized (or even better than that), learned through bitter experience that there was no way that those in power could or would accept, publicize, and/or adopt our theory and findings.

The next step was obvious. We had to begin to plan how we could pool our talents and knowledge in order to counter the exclusive control Perot and the media were exercising in defining ETMs. All of our visions and experiments were far more imaginative, sophisticated, successful, and empowering than anything presented by any politician seeking to use ETMs to get elected. Furthermore, they were well beyond the critique—and perhaps even the comprehension—of the old paradigm mass media.

THE 1993 FORT MASON CONFERENCE: THE SYNERGY BEGINS

Several of us decided to organize a conference that would bring many pro-teledemocracy people together to design an "advanced" or "comprehensive" model of ETMs, consistent with "new paradigm" thinking, one combining the core values and key features of the best experiments. Since most of the teledemocratic practitioners had developed and tested their systems at either the community, local, regional, or state level, we thought it would be useful to construct an advanced design of ETMs that could be used at the national level as well. However, it was equally important to start working together. A united voice might eventually overcome our autonomous sounds of silence. Working together might produce unique opportunities for bringing about the democratic transformation we all wanted. The frustrations we experienced in the 1992 presidential campaign provided a strong impetus for us to begin a process of synergy.

Theory, Participants, and Process

Together with Robert Horn, director of the Electronic Democracy Project for the Meridian International Institute, we organized a conference at Fort Mason in San Francisco during two days in March 1993. Our mutual goal was to discuss how to develop the "next generation" of "advanced" Electronic Town Meetings. It was agreed that there had already been sufficient ETM experimentation at the state and local level to provide the foundation to build the next generation of a national Electronic Town Meeting process that would include interfaces with regional and local Electronic Town Meetings. The organizers were distressed that Perot, the entire American political spectrum from Left to Right, and the national press largely ignored the experience and data gained from numerous ETM projects across the United States (Hawaii, Alaska, Georgia, New York, and California) so they were determined to utilize the expertise of many of those innovators to help evaluate the process and to help create an empirically based, incremental model for a national ETM.

Thus, this meeting was a working conference in which those attending were specifically invited on the basis of their previous experience or interest in ETMs. Invitees were a mixture of practitioners (who had developed and conducted ETMs), academics (who had studied them), foundation representatives (who were sponsoring ETM projects), cable and business executives and entrepreneurs, professional facilitators, and computer specialists. The goal was to ground the conference in theory, which would then guide the designing of a model or models that could be used for further experimentation at the national level.

A number of conference attendees were skeptical about the agendas of some of the other participants. Practitioners expected petty haggling from academics, whom they suspected were bent on endless esoteric discussion and eternal inaction. Academics looked askance at practitioners, whom they perceived as barging ahead too quickly without due consideration of social and political implications. Foundation representatives expected self-promoters to hound them for money. Some worried that the entrepreneurs would pick their brains and then run off to bastardize the process for financial gain.

Recognizing the potential clash of priorities, the organizers agreed on a process that was designed to facilitate consensus. First, there were a number of professional facilitators present to guide the discussions. The conference organizers had experience that emphasized consensus development. Several participants had mediated discussions in ETMs, computer conferences, government and business organizations, and large meetings. Indeed, some were professional mediators and arbitrators.

Fortunately, the mixture of people and process worked. What came out of the two-day interaction was a great deal of agreement on (1) theory, purposes, and core values of a national ETM process; (2) the operational components of ETMs at the national, regional, and local levels; and (3) how well we all got along and collaborated.

Proponents of ETMs use diverse theoretical routes to reach the same destination. For most, many of the paths merge at some point. This leads to substantial agreement about the purposes and design of ETMs.

For example, participatory democrats, who study, design, and/or operate ETMs, see great value in enhancing and encouraging citizen participation. In their view, as citizens are engaged, they build a sense of community and develop a feeling of ownership in the decisions that then become easier to implement.

ETM proponents who distrust direct public power and focus more on citizen-enlightened elite decision making acknowledge that even wise decisions made by remote elites can be overturned or obstructed by citizens who have been excluded from discussions and who are suspicious of such a closed process. Other advocates of ETMs favor them because the American representative system is so unrepresentative of the diversity in the United States. Their view is that regardless of the possible good intentions of a representative trying to represent diverse constituents, one's life experience serves as a filter that blocks or screens information to fit one's own perceptions. When representatives are predominately wealthy, white men, they often "don't get it" when trying to represent the disadvantaged, minorities, or women.

Other friends of the ETM process share concerns espoused by Thomas Jefferson and John Dewey and envision ETMs as a means of educating citizens, teaching responsibility, and creating a vast population of practicing democrats. Yet others are influenced by Abraham Maslow's process of self-actualization and Erich Fromm's view of social pathology. They view ETMs as mechanisms to be utilized in the process of self-growth and fulfillment.

In other words, the purposes of ETMs are largely based on one's theoretical and/or value-based starting point. But despite the great variety in value preferences of the participants in this conference, a general consensus emerged on the purposes and core values of ETMs. While there may be disagreement on the ranking of importance of the purposes, there was little to no dissent on the purposes that fall under four major categories: (1) community development; (2) expand the democratic franchise; (3) enhance the democratic process; and (4) improve public outcomes. Table 5.1 presents those major groupings with a number of objectives that all agreed were subsumed with them.

Community and Local ETM Handbook: Inventory of Problems and Useful Technologies and Techniques

Many of the participants in the working group on Local-Metropolitan Town Meeting Design had experience with conducting citywide or statewide Electronic Town Meetings: Mike Hollinshead (Alberta, Canada);

Table 5.1
Purposes of Electronic Town Meetings

Community Development	Expand Democratic Franchise	Enhance Democratic Process	Improve Public Outcomes
Expand public space	Enfranchise the powerless and apathetic	Expand the deliberative capability	Enable individuals to have influence over their lives and circumstances
Enable people to effectively and collaboratively address common social, political, economic, and community issues	Be accessible and user-friendly to all groups of people and their capabilities	Facilitate informed dialogue among citizens, experts, and government officials	Enable individuals to participate in developing a more inclusive polity that will yield more equitable results
Create new or reinvigorate old communities	Enable and encourage new leaders to emerge	Increase the capacity for dealing with complexity by all members of society	Identify more stakeholders in policies to reduce resistance to implementation
		Maintain a *neutral* facilitation process	Maximize the response of political leaders to citizen input
		Enhance learning and listening of all involved	
		Present a wide range of balanced information and opinions from a broad base of resources	
		Be interesting, engaging, and entertaining	
		Involve citizens in agenda setting, planning, and the direction of society	
		Discourage demagoguery	

Christa Slaton (Hawaii Televote and Honolulu Electronic Town Meeting); Ronald Thomas (the Savannah ETM); and Kirk Bergstrom (Los Angeles Televote). The group was assisted by professional mediator Geoff Ball, who had facilitated various interest groups in arriving at a consensus agreement in the San Francisco Estuary Project.

Based on the experience of the practitioners and the probing of the theorists and visionaries, the group identified a complex set of variables that need attention in the design and successful execution of community or local Electronic Town Meetings: (1) scenarios; (2) stakeholders; (3) components; (4) dimensions; (5) technologies; (6) technological constraints; (7) financial obstacles; (8) political constraints; (9) successful elements of design; and (10) unresolved design issues.

What follows, then, is a short description of what all these ETM specialists agreed upon. We present it as a general guide or handbook for future use for those interested in continuing and improving upon the work of the ETM pioneers in their local communities, towns, and cities. We also present it as an illustration of the kind of synergy that began to grow at the Fort Mason conference in 1993 and that continues to evolve in the 21st century.

(1) Scenario Selection

What will be the subjects of Electronic Town Meetings or which issues will be appropriate for the scripting of ETMs? There are a multitude of potential scenarios for local ETMs. Subjects of various ETMs that have been conducted by the participants included planning for sustainable "smart" growth, health care reform, budgeting, and transportation. Various avenues for selecting ETM scenarios or subjects for discussion include:

(a) Conduct a scientific deliberative public opinion poll to determine public sentiment and find out what the citizens want to discuss.

(b) Select a dominant single issue, one that has been discussed for a long time and remains unresolved.

(c) Engage the citizens in planning for the future or in establishing exercises that establish public priorities.

(d) Use ETMs as an educational tool to increase knowledge on selected issues and then ask for a prioritization.

(2) Stakeholders

Who may be the major stakeholders in ETMs?

(a) Government (local planners, representatives, mayors, administrative agencies, etc.);

(b) Citizens impacted by the issue;

(c) Resource owners (large landholders, manufacturers, etc.);

(d) The media providers (newspaper, radio, television, cable companies);

(e) Private organizations (businesses, service clubs, etc.);

(f) Nonpartisan public interest groups (e.g., League of Women Voters);

(g) Schools and universities;

(h) Technology providers (computer companies, telephone companies);

(i) Under-represented groups (poor, minorities).

(3) Components

What are the elements of the ETMs that are necessary to make them work as intended?

(a) Publicity, education, and entertainment to maximize public participation and interest;

(b) Public agenda setting;

(c) Clear issue framing;

(d) Multiple channels for participant input;

(e) Linking face-to-face meetings with electronic meetings;

(f) Professional facilitation;

(g) Random polling (conventional and deliberative);

(h) Readily accessible information;

(i) Trained volunteers;

(j) Feedback process;

(k) Evaluation of process and content;

(l) Coordination of components a–k.

(4) Dimensions

What dimensions of ETMs vary from case to case?

(a) Cost;

(b) Time frame;

(c) Sophistication of production (depends somewhat on issue complexity);

(d) Cultural differences;

(e) Language;

(f) Available technology;

(g) Expertise;

(h) Political support.

(5) Technologies

What are the available and desirable technologies to incorporate in ETMs?

(a) Television (commercial broadcast, public, CATV, public access);

(b) Radio (network, local);

(c) Newspapers and magazines;

(d) Newspaper issue balloting;

(e) Talk and call-in TV and radio shows;

(f) Multisite hook-ups;

(g) Graphics (computer and otherwise);

(h) New signaling systems for high-capacity call counting;

(i) Interactive electronic technologies (consensors, keypads, PCs);

(j) Two-way television teleconference and teleconferencing satellite;

(k) Computer bulletin board, Voice-mail;

(l) Structured telephone and/or computer conferencing for issue framing;

(m) Computer programs that facilitate interaction;

(n) Computer networking (e-mail lists, chatrooms);

(o) Interactive and continual polling (random, 900 number, 800 number, encrypted Internet voting);

(p) Public electronic meeting rooms;

(q) Bubble scan—public screen;

(r) Video programs, minidocs, informercials, and slide shows;

(s) Community production facility and support;

(t) Facilitation and mediation;

(u) Fax machines;

(v) Anonymity and privacy options.

(6) Technological Constraints

What are the barriers or other obstacles that designers of ETMs have faced in regards to technological boundaries?

(a) Limitations on how many people can talk on a channel at a time;

(b) Access by people who are not comfortable with technology or do not have it;

(c) Technological resources that have previously been incapable of meeting the demand for input (system overload).

(7) Financial Constraints

What are the barriers or other obstacles that designers of ETMs have faced in regard to financial limitations?

(a) Budget constraints often limit options;

(b) Funding sources may want to control the agenda, information, and questions or utilize certain technologies for their own economic or political gain.

(8) Political Constraints

What are the constraints or other obstacles that designers of ETMs have faced in regard to political institutions?

(a) Power imbalances must be recognized and addressed so that the ETM does not reinforce existing power imbalances;

(b) Resistance will come from some who currently hold power and want to retain it;

(c) Professionals want to control too much;

(d) Media resists change in present one-way, nonlateral political communication system;

(e) Politicians may ignore information gathered through the ETMs;

(f) People anxious about experimenting with new communication technologies may feel they are incompatible with traditional town meetings.

(9) Successful Elements of Design

What are the features of ETMs that have been conducted that practitioners and researchers have concluded are successful features that need to be included in future ETMs?

(a) Random sample surveys or scientific face-to-face deliberative polls for participants to frame the issues, determine the agendas, and develop the questions;

(b) Providing feedback loops that involve continuous input by participants;

(c) Attractive visuals and graphics (logos, ads, PSAs);

(d) Maximize variety in media (e.g., combining newspapers, TV, radio, telephones, etc., in the ETM);

(e) Maximizing channels of communication of participants (e.g., combining TV and radio call-in shows, face-to-face meetings, delphi questionnaires, Televote polls, letters to the editor, e-mail, etc.);

(f) Allowing a wide variety of times and places for input;

(g) Inclusion of simulations, "what if" games, acting groups, computer simulations;

(h) Role playing—presenting "step into others' shoes" scenarios;

(i) Including local cultural flavor;

(j) Entertainment, political satire, music, rap;

(k) Facilitators who are sensitive to all voices and willing to be surprised;

(l) Moderators who can move conversation forward and piece together elements of consensus;

(m) Anonymous input on selecting options, particularly on sensitive issues;

(n) Composite video presentation of various voices/stories at the beginning of the program;

(o) Diversity in programming (e.g., documentaries, expert panels, debates, animation, computer graphics, cartoons, call-in shows, etc.);

(p) Real-life stories (person-on-the-street interviews; home interviews, etc.).

(10) Unresolved Design Issues

What are remaining problems to be improved or resolved in ETM design or which features of ETMs have had mixed success?

(a) How to avoid "ballot" stuffing—fail-safe voter registration and voting system—and how to assure that vocal minority does not dominate;

(b) How to increase community involvement and diminish isolation of marginalized individuals and groups;

(c) How to better sustain interest and participation over the long haul;

(d) How to aggregate, distill, and distribute all the information gathered from ETMs in the best ways possible;

(e) How to further increase people's thinking capabilities and understanding of the complexities of issues;

(f) How to involve even larger numbers of people in a deliberative process that is composed of an exchange of ideas, not just numeric or yes/no responses;

(g) How to improve advertising and promotion of ETMs so as to maximize diversity and broad-based input;

(h) How to move toward consensus and how to determine what is the "best consensus possible";

(i) What is the proper relationship between random samples and self-selected samples;

(j) What are the best ways to ensure the independence, integrity, and credibility of the organizers and operators of the ETM;

(k) How to avoid public attention diverted from issue discussion by "personalities" and slick public speakers;

(l) What are the preferred methods to train and select moderators and/or facilitators;

(m) How to deal with censorship—who decides what gets on the air;

(n) How to deal with advocacy groups or individuals who want to use the ETM process to attain personal goals;

(o) How to ensure the funders do not control the process—unless the public funds the process directly;

(p) What are the best strategies to make ETMs a meaningful component of representative democracy and/or to enhance the initiative and referendum processes;

(q) How to ensure that the results are used by those in power and not ignored or diluted to irrelevancy.

Slaton addresses how a number of these issues were dealt with in experiments in Hawaii, New Zealand, and Los Angeles (Slaton 1992, 123–172). Ben Barber, in *Strong Democracy* (1984), also proposes a number of solutions to some of these problems. Furthermore, there is considerable data from the individual ETM experiments that provide insight into how many of these various unresolved issues have been handled for better and for worse in the past. Many of these issues, however, are dependent upon larger questions, such as who is sponsoring, funding, and designing the project. Some options will be discussed later in this chapter.

National ETM Design: Post-Newtonian Architecture for an Ultra-Democratic Space

Participants in the National Town Meeting Design Group included several individuals who had experience in local, state, and even one national Electronic Town Meeting and professional facilitation, as well as a few teledemocracy visionaries. Their goal was to develop a design for a complex model for a national Electronic Town Meeting, one that would adapt the successful components at microlevels to the macrolevel and put them into motion.

The Dynamics of the Design

The results of their work are depicted in Figure 5.1. It is fairly obvious that this depiction of a national ETM is far more complex—and perhaps strange—than any programming previously presented by politicians and/or the media as TV Town Meetings or ETMs. Compare it to Ross Perot's model! Compare it to any so-called Electronic Town Hall Meeting called by any political party, foundation, TV network, or political candidate or leader. Nothing resembles it because none of what has been done nationally by politicos or the corporate-owned media has genuinely embarked upon the mission of constructing citizen-empowering ETMs. The synergy developed at the Fort Mason conference was eminently successful at designing such an endeavor because of the mutual commitment to apply new ICT to citizen empowerment. Thus, the final product integrated all the then-known and previously tested technologies and techniques available at the time and tried to address all the pitfalls and

Figure 5.1
National Electronic Town Meeting Design

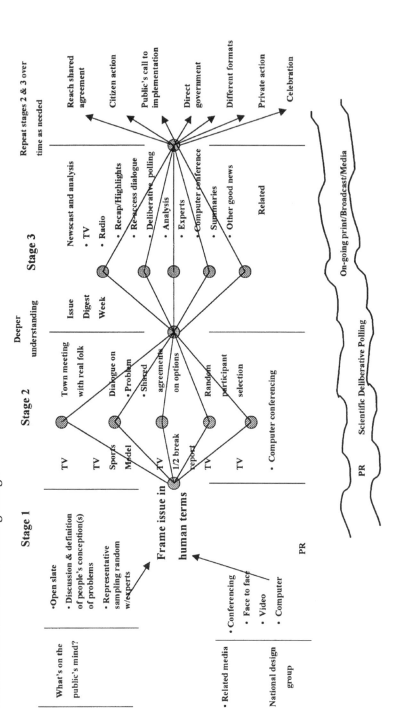

pratfalls that individual ETM experiments had encountered and experienced over the years.

As one can readily visualize from the diagram, the national ETM model involves a multimedia, multitiered, multiphased process that incorporates multiple, overlapping technologies designed to engage numerous segments of the public in education, thought, discussion, and deliberation of issues and voting on them. From the first stage and moving into the second, the public is involved in setting the agenda (determining which problems or issues should be discussed and in what order of priority). Electronic meetings are supplemented and enriched by periodic, ongoing, face-to-face meetings—and they are continually informed by ongoing scientific deliberative polling processes, which in some models are the central feature of the ETM itself.

As one moves from Stage 2, which uses a variety of programming formats to present information and a wide array of expert opinion on the top issue or issues selected from the public's agenda, to Stage 3, the emphasis is increasingly placed on delving deeper into the complications and trade-offs involved in the issue(s) and synthesizing input and feedback from participants. A deliberative process is enhanced by a series of assessments, analyses, and reevaluations of previous inputs.

Stages 2 and 3 can be repeated over and over again at various levels (local and/or national) and by way of competing Electronic Town Meetings before moving into the final stage. This terminal phase of the model is the key to success, because it aims at a consensus or a shared agreement on how to best resolve the issue and how to choose the most appropriate action to administer the most popular public policy choices.

We also all agreed that various or all components of the national ETM process were capable of being utilized as needed to evaluate the impact of the policy, and to reconsider the problem anew if the first direction did not arrive at a satisfactory solution. As in any mediation process, "final agreements" can be renegotiated or remediated. And finally, we agreed that the national model is intended to work in collaboration with local ETMs, not to replace them.

Finally, one might say that Figure 5.1 is a peculiar looking model. We agree. However, we see it as being consistent with post-Newtonian physics and the New Democratic Paradigm. It is replete with overlapping processes and redundancies—all of which are highly functional for the "messy" process of post-modern democracy.

What we are doing is creating the architecture for a new type of public space—one conducive to a new type of democratic discourse and decision making. There is a parallel to the new construction boom occurring in Berlin, Germany, where a new wave of public planners and architects are building a 21st-century democratic capital in a nation haunted by a history of authoritarianism. The form of some of these novel buildings defy and dazzle eyes conditioned by classic design. That is why Figure 5.1 looks so "different." Notice it is not a "top-down" model. Notice it does not seem "even." This is similar to the observation that one contemporary architect made about one of these new structures in the new Berlin, that it was a "revolutionary, democratic asymmetrical organicism" (Kramer 1999, 53). Somehow, that seems to fit snugly with the structure of the new democratic communications system depicted above.

Infrastructure and Strategies Group: How Best to Fund and Sustain an Authentic, Independent ETM Process

Throughout the conference, one nagging issue kept bobbing to the surface. It created an undertow of high anxiety and was one of the leading concerns that drew us together in the first place. This was the two-pronged question that all the practitioners faced time after time: Where will the money to finance the ETM come from, and after it is over, how will the ETM process survive? After all, resiliance and resources—as much as values and design—go to the heart of the strength and credibility of the entire ETM empowerment process.

Who should sponsor, finance, and conduct the ETMs—government, private commercial media companies, public television, public interest groups, universities, private foundations, politicians, political action committees, all of the above, some of the above, or none of the above?

This is much the same dilemma illuminated by the Gamma Group in Montreal (Arnopoulos and Valaskakis 1982) and Benjamin Barber (1984): *What is the best institutional structure in a modern ICT society to maintain the most independent, unbiased, inclusive, impactful system of ETMs?* How can we hire and insulate a cadre of "democratic technics" who are dedicated to providing the best teledemocratic process and have no hidden policy agendas?

Table 5.2 presents a rudimentary chart drawn up at the Fort Mason conference of potential models for a national ETM infrastructure, one that can serve local, state, or regional ETMs as well. Models are categorized as either private or public and either profit or nonprofit.

Designs falling under a private, nonprofit infrastructure would be developed by such groups as foundations, public interest groups, or political parties. An excellent recent example of this type was conducted by Carolyn Lukensmeyer for the Pew Charitable Trust, 1997–1999. It was the first U.S. nationwide ETM and integrated multicity face-to-face forums via television conferencing and electronically facilitated interactive discussion (Americans Discuss Social Security 1999). Public, nonprofit ETMs would be sponsored by organizations such as a presidential commission (e.g., Commission on Presidential Debates); a government agency (e.g., a future Congressional Office of Public Opinion Research

Table 5.2
Electronic Town Meeting Infrastructure Models

	Nonprofit Models and Examples	Profit Models and Examples
Private	♦ Foundation (Kettering, Public Agenda, Pew) ♦ Public Interest Group (League of Women Voters) ♦ Independent Membership-based Research Organization (Consumers Union)	♦ Commercial Over-the-Air TV Station, Network, Media Company ♦ Corporate Sponsor ♦ Private Cable Station or Network ♦ Marketing Firm ♦ Independent ETM Corporation (ETMCo)
Public	♦ Independent Commission (Commission on Presidential Debates) ♦ Independent Government Agency (Congressional Office of Public Opinion Research and Assessment) ♦ Public TV Station/Network (C-Span; California Channel) ♦ Independent Community-based Organization (Bay Voice) ♦ University (Honolulu Electronic Town Meeting)	♦ Public-Private Corporate Entities (Post Office, Amtrak)

and Assessment); public television (e.g., PBS or a new kind of U.S. government-owned but independent citizen service TV network); an independent community-based group (e.g., Bay Voice); a university (e.g., Honolulu Electronic Town Meeting, New Zealand Televote); or an independent membership research or discussion organization (e.g., Consumers Union, League of Women Voters, etc.). Private, profit groups would include organizations such as commercial broadcast television networks or stations, corporate sponsors, private cable networks, and/or marketing agencies.

However, this taxonomy still does not solve the main puzzle. Both theoretically and practically, the Fort Mason conferees agreed that funders—regardless of political orientation or profit/nonprofit and private/public status—have an irresistible urge to manage the process, as well as the outcomes. Power holders usually understand the potential threat to their own status by empowering those who truly want to empower citizens. Many experiments of the past two decades have lacked sufficient funding to produce the quality programming envisioned in their designs. Projects often have relied on volunteers and donated media time and facilities. In addition, no ETM project to date has been able to achieve the financial support, regardless of the level of success on the other variables, to continue "permanently" as an *ongoing* project to improve on its design and/or to engage a particular public in further developing public agendas and/or policy.

Trying to experiment with New Democratic Paradigm systems is not easy in a world dominated by those who embrace the assumptions and philosophy of the old democratic paradigm. But this has always been so and despite this natural resistance to democratic change, change has come sooner or later—but it will always come. As we have stated in Chapter 2, there will be other democratic surges in American history, and they will occur several times in the 21st century. There will be many sources of energy in this movement, which will continue to gain strength through a wide variety of synergistic fusions.

This kind of inexorable forward movement is detailed extensively in James MacGregor Burns and Stewart Burns's book, *A People's Charter: The Pursuit of Rights in America* (1991). They, like us, believe that the American people have an innovative political spirit and that the people are often far ahead of political elites. When frustrations reach a certain level in American politics, "moral forces" and "social resources" propel citizens into demanding to be heard and compelling the political leaders and system to respond.

In the modern context, as the new millennium follows a century that featured several separate, but interdependent, democratic surges within its 100-year time frame—the Populist and Progressive movements; the Women's Suffrage movement; the New Deal; the Women's Liberation Movement; and the Civil Rights Movement—we know that some new citizens' movement will demand new kinds of democratic advance. What will it be? At this point in time, nothing else seems more likely in the age of ICT than "teledemocracy."

So, the question at this point is not whether genuine ETMs will exist in the 21st century, but what will be their operative design and which will be the optimal institutional structure to guarantee their independence, influence, and resilience? That lingering question was not answered at the Fort Mason conference. However, the spirit of cooperation that infused it, also inspired and fired up a number of collaborative organizational initiatives and experiments soon thereafter. One, in which we became active participants, was to form a commercial enterprise devoted to producing ETMs for a profit. We called it "the Electronic Town Meeting Company," or ETMCo. It is still alive and kicking, although it has metamorphosed of late.

THE ELECTRONIC TOWN MEETING COMPANY (ETMCo): CAN CITIZEN EMPOWERMENT SELL?

During the San Francisco conference in 1993, a small group of us decided that perhaps the best way to develop and sustain an organization that could conduct independent, high quality "comprehensive ETMs" on a regular and continuing basis was via a highly unorthodox and untried method. After all, just about all other types of organization had been tried: nonprofits; media companies; governments sponsored projects; university-based projects; foundation seedings. All of these, despite a high level of success in reaching their stated goals, had been one-shot deals. The government and/or media and/or foundations sponsor, for one reason or another, did not see fit to underwrite another ETM experiment.

That untraveled road was to conduct ETMs as a business. Those who were opposed to this approach—and they were many—fell into two groups. The first group felt this approach was tainted. In their opinion, nonprofits are a more ethical way to run an organization devoted to the public interest. They also did not like the idea of making democracy into a commodity. The other group was more practical in its opposition. They predicted it would not work. In other words, we would never find investors, but even if lightning struck and we did, electronic democracy would not make money for the investor or the company.

We understood these objections and, frankly, each had considerable merit. Still, our thinking was that since no polity, TV station, or private foundation was committed to financing these projects, why not at least *try* the commercial route? All we really needed was one person or one group of people somewhere on the face of the Earth, with a sufficient level of discretionary capital, who understood and accepted the New Democratic Paradigm, and was willing to invest in testing various combinations of its field-tested elements. If we were correct in our assumption that one such person (or group of persons) existed, he, she, or they would not only advance the development of this highly innovative democratic political communications system, but also might even "do well by doing good."

This subset of the Fort Mason conference agreed that the business model was a promising route to producing a series of teledemocratic projects over time, for a number of reasons. For one thing, if such a political communications process was truly empowering, enlightening, educational, and entertaining, why couldn't it make money? To insist that the average citizen only spends money for frivolous and escapist media products is old paradigm thinking. Why couldn't ETMs be marketed like a movie or a television special—with hefty public relations and advertising budgets to attract a large participatory audience? Successful American cable TV companies make a reasonable profit by gaining less than a 1% share of the American TV audience. As we have noted earlier, many of the interactive TV experiments had done much better than that—even winning their time slots. Why couldn't such a company re-invest its likely profits into promoting and expanding its offerings to other communities in the United States and elsewhere?

As a private, for-profit company, there were a number of potential "revenue streams" that could keep the venture "in the black." For one, 1993 was the height of the "privatization" frenzy in the United States and England. Governments at all levels were doing a lot of "partnering with" and "outsourcing to" private commercial companies to do what they, the governments, had been doing for a long time with mixed results. Using a business model was seen as being more "efficient" and "productive," an alternative to strict government monopolies in transportation, public works, and education—even prisons. Governments were widely viewed as being inefficient in these areas and they were certainly ineffective in getting people to pay attention to public matters. By contracting to a private company, governments could provide a multimedia, multiphased project to put them in much closer touch with citizens who were already alienated from and suspicious of politicians and bureaucracies.

Another source of money that we all saw as being eminently tappable was having ordinary citizens and TV viewers pay directly for a variety of interactive media services. For example, many American TV stations were adding telephone call-ins on issues (self-selected sample polling) to their news programming (as we mentioned in Chapter 4). By using a 900-number dial system, they were charging people to vote on all kinds of superficial questions where the results were instantly sucked into a black hole, never to see the light of day again. In addition, a couple of these projects, one on CBS national programming, had attracted over 25 million callers wanting to "vote" on President Bush's ritualistic State of the Union message in 1992. There were a spate of examples of how a lot of money could be made by adding this to our ETM programming— particularly since the key polling was being done by at least one method of scientific deliberative surveys.

Yet another possible source of revenue was advertising. After all, the American model of BBC is the Public Broadcasting System. On PBS, it is a long-standing tradition to raise money from the corporate sector by selling very discrete, low-key ads. This has not, according to what we know, compromised the "independence" of PBS and/or the quality of its productions.

So, with the "comprehensive ETM" design from the Fort Mason conference in tow, plus an agreement among several of us to give the business option a try, we formed a private corporation in the state of Washington called the Electronic Town Meeting Company, or ETMCo. One of our partners, Larry Greene, was a "new paradigm" businessman who was president of a multimillion-dollar telemarketing company headquartered north of Seattle. He agreed to be president of ETMCo and to perform the incorporation chores. Once all the paperwork was done and a modicum amount of money was raised to pay for the incorporation, we were in business.

The Democracy Channel and ETMCo

Our first project involved a cable TV executive who participated in the Fort Mason project. Together we worked up a plan to have ETMCo serve as a "production unit" for America's largest TV cable company at the time. That company's owner had recruited this executive to set up 10 new channels, one of which he wanted to be "an electronic commons" where all cable viewers in his system could tune-in for information, discussion, and voting on major issues of the day. It seemed like a natural fit between that media company and ETMCo. We called our proposed cable channel "the Democracy Channel."

As fate would have it, just about that time, the U.S. Federal Communications Commission (FCC) socked the entire American cable industry with a sizable price rollback. In all honesty, cable rates had been rising at an unconscionable rate for years and American consumers were sick of it. So, heavy pressure was put on the FCC to do something about it, which they did. The owner of the large cable TV company that was nearing some kind of deal to start the "electronic commons" became enraged at the federal government for this precipitous reduction of his profit margin. He changed his mind and decided, instead, to convert his new political channel into one that would be openly and avowedly hostile to all government regulation of the media.

Therefore, instead of ETMCo becoming allied with a "democracy channel" providing authentic ETMs, the new channel was handed over lock, stock, and barrel to Republican Speaker of the U.S. House of Representatives, Newt Gingrich. Oxymoronically, they named this avowedly right-wing, conservative cable TV channel "National Empowerment Television." Sad to say, the only people it empowered were those who already had plenty of it.

Shortly thereafter, though, we thought we had struck oil again. The

Markle Foundation in New York City agreed to fund a conference among the partners and several potential ETMCo subcontractors in Snowmass, Colorado, in the fall of 1994. The goal of their generosity (a $60,000 grant) was for us to work up a full-scale business plan for ETMCo—complete with a more detailed set of operations for a multiphased, multimedia ETM along the lines suggested by the participants in San Francisco.

That business conference lasted for three days and was divided into two groups: the ETM advanced-design group and the business-plan group. Discussions were intense and what emanated was a full-scale business plan attached to an even more refined and sophisticated model of an ETM process. We believe that the ETMCo design optimizes citizen empowerment at any level of government. It includes all the successfully tested components discussed in Chapters 3–5, but adds or emphasizes several new features. For example, in the ETMCo model, the Televote method of scientific deliberative polling is at the center of the entire ETM process. In other words, all aspects of the ETMCo process interface with the Televoter "random citizen legislature" from beginning to end. Also, because of the input of Peter and Trudy Johnson-Lenz, long-time pioneers in the development of computer conference "groupware," facilitated computer consensus building plays a central role in the process of Televoting and throughout the entire ETM.

How Successful Was ETMCo?

At this writing—at the advent of the year 2000—we would say that the ETMCo idea hatched at the 1993 San Francisco conference had a smidgeon of success, albeit not in (yet) attaining its goal to become a profitable and ongoing commercial enterprise dedicated to serving the public interest. Its greatest accomplishment, so far, was in refining the San Francisco model at the Snowmass, Colorado, conference. We believe that this model is by far the most consistent with New Democratic Paradigm thinking. We like to call it a "21st-Century Democratic Political Communications System." It combines all of the successfully tested elements of ETMs—interactive TV, conflict resolution, computer facilitation, and scientific deliberative polling—in a reasonable time frame to produce an extraordinary mix of refined and deliberated public consensus. We have no doubt it would perform well and at a reasonable cost. We will also discuss some of its most promising governmental applications in Chapter 7.

Perhaps its greatest benefit to our journey into teledemocracy and the New Democratic Paradigm, however, was that it kept us working in a movement that, for the time being, was stalled by stiff opposition. ETMCo gave us a base of operations, some direction, and the impetus by which we could continue to promote teledemocracy as the 21st-century system of democratic political communications. Through it, we have made lots of new acquaintances, friends, and colleagues.

However, it was just about that time when something unimagined and unpredicted burst upon the political scene, an ICT development that rocketed everyone into a new dimension of teledemocracy networking—one with which we were just tinkering. It was like being handed electricity after a lifetime of whale oil. This new gadget propelled us beyond ETMs, beyond scientific deliberative polling, and into more broadly defining and promoting teledemocracy. It handed us the means and wherewithal to help synergize what we came to call "the Global Democracy Movement." Best of all, this new break, this source and resource of limitless social energy, required the gratuitous assistance of neither an altruistic trillionaire nor an idealistic politico (two more oxymorons), but guaranteed us rock-solid independence in executing our newly revealed mission.

6

Beyond ETMs: Synergizing Future Teledemocracies via Computers

In Part II, we have been discussing how we—and others—have been experimenting for what seems like ages with a wide range of interactive ICTs to empower citizens in modern representative democracies. The designs and the technologies we personally chose and mixed were all guided by what we understood to be implicit within the New Democratic Paradigm. However, all our excursions were taken prior to the materialization of the fondest dream of even the most ardent advocates of future electronic democracies: personal computers as a self-contained, user-friendly, two-way, lateral, multimedia information and communications system, or, as it is now universally known: the Internet (in its post-1995 reincarnation).

In Chapters 3–5, those interactive ICTs that were the heart and soul of our vision were the old standbys: telephone, the radio, and TV. Computers, when added to our ICT mélange, were—at best—complementary to the more citizen-friendly and omnipresent ones we embedded in our systems. However, this should not be taken as evidence that we thought computers to be unimportant or irrelevant to the future of new paradigm teledemocracy. After all, it was our aim to include those ICTs that empowered *all* citizens. Computers, up to recent days, intimidated the average citizen as much as they cowed us. So for most of our journey into the New Democratic Paradigm, computers did not play a central role.

On the other hand, whenever any computer whiz (or whizzes) wanted to join our enterprises and add computers to the media superstructure, we were routinely amenable. We embraced their efforts within our scheme and let them set things up and run them according to our mutual, teledemocratic theories. So, in the first part of this chapter, we will review several of those experiments, which we designed or advised, that utilized computers as an ICT component within our blueprint.

The second part of this chapter, however, portrays our own personal growth in the age of personal computers. Being denizens of the hollow but hallowed halls of academe since the 1970s, we have been well aware that the Internet was around long before the mid-1990s—when we first began to reap the rewards of its e-mail and Web-browsing properties.

Of course, it was not until early 1995 that Netscape came along and concocted what we call "the New Internet." This transformed the Internet into something not only less daunting to a cyberphobe like Becker, but also into a multimedia contraption that was mesmerizing and powerful. At last, there were: (1) no cards to punch; (2) no trek to the computer lab to pick up print-outs; and (3) no undecipherable codes to commit to memory. All we had to do was point and click. There were no more lengthy, faint, eye-watering texts. Now the content had vibrant colors, classy graphics, and nifty animations to seduce the average citizen into long seances with glowing screens.

The New Internet delivered what had been vaguely promised for so long. If Becker (who still does not know how to program a VCR) could take to it, and enjoy himself to boot, then so could anyone with an IQ and EQ (Emotional Quotient) within two standard deviations from the norm. Since then, the computer has become crucial to our own vision, thinking, design, work, and teledemocratic politics and political science. What follows is the tale of that evolution.

FROM CON-NET TO THE NEW INTERNET

Back in 1977, we first started thinking hard about how to weave together a wide array of theories on participatory democracy. We also understood that if we were truly going to empower citizens at city, state, and national levels of governance, we had to find new ways to use the citizen-friendly ICTs of the time to do that. As good fortune would have it, at that very moment, a rare opportunity came knocking, the very same one that stimulated us to launch Televote (the scientific deliberative poll). However, there is much more to the story that needs telling.

The state of Hawaii, upon becoming the 50th state, held its first state Constitutional Convention (or ConCon) in the late 1950s. The state constitution that emerged included a provision that mandated a highly unusual referendum every 10 years. This automatic referendum was very progressive and equally simple. It asked the citizens whether or not they wanted a new constitutional convention to discuss amending or rewriting the existing constitution. The people could vote thumbs-up or thumbs-down—and if the vote was in the affirmative, then a new constitutional convention (ConCon) would be convened the following year.

Thus, in 1968, a year after the people of Hawaii voted "yea" in the first such referendum, the second Hawaii State ConCon was held—albeit with humble results. Then, in 1977, that same referendum appeared on the ballot, and once again the people voted to reexamine the constitution. Thus, a third ConCon was scheduled for the summer of 1978.

This time, however, many people saw the new ConCon as a golden opportunity for drastic and dramatic change in the ways things were done in Hawaii. After all, this was the mid-late 1970s, shortly after the tumultuous Vietnam War—with all the lies the government had told still fresh in minds of many citizens—and hard on the heels of the Watergate scandal—with all its lies. At this time Hawaii was in the midst of an unchecked and chaotic construction boom that had transformed the main island of Oahu from a sleepy Pacific backwater into the Polynesian kid brother of Los Angeles.

In other words, momentum had gathered for doing *something* about government being out of control—not mere patchwork this time, but crafting systematic and significant alterations deep into the political fabric of the state of Hawaii. With popular suspicion of government and big business at stratospheric levels, there were strong emotions about empowering citizens; making government more accountable; giving the native Hawaiian people more of a say in government; and making sure government did not try to sneak nuclear power into Hawaii, just to name a few. There was also widespread agreement that the delegates who were to be elected to the new ConCon, unlike those who comprised the first two ConCons, should not be members of Hawaii's established political class. They should be just plain everyday Smiths, Takemotos, Wongs, Apos, and so forth.

As we noted in Chapter 3, the tenor of the time also seemed ripe to address another major structural change that had been hotly advocated at the first ConCon, but with scant success. This was to amend the Hawaii state constitution to add the power of citizens initiatives and referenda, that is, to insert direct democracy at the state level. As noted before, this latter proposal became the "hot button issue" of the 1978 ConCon.

The Constitutional Network: Close, But No Cigar

Constitutional conventions are not the optimal vehicle to raise the dander of citizens over politics. After all, for the most part, citizens do not really understand or care much about the basic theory and structure of representative government. How often have you heard department store clerks or TV pundits debate the relative merits of unicameralism vs. bicameralism? And what radio talk show entertains spirited call-ins over whether judges should be appointed, elected, or selected by a "merit system"? Even the issue of whether to bring initiative and referendum to Hawaii—a form of democracy that has proved to be extremely empowering to citizens wherever it exists—was not something to seed and nourish citizen enthusiasm. In fact, all the conventional scientific public opinion polls held in late 1977 and early 1978 showed that a majority of citizens in Hawaii did not have the foggiest clue about what those words meant.

As we described in Chapter 3, one of the ways we decided to tackle this dilemma (how to empower citizens to empower themselves) was our re-invention of Vince Campbell's Televote method of "civic communication" as a scientific deliberative poll. The only electronic technology wired into this process was the telephone. However, a number of people around the University of Hawaii those days were hyping the latent potential of the computer for empowering citizens as well.

Those were the exploratory days of computer conferencing and networking (ARPAnet, Peacenet). Of course, this activity was the almost exclusive preserve of the so-called computer geeks and nerds.[1] They had their intimate networks scattered about the country and the globe and delighted in their monopoly of expertise about how to use this esoteric technology. Most political scientists at the time—certainly including ourselves—were about as familiar or interested in this kind of machinery as we were in ballistic missiles or seismographs.

So, when some of our computer-adoring colleagues started telling us how remarkable it would be to use computers to enlighten the ConCon delegates and also engage citizens in the ConCon, we were skeptical. (Who did they think they were kidding?) But they persisted and the more they waxed eloquent, the more it began to dawn on us that perchance this might work.

Their idea had several facets. First, there was the computer network that would link a number of experts in the fields of political science, constitutional law, nuclear power, the rights of indigenous people, environmental protection, ad infinitum, into a computer conferencing system that we, at the University of Hawaii, would offer pro bono to the various ConCon committees that were supposed to be investigating these subjects. In other words, the forthcoming "Hawaii grass-roots citizens ConCon" would have at its fingertips a 100% absolutely free network of experts who would testify from around the world on any subject dear to the heart of any and all delegates. It certainly sounded like a great bargain. Wasn't this an offer the ConCon could not refuse?

We were convinced that if we could raise the money, it was eminently feasible to set up a system of citizen-conferencing centers around the entire state of Hawaii—at least one on each of the six major islands. In each of these centers we would install a cable TV production and distribution system that would broadcast live the events at the ConCon that day. In addition, we would videotape testimony so that citizens who came to the center could communicate directly with those at the ConCon in downtown Honolulu, but also horizontally with other centers around the state.

But the main feature was that we would also have at least one or more computer terminals in each center, staffed by paid computer experts who would be on hand at all times to help citizens use them for their purposes and at their convenience.

So, people who were keeping abreast of what was happening at the ConCon via the TV, radio, and newspapers would be able to visit these centers to ask questions, provide information, express their opinions, and, yes, even converse with people in other centers around the state on all major issues under consideration. All these remote centers would be connected with the central computer system at the ConCon itself. This would provide a two-way and lateral system of information and opinion exchange between concerned citizens all around the state and could enliven and enrich the hearings and generate and stimulate debate at the ConCon.

Thus, the idea of the Constitutional Network (*Con-Net*) was hatched. The next step was to develop a nonprofit corporation, one that had a community-based board of directors who could help us gain the key financial and political support that was necessary. This was done and Con-Net became a reality.

We then began an extensive public relations campaign that gained us supportive reviews. For example, the *Honolulu Advertiser*, the major morning newspaper in the state, had this to say in a flattering editorial that they titled "ConCon & Openness":

> There are also those who see a much greater potential for using available new technology to, in effect, decentralize the Con-Con—to take the proceedings to the public and also bring the public into the decision-making process . . . a Con-Con is supposed to be an occasion for a serious re-examination of the basic system with an eye to the future, as well as to present problems. *Both public confidence and progressive thinking call for as much openness as possible using the best available technology.* (*Honolulu Advertiser*, March 2, 1977; emphasis ours)

We also sought outside, mainland publicity to help us gain national visibility, which we felt was necessary to attract some financial support.

So, we dispatched our brochure to some progressive outlets and one, the environmentalist magazine *Rain*, gave us some positive publicity as well.

> The Constitutional Network, Inc. (CN) is a private non-profit corporation devoted to establishing an integrated grid of appropriate communications and information technology—a three-way system that will work something like this:
> ... At each of the 21 centers, videotape cameras and production equipment will be available for personal, group and community usage. People in every area will be encouraged, trained and assisted in making issue-oriented statements on videotape. These statements will be played on the second CATV channel—another aspect of the people-to-people exchange.
> ... Each center will also have two computer terminals open for public use. These will be of the typewriter keyboard/TV screen variety, and there will be staff available to help people learn to use them, or to serve those who don't want to learn but who want to help. The computers will be mainly used to establish "computer conferences" between the centers on various issues. But best of all, citizens will be able to plug into the conference by staying at home and calling into the center in their area.
> ... What is more, since the computer network will be hooked into national (and international) sources, CN will be able to provide research and informational assistance to all interested citizens on any and all issues. The citizen can either go to the center near him or pick up the phone and make a request. ("The Constitutional Network" 1978, 10)

What happened thereafter is instructive. Despite the practicality and affordability of the design, plus a $25,000 grant from the Office of the President of the University of Hawaii to breathe life into the computer-expert conferencing system (as well as the new Televote poll), plus excellent publicity at home and abroad, the collective leadership of the 1978 Hawaii State Constitutional Convention declined to accept our gift.

We had simply requested a room at the building in which the ConCon was being held so that we could install our computers and staff—free of charge—and service the needs of any delegate or ConCon committee that might wish to utilize the skill and knowledge of a long roster of experts who had registered as computer-consultants in our system. Although they did provide a special room to us for the Televote poll results to be collated and hand-delivered to the delegates in their offices, the answer was "no" to Con-Net. Why? No reasons were tendered. We could only surmise that expert opinion on such issues, even when costless and priceless, was not something the leadership thought was important to the deliberative process of the 1978 "citizens" ConCon.

As for the 21-center part of the plan, despite a concerted effort by the board of directors that produced and distributed literature and video-tapes that described our system; appeared as speakers at pre-ConCon panels and workshops and before community and neighborhood boards; and presented our views on radio and TV, "not one funding source could be tapped in Hawaii or throughout the United States to foot the bill for this experiment" (Becker 1978, 300). Not a single soul in Hawaii state government offered to help. So, in terms of making this dreaam of a two-way, lateral system of information and communication between the citizens and government in Hawaii come true, we did not get to first base. However, as the article in *Rain* concluded: "By developing the idea, establishing the corporation, distributing information about it, and ad-dressing various civic and community organizations, the Constitutional Network is dramatically raising consciousness about the dangers in our present political system and is presenting a real alternative" ("The Con-stitutional Network" 1978, 10). For the time being, we had to be satisfied with that.

Alaska Proves Our Point

Little did we know that a nearly identical experimental system was actually being tested in the other non-contiguous American state, Alaska, at much the same time (1978–82). Called the Alaska Legislative Telecon-ference Network (LTN), it operated in a similar fashion to what Con-Net had envisioned. Fourteen centers around Alaska were linked to the capitol. Each installed computers in them to interact with state officials, legislators, and/or congressmen via a two-way computer teleconference.

This system (LTN) proved to be immensely effective and popular. By way of example, in the first four years it was in operation, *citizen usage doubled each year*. Additionally, follow-up surveys revealed a high level of user satisfaction, for example, approximately 75% used the system more than once. This is known as voting with one's feet. It is a far better indicator of satisfaction than anything users might say about how grat-ified they were. Furthermore, about 75% told the interviewers that they were able to express themselves "very well" via the computer.[2]

Indeed, the system proved to be such an efficient, interactive tool be-tween legislators and constituents that the state legislature subsequently decided to add a videoconferencing capability to it—making it close to a carbon copy of the system we proposed in the Constitutional Network. Thus, the biggest difference in these two projects was that in one state (Alaska) there was tremendous foresight, a spirit of innovation, and a willingness to invest capital to achieve such a vision among those with power—while in the other (Hawaii), there was a total lack of each.

It was not until well after the Hawaii ConCon had concluded that we learned of the success of the Alaskan experiment. Such news elated us because we realized just how well our system would have worked in Hawaii if we had obtained even a modicum of help from anyone with dollars or political power. What a strange twist of fate that an Alaskan team would validate our hypotheses at the same time we could not raise the money to test them. Any doubts we had about its workability were answered affirmatively by the Alaskan experiment.

Southern California Association of Governments (SCAG) and the Los Angeles Televote: The Next Stage in Our Evolution

Our next brush with computer conferencing came indirectly through our role as advisors on the Los Angeles Televote project sponsored by the Southern California Association of Governments (SCAG) in 1982. We had just completed our first two experiments integrating the Hawaii Televote method of scientific deliberative polling in two Electronic Town Meeting projects, New Zealand Televote (at the national level) and the Honolulu Electronic Town Meeting (at the city and county level). We had learned that putting a scientific deliberative survey at the core of an ETM worked quite well—by helping keep the random sample involved over time and helping attract large numbers of citizens into the discussion and deliberative process via the use of many multimedia techniques that were coordinated with the Televote process.

During one of our lectures on this at the University of Hawaii, a graduate student in the Alternative Future Studies Program named Kirk Bergstrom approached us. He said that he was going to work for a member of the Los Angeles City Council (Pat Russell) and that she was very interested in new methods of teledemocracy to involve citizens more directly in important governmental decisions. Russell was also the president of the Southern California Association of Governments (SCAG), which, as we noted in Chapter 3, was looking for novel ways to inject public input into a number of "hard choices" they had to make about the upcoming Los Angeles Summer Olympic Games of 1984. Bergstrom asked for our permission to replicate our Televote-ETM model for SCAG. We agreed. Becker and Jim Dator, the political scientist who also played a key role in the Honolulu Electronic Town Meeting Project, were invited to serve in an advisory capacity on the project. They lent their expertise throughout the project.

Essentially, Bergstrom used virtually the exact same model we developed in our Constitutional Network, New Zealand Televote, and Honolulu Electronic Town Meeting projects (the same elements included in the "comprehensive ETM" model developed years later at the Fort Mason conference). The key features in Los Angeles Televote, once again, were a Televote scientific deliberative poll at the core; interactive TV and interactive radio; newspapers that ran stories and Televote-style surveys that solicited input from self-selected samples of their readership; and so forth.

One key addition to the mix that Bergstrom added was a computer-teleconferencing system that included a large database. The database was accessible to those who participated in the computer teleconference—an item that uncannily foresaw how informed deliberations could be carried out in the future on the New Internet.

Consider Bergstrom's contribution to the LA Televote model in light of the ETMCo model developed many years later:

> The Los Angeles Televote ballot was made available to Los Angeles residents on The Source computer data base. . . .The Televote ballot was entered . . . as an interactive file, meaning computer users could read about the ten Televote issues and then register their votes and add comments via their computer terminal. The idea was to stimulate an electronically annotated exchange between users in which participants could not only respond to the ten proposed questions, but also to the comments and suggestions of others.
>
> . . . In addition to television, computer networks appear to be particularly well suited to two-way political communication. Large amounts of information on issues can be filed, and citizens can access, interact with and respond to this information at their leisure. (Southern California Association of Governments 1983, 8)

The results of this experiment were phenomenal in a number of ways. First, SCAG used the results to help set up several plans to control traffic at the Los Angeles games, all of which helped reduce traffic at that time to relatively normal ranges. Second, four of the items on the Televote brochure were actual citizens initiative ballot issues. The opinions of the Televoters in the survey, aided and abetted by the entire ETM process under way at the time, fell within $+/- 2\%$ to 4% in predicting the actual, final vote during the election. This is all the more surprising since there were only 400 Televoters—a number that only promises a level of $+/- 5\%$ accuracy in ordinary polls.

Despite the success of utilizing computers for citizen interaction in the Alaska LTN and Los Angeles Televote experiments—as well as successes elsewhere—we still did not begin to appreciate computer teleconferencing as an essential ingredient in the ETM mélange until the 1994 Snowmass, Colorado conference. It was there, with the help of some new collaborators, that we began to grasp the full potential of computers in the Televote scientific deliberative polling process.

The ETMCo Design: The Televoter-Computer Dynamic

By the time we assembled our ETMCo group at Snowmass, we were quite certain where computers fit in our model. As a source of reasoned discussion and communications, they were in the secondary discussion circle—along with interactive TV, radio talk shows, self-selected polling, and the like. In other words, they were to be part of the general consciousness raising about the issue at hand, but were tangential to the deliberative processes of the scientific sample(s) at the hub of the ETMCo process.

We were somewhat familiar with the work of Peter and Trudy Johnson-Lenz, but it was not until this conference that we closely worked together. As we noted in Chapter 5, they, too, had been experimenting with novel teledemocratic practices since the mid-1970s. Unlike us, however, their expertise was with computers as a communications device.

The major focus of their work over the years utilized the computer as an instrument to help groups arrive at a consensus on resolving complex problems. They had developed software (which they copyrighted as "Groupware") that would help such groups sort through information, ideas, and shifting positions over time with the help of professional facilitators. They had been using the Internet for years to host their unique computer conferencing techniques and had successfully applied their theories and processes in many different kinds and sizes of groups and venues.

During one intense meeting of the design group, the Johnson-Lenzes made it clear to us that computer conferencing had a much more decisive role to play in the emerging ETMCo model than we had originally foreseen. After all, although the Televote model we developed from 1978 to 1985 had improved over time, it still had some weaknesses—particularly if it was to become part of such an advanced system of ETMs as was projected by this new design group.

Perhaps its major shortcoming was that it would be a static process in the midst of a very dynamic and changing opinion-forming environment. As we had structured the Televote process, the Televoters receive a printed brochure in the mail and have time to think about their opinion, plugging themselves into the outside discussion if and when they choose. Then they fill out the questionnaire and we collect the results.

But what if they want new information relevant to their concerns? What if they participate in their own personal discussions and hear new options they prefer over the ones already printed in the Televote brochure? With the model we developed, nothing could be done about that.

They had to answer the questions provided in the brochure—which they received at the start of the deliberation process. Those were the rules of the Televote game: no change of mind was possible; no fresh alternatives could be considered; and there was no facilitation of the Televote process itself. The "core" of the ETMCo process, then, would be a rigid scientific deliberative survey in the midst of many mediated discussion processes that would be unearthing new data and fresh ideas about how to resolve the issue(s) under scrutiny. The Televote process needed to be updated and renovated to fit into a more dynamic and fluid outside environment.

The Johnson-Lenzes had incorporated themselves as The Institute of Awakening Technology and they were true to their name. If what we needed was a way to help the Televoters evolve their thinking about the issues themselves or among themselves, then why not via computer support for collaborative work and decision making, or what they call "computer augmented dialogues," the essence of the Johnson-Lenz formula (Johnson-Lenz 1992, 1)?

Of course, very few of the Televoters in 1994 would have PCs in their house or access to them at work—since they were a representative sample of the population. But we were developing models for the future—for 21st-century teledemocracy—when it was possible that computers would be as omnipresent in living rooms as TV sets.

But what about the interim period—when very few Televoters would be "online"? Several ideas were brainstormed. The main one, part of the ETMCo model, went something along the following lines.

If we could have computer experts staff remote centers—as in the Constitutional Network or the Alaska LTN—why could we not have a computer-resource team collaborate with the Televote staff to interface with the Televoters? In other words, we could have a team of experts and/or ordinary citizens who were online to have informed, facilitated discussions on the issue(s) at hand and then have the Televote staff update the Televoters at home on the progress of that discussion. The new Televote brochures would have to leave room for flexibility—for new alternative solutions—to accommodate shifts in the discussion and changes of alternatives and minds. Another possibility was to have the Televote staff itself be computer experts who would play a dual role and themselves interface the computer conference with the Televoters. All of these additions would meet the prerequisites for sound "teledemocratic" practice advanced subsequently by two Finnish experts on this subject: "Citizens should not only react to preselected information but as the teledemocratic discussion proceeds, they should be able to create new alternatives and redirect the whole process, if needed" (Savolainen and Anttiroiko 1999, 41).

When we left the Snowmass conference in October 1994, we were convinced that any future ETM-Televote project needed computers at the

Televote core. We assigned them that location in the new, advanced ETMCo model—which we saw as the ultimate multi-interactive system to advance citizen empowerment via the New Democratic Paradigm. What we did not foresee was the leading role computers would come to play in catalyzing a global teledemocracy movement of which we (and our experiments) were but one small part. We also did not realize then that computers would become the principal instrument in changing our role in the evolution of global teledemocracy.

THE "NEW" INTERNET AND THE NEW DEMOCRATIC PARADIGM: TELEDEMOCRACY ACTION NEWS + NETWORK (TAN+N)

It was not until mid-1995, though, that the computer-communication revolution caught up with us, or, it might be better to say, that we finally caught up with it. Our first personal plunge into the science-fiction communications capability of the computer was via e-mail. Until then, we were burdened by the limitations of "snail mail," fax, private couriers, and telephone as the major ICTs to send messages and text to colleagues and compatriots. But e-mail was entirely different—allowing us to transmit messages and text cheaply, instantaneously with a flick of a forefinger to innumerable colleagues around the world.

The main breakthrough, however, came around the springtime of 1995 when Netscape developed its unprecedented browser system that added color, graphics, audio, and video to Web sites and offered this captivating array of choices to anyone to "surf" around the Web with ease. An infinite technicolored vista of information and communication dawned. Better yet, this new system allowed just about anyone to set up his or her own full-service Web site. All of a sudden, we realized that with just a little help, we could become multimedia producers in our own right and that we were at the threshold of a universal, blink-of-an-eye electronic distribution system.

The Unique Properties of the Web

There has never been anything like this New Internet. This is the first time in the pockmarked history of humankind that a system of mass telecommunications has had (1) *no owners*—neither capitalist nor state; and (2) *no gatekeepers*—no station managers, no editors, no pyramid of authority. This new global system of interactive ICT was absolutely, totally, 100% *uncontrollable and chaotic.* You could "publish" anything you wanted or even create a "virtual movement" if you had a personal computer (PC), a modem, and some knowledge of Hyper Text Markup Language (HTML)—or knew a colleague learned in that language who was willing to lend you a hand and mind. With those assets as capital investment, anyone could "share" in all the fonts, graphics, colors, and animations that were already on the Web as well as the global system of distribution.

With all this freely available, all you had to do was design the "Web site," including whatever content your heart desired, FTP (send) it to your server (which was free if you happened to be a professor at a university that provided it to you)—and you reserved an immortal presence in cyberspace. Better yet, each dwelling in this parallel universe is as equally easy to discover or reach as anyone else's—including such political economic mastedons as global corporations, global NGOs, national political parties, national or state governments, and so forth. In this sense, all Web sites are equal. Type in the URL (Uniform Resource Locator)—the Internet address for the Web site—and you are magically transported to the "homepage" of your choice.

Having your own Web site, plus the e-mail function of the Web, constructs a perfect bilateral, multilateral, multimedia smorgasbord of telecommunications, where you can help yourself to illustrated text, huge data bases, audios, and videos. Moreover, your Web site is automatically reachable by citizens armed with the prerequisite arsenal (PC and modem)—of which there were already approximately 100 million users worldwide in 1999 and estimates of 320 million users by 2002.

TAN+N: Synergy as the Primary Mission

At long last, the computer had become the indispensible vehicle on our journey into the New Democratic Paradigm. It would now permit us to convey our ideas and experimental data sans the drawbacks of traditional publishing (entreating publishers; haggling with editors; hoping some professors decide to foist our book on their captive audiences, in other words, students; about a year's time lag for publication; and third-rate promotion). It would let us reach a much broader audience and encourage all kinds of people all over the world to question us or contact us about our ideas at their whim. At last, what we wrote and cyberpublished would not be fated for special delivery to a few hundred dingy, musty, out-of-the-way book graveyards called university libraries.

But what should we put into the Web site, what should we call it? If we followed the trend set by most people or organizations, we would have put our names on the cybermarquee, something like the "Ted Becker and Christa Daryl Slaton Web Site." Or, if we wanted to shine the spotlight on our own work, it might have been best to call it "The Televote Web Site" or "The Electronic Town Meeting Web Site." Actually, none of these crossed our minds.

Perhaps it was our recent experience collaborating on designing the comprehensive ETM models in San Francisco and Snowmass. Interacting with so many people as dedicated as ourselves to helping develop a more citizen-directed democracy was encouraging. It was also exhilarating to find out we were part of some kind of "teledemocracy group"— people thinking along the same lines but with so many different perspectives, talents, and experiences. We had begun to see that we were, after all, just one segment of a more encompassing movement. This did not mean that our own work, our own theory, had to take a backseat to anyone else's. It meant that we were beginning to locate ourselves in a different position, one that was linked to others and contributed to an enormous network of teledemocratic theorists, researchers, and activists.

So, when one of our colleagues at Auburn University, Charles Spindler, who was already heavily experimenting with the New Internet, kept urging us to establish a Web site, the first thing that occurred to us was to make it a generalized one, one that was not specific to our pet projects, but one that would promote and link them to all the other work we had encountered in recent years. It seemed only natural that the Web site's conceptual umbrella had to cover all authentic teledemocratic projects from around the world.

The other principal feature that had to characterize our Web site also was clear. This Web site could not just be an information and data base about teledemocracy and the New Democratic Paradigm. It should be used—consistent with the exciting, new properties of the New Internet— as a communications and organizational center. The Web site had to not only link our work with compatriots electronically and stay in touch on a regular basis, but most of all, it had to give us the wherewithal to organize—and synergize—projects with like-minded people around the world, in real time, on a time delay basis, or both simultaneously. Bucky Fuller, Erich Fromm, and Hazel Henderson were right. A new form of electronic democracy was going to be the wave of the future and it was going to be facilitated by something that they could only imagine: that fortuitous invention called the "Internet."

In retrospect, it seems to us that the dearth of communication and cooperation among the emerging teledemocratic community had been at least as difficult a stumbling block to overcome as was the implacable resistance of old paradigm political and media elites. Why was there so little communication and collaboration among us? In its most malignant form, it was the triumph of egotistic researchers trying to outdo others— boasting how our way of empowering citizens was the best or first. In its most benign form, we labored with blinders on, in blissful ignorance of the progress of others. Each person or group, though, preached to congregations of disbelievers about how their own unusual experiments and extraordinary thinking were the way to the promised land of a more virtuous representative democracy. But what the outside world beheld were solitary missionaries—standing alone—which diminished the power of their message.

What if we had known of the Alaska LTN when we were advancing the cause of the Constitutional Network—and vice versa? What if we had been cognizant of the work being done by Ned Crosby at the Jefferson Center in Minneapolis and of Peter Dienel's work on his *Planungszelles* in Wuppertal, Germany, when we were developing the Televote method of polling? The results they were finding and accumulating reinforced everything we said and tried to do. If nothing else, knowing all this was occurring in so many places around the world would have given us all an extra psychic boost and a sense of transcending ourselves, being part of an international transformational movement.

Of course, all sciences develop in much the same way. Several cutting-edge experiments often are being conducted at approximately the same time and in much the same way. The development of the science is often hindered by classic egomania and traditional modes of communication. That was one reason the Internet was developed in the first place. The U.S. Department of Defense could see that independent university- and institute-based researchers under contract on a wide variety of weapons systems were being hampered by not knowing what was going on in their research area by other researchers working on other parts of inter-related systems. So, the computer communication network was designed to speed things up and to synergize the completion and refinement of these systems by sharing new techniques, data, and analysis in a super-compressed time frame.

Why, then, couldn't the New Internet be used in like fashion to accelerate research and action designed to further the realization of the New Democratic Paradigm? Furthermore, this information could be shared and synergized not only among the action theorists and experimenters themselves, but also with those people in the general population who harbored similar values and ideas.

It became clear to us that the New Internet was a marvelous engine to promote—and hopefully increase the momentum and velocity of—the entire global movement devoted to transforming representative democracies into much more citizen-accountable systems and self-governance, particularly through the use of contemporary ICT. What was right in front of our eyes was an imminently reachable worldwide cybernetwork of teledemocratic centers and projects.

That is why we decided to name the Web site *The Teledemocracy Action News + Network* (www.auburn.edu/tann) and why we gave it the motto: "The Website of the Global Democracy Movement." Thus, the New Internet had not only advanced our work in conceiving better teledemocratic systems for future use and applications, it had added a whole new sense of purpose for our work as at least two network coordinators.

THE THEORETICAL AND INFORMATIONAL
COMPONENTS OF TAN+N: REFORMIST TO
TRANSFORMATIONAL

Since our aim was to boost this new global democracy into cyberorbit, we knew we had to be forthright about the theory and ideology that guided TAN+N. By declaring the concepts and values inherent in the New Democratic Paradigm—and what we meant by teledemocracy—we would be able to distinguish this Web site from many others (that might sound the same) and decide which projects and people we would include and exclude.

Thus, as the first order of cyberbusiness, we posted two editorials proclaiming our prodemocratic values and that our cardinal aim was to transform (not merely reform) representative democracies primarily through electronic telecommunications technologies and systems. In these editorials we were candid about the salience and significance of what we called "genuine" and "authentic" citizen-empowerment projects. We defined those to include projects where citizens actually made a difference in governmental decision making and its outcome, or which were designed to change a political system so that citizens could directly impact on either their representatives or on the administration of laws.

The TAN+N Evaluation System: Separating Cyberwheat
from Cyberchaff

Thus, we reserved the right to ignore and avoid as "un-newsworthy" a type of cyberpolitics that we consider to be the cyberchaff of cyberspace. These are the Web sites of big-money political candidates, mainstream parties, or establishment special interest groups—where there is a motherlode of information about the candidates or parties and e-mail access to them. Sites like this are not part of TAN+N because they are, in our view, cyberpolitics-as-usual. And since politics-as-usual, in our view, is dis-empowering to say the least, emulating it on the Web does not change anything for the better. Actually, such Web sites are akin to public relations—they aim to shore-up, reinforce, and *cyberlegitimize* a system that specializes in creating the "necessary illusions" so vital to the status quo. They aim to co-opt and appease.

A second tactic to make this Web site into an effective transformational cyberagency was to deter the legions of true believers who might think TAN+N had something to do with the mainstream, humdrum party and electoral charade that is all over the Web. One way to accomplish this was to limit the unobtrusive cybercues that advertise our site to search engine robots scouring the web to "Teledemocracy," "Direct Democracy," "Televote," "Electronic Democracy," "Electronic Town Meetings," "Deliberative Polling," and "Citizen Empowerment."

Our explicit goal, given our paltry resources, was for light traffic. We sought only those who were genuinely interested in or intrigued by the work we were doing and promoting. We think we have been quite successful at that because in five years we have had over 30,000 "hits" or visits. We have also received an outpouring of moral support; generous offers to link our site with other sites; earnest and incisive questions about how to treat a wide variety of problems concerning teledemocracy; offers to help us out or to ask us for help; an avalanche of invitations to conferences and cyberconferences; and a surfeit of information about like-minded projects. We have more than we can handle. In fact, when we get e-(junk)-mail solicitations from Web companies promising to triple the traffic on our site, we make a beeline to the delete button.

The third technique we used to crystalize the theory and ideology that was the foundation of this Web site was our "rating system." We decided to award up to six degrees of "citizen empowerment" to each and every project we included in the site's database—with one blue and gold lightning bolt being equal to each degree of empowerment. In our system, one bolt equals the least empowering and six is the most. Actually, there are three levels of empowerment, each with two degrees of separation within it.

The bottom level of citizen empowerment is "Reformist," which gets either one or two bolts. This indicated that—to our way of thinking—the experiment or project improves the role of the citizens within the present parameters of the representative democratic system a trifle or a bit. If a project gives citizens valuable information about how their representatives think or vote or affords voters an opportunity to talk with officials online or provides them a cyberlobbying service, it helps empower citizens a tad. Citizens can now be better and more effective actors within the present system. In our view, that makes the project first-degree "Reformist," which rates one bolt.

Second-degree "reformism" actually alters the present system slightly in some way that makes it more effective within its own frayed theory and ideology. So, one of the embarrassing problems in modern representative democracy is the declining interest in voting, which helps make the demographics ever more tilted toward older, richer, whiter, and more conservative voters. Some of the projects included in TAN+N are designed to make the balloting process more voter friendly in order to swell and equalize the voting population (1) by inducing more people to vote and (2) lengthening the voting process to give people more time to think about for whom they want to vote.

A good illustration of this is the state of Oregon, where the electorate recently voted (in a citizens initiative) to give themselves the power to vote by mail over several weeks. This improves the present system by making it more convenient and less intimidating to citizens. In a special election a few years ago that used this method, an all-time record was set for an electoral turnout in Oregon, and it was half as expensive to operate as the traditional ballot box and/or voting machine method. (True to form, this impressive turnabout in citizen interest and government efficiency was barely mentioned in the mainstream mass media.)

Another example of a two-bolter was how the Liberal party of Nova Scotia (Canada), Conservative party of Saskatchewan (Canada), and Reform party (United States) all allowed registered voters in their party to vote for their preferred party leader by telephone after watching televised nominating speeches at their party's convention. This increased the quantity and quality of ordinary citizen participation in an important party affair—again bolstering the present party system's method of picking leaders—by making structural changes in how things were done within that system. In our rating system, these kinds of projects are worth two lightning bolts. They do afford citizens a better shot at influencing who rules, but that is all. This becomes a more important kind of systemic change if (and when) it becomes commonplace in citizens referenda and initiatives (to be discussed in Chapter 7).

Projects in the middle category, "Transforming Representative Democracy," score higher on our empowerment scale because they are intended to and actually change the power equation between the citizenry and their government. They do this primarily by constructing new ways to make citizen opinion *impact government*. In other words, they do more than help the party system or provide more/better information and communication and discussion between citizens and government and/or make it easier to vote. They either influence governmental decision making directly or indirectly (three bolts) or compel governmental compliance with the wishes of the public (four bolts).

Examples of the former are the scientific deliberative polls in the United Kingdom and Germany (described in Chapter 3) where direct influence on official decision making was expected by the public, the participants, the press, and to a large degree, the government agencies involved. Another illustration was the Honolulu Electronic City Council Hearing that we described in Chapter 4—where direct influence was neither welcome nor expected.

An excellent example of a four-bolter was an experiment performed by the Reform party of Canada. This was a real-life application of the "Choosing Our Future" type of scientific deliberative TV poll, also described in Chapter 4. Michael Hollinshead, the leading Canadian consultant on teledemocracy, helped design this extraordinary project where five Reform party MPs (members of the Canadian national Parliament) from the Calgary area publicly agreed to be bound by the results of this experiment under certain conditions.

First, they recruited a random sample of Televoters from each of the five parliamentary districts they represented. Each of the Televoters in the five districts agreed to watch and vote in a live TV ETM on the issue of "physician-assisted suicide in Canada." These ETMs were conducted with a live studio audience. The format included documentary films on the subject; a discussion among experts present in the ETM studio on the subject; and questions and discussion among those in the studio audience—all of which was moderated by a well-known TV personality in the Calgary area.

Second, during the ETM a variety of questions on the topic were flashed on the TV screen to the viewing audience, but especially to the Televoters across the Calgary area for their consideration and vote. When the Televoters called on their dedicated lines, the scientific deliberative polling results were then shown in colorful graphics for everyone at home and in the audience to see, including, of course, the five MPs.

After the ETM concluded, there was an overwhelming majority of Televoters (about 70%) who favored changing the law to permit doctors in Canada to help terminally ill people end their excruciating pain, albeit under several clearly ennumerated preconditions that were all an integral part of the ETM discussion. In addition, other conventional scientific polls and mail-in ballots from constituents pretty much showed that this sentiment was widely shared among those who lived in the Calgary area, including the representative sample in the ETM. Thus, the five MPs— each of whom was personally opposed to permitting physicians to write this kind of lethal prescription—restated their public vow to vote as their constituents wished when that issue came to the floor in the Canadian Parliament. Naturally, since the ruling Liberal party was (and remains) programmatically opposed to such a revision of Canadian criminal law, such a proposal has not seen the light of day to this time, despite the high probability that a national ETM on this subject would lead to a similar result (according to most conventional scientific polls conducted in Canada). As we have repeatedly shown throughout this book, alleged "representatives" of the people are much too bogged down in old paradigm thinking and their self-serving party politics to defer even to clearly demarcated and precisely calibrated desires of a well-informed, avidly concerned, and (at least an equally) moral public.

The highest ratings in TAN+N are awarded to projects we consider "Transformational"—in other words, those that help representative democracies evolve into more direct democratic forms or that shield the direct democratic aspects of a system against attacks that would cripple its use and usefulness. Thus, a five-bolt project is ETMCo. The reason for this lofty ranking is that both the intent and the process itself are to craft the most democratic form of political communications humanly and technologically possible. Although the ETMCo process could be used to reinforce the representative system, its main purpose is to be a transitional use of ICT, which would work best when plugged into more direct forms of democracy—as we will show in Chapter 7.

Organizations that are actively involved in the real, tumultuous world of politics—including the politics of cyberspace—and that practice direct democratic politics win the six-bolt accolade. A superb example of this is the Initiative and Referendum Institute (IRI) in Washington, D.C. (www.iandr.com), which wins six bolts hands-down. This organization commits the lion's share of its resources to political and legal strategies and tactics whose intent is either to (1) expand citizens initiatives into states where they are not yet permitted or (2) defend citizens' rights to invoke the initiative process in court against political pressures from politicians whose intent is to curtail this right.

We think it is important to note that IRI has majority representation on its board of directors from that corner usually considered—in the American political spectrum—as being "very conservative." Its director, M. Dane Waters, however, is quick to note that in his view, the initiative and referendum process is neither partial to the Left nor the Right in its usage or degree of success. Much evidence from around the world backs him up on that. Thus, in an conference celebrating the 100th anniversary of citizens initiatives in America that IRI hosted in Washington, D.C., in May of 1999, a panoply of "liberals," "conservatives," "radicals," and "moderates" were in colorful display on the panels.

Another group that rates the six-bolt honor is one that has its homepage on TAN+N. This is the International Congress on Direct Democracy—founded in Prague, the Czech Republic, in the summer of 1998. This "virtual organization" is devoted to promoting all aspects of direct democracy throughout the world by publicizing, supporting, and being part of any kind of development along these lines. It produces a newsletter (in part online); maintains an e-mail membership list that anyone can access individually or collectively; posts a message board that has attracted a great deal of discussion on a number of topics related to global direct democracy; publishes up-to-date news on developments in the movement; organizes regular bi-annual conferences (the second will be in Athens in June 2000); and synergizes collective projects among the membership, ranging from co-authored books to fund-raising campaigns.

How Successful Is TAN+N?

From our point of view, TAN+N has been an unqualified success, particularly since it is almost entirely a voluntary organization with few resources to keep its motors going. Its avowed goal, as we have stated above, has been to help galvanize a broad movement throughout the world dedicated to instituting or expanding on what we believe to be teledemocratic and direct democratic processes. Our objective has been to bring academics, activists, and political leaders together. We know we have made substantial progress toward achieving this goal. There are numerous ways in which inventors and direct democratic activists have come together on or via TAN+N. And, from our unique vantage point, we see exponential growth both in size and momentum.

We also are particularly pleased by the degree of interest and/or curiosity of ordinary citizens from around the world who come into the Web site for information, to clarify their thinking, looking for support for individual projects, and/or seeking to work with or join up with some of the organizations represented on TAN+N or to help TAN+N itself. From the time we went up on the Web, we have had no dry spell. Our average number of visits per day is approximately 15 to 20. Our average number of "hits" to our homepage is roughly 450 to 550 per month. Our annual total is somewhere in the range of 5,000 to 6,500.

We realize that these statistics are pitiful compared with those amassed by *Playboy* magazine, the CNN Web site, or what even a pint-sized city government attracts. Moreover, we suspect that as a political informational and organizational device, we get much less usage than a run-of-the-mill "hate" group in America or elsewhere. None of this detracts from the fact that TAN+N, rated as being among the top 5% of all Web sites in the world by Lycos—a leading web search engine—successfully promotes "teledemocracy" and the New Democratic Paradigm. These are not concepts in normal political discourse anywhere in the world—in politics, in government, in the media, in universities, in cybercafes or coffeehouses, in academic conferences, in kitchens and living rooms, or around water coolers and office coffee machines—yet!

Nevertheless, in the time span from August 1998 to August 1999, TAN+N had visitors from 70 nations and approximately 6,000 hits altogether. This is far more attention than most academic books ever receive. Without TAN+N would many thousands of people worldwide be familiar with the growth of global scientific deliberative polling? Hardly.

It must be remembered that TAN+N is only a toddler—just as the New Democratic Paradigm is in a prolonged infancy. The debate is yet to be joined. The synergy between the components is only beginning to occur. The Web site is playing its role, sparking the kind of energy for which it was planned and constructed and is reconstituted on a regular basis. We have come to see it as an instrument that in its own way is helping form that "critical mass" of teledemocracy that will catalyze a quantum leap in the future acceptance of New Democratic Paradigm political science, conventional political thinking, and everyday political life in the 21st century.

In the final part of this book, we will try to put all those teledemocratic and direct democratic components together—most of which are in TAN+N—and demonstrate how they seem to be gaining in power and cross-fertilization. We will also discuss how we see them being applied, potentially, in the future. In the meantime, TAN+N will continue reporting on these developments, adding new ones as they happen and helping involve more and more citizens around the world in the development of all aspects of the New Democratic Paradigm. To keep updated, just keep logging on.

NOTES

1. Computer experts themselves use and define these concepts. "Geek is a subset of nerd. They are all technical people, but in general, geeks are closer to the hardware." This definition can be found in "Questions for Robert X. Cringely," *New York Times Magazine*, November 22, 1998, p. 25.

2. Actually, this is extraordinarily similar data to the seminal research by Amitai Etzioni on electronic deliberation over the telephone in his famous "Minerva Project" experiments in the early 1970s. See Amitai Etzioni, Kenneth Laudon, and Sara Lipson, "Participatory Technology: The MINERVA Communications Tree," *Journal of Communications* (Spring 1975): 64–74.

PART III

The New Democratic Paradigm in the 21st Century: Another Step in the Right Direction

So how is the future of teledemocracy taking shape? Given the indisputable fact that no one can know definitely what is going to happen in her or his own personal life—even by the next morning—why fret about the macro-political world circa A.D. 2025? Isn't this pure, unadulterated gall, a colossal waste of time?

After all, who in 1899, the culmination of the past century, could have imagined the ghastly or pleasant surprises that awaited humankind on the peaks and in the valleys of the 20th century:

- World War I;
- The collapse of international capitalism and the global depression in the 1930s;
- World War II and the Holocaust;
- A decades-long cold war and nuclear stalemate between capitalism and world communism;
- The emergence of the European welfare state and social democracies;
- Dalliances with world governance (League of Nations; United Nations; New World Order).

No one. So, why try reading the tea leaves of the 21st century before the tea has been brewed?

One of the inherent problems in such forecasting is that no one can foretell what kind of catastrophes are in store for the human species in the coming decades. We have said earlier in this book, several times, that we see democracy as the *normal* wave of the future. Of course we cannot prove that, or be certain that such will always hold true, even if that had actually been the case throughout human history. Some entirely new abnormalities might becalm the wave of democracy for centuries to come. More likely, though, that wave can be disrupted or even divert by some great calamity or series of them.

Historian L. S. Stavrianos discussed the possibilities of a vast, lengthy civil unrest about 20 years ago in his book *The Promise of the Coming Dark Age* (1976). He observed then that many of the most intractable problems we face today are really holdovers from days of yore, for example, "war, hunger, racism, ignorance" (Stavrianos 1976, vii). But there were several modern developments, when added to the ancient ones, that he saw as combining to cause general global desolation and destitution in the near future. These included "(1) economic imperialism; (2) ecological degradation; (3) bureaucratic ossification; (4) a flight from reason" (Stavrianos 1976, 7). Like many others today, Stavrianos foresaw that our present technologically dependent systems are neither economically nor ecologically sustainable at the present rate of growth, and that strife and pestilence were likely to once again settle over much of the Earth's surface. In his view, even such a devastating prospect did not toll the death knell for democracy.

In point of fact, Stavrianos thought just the opposite would occur. From his take on history, even if a series of political-economic-environmental cyclones lash our planet for years on end, salvation will not result from regressing into highly authoritarian and hierarchical systems presided over by the usual suspects.

The main reason for this is that the intellectual, scientific, and technological achievements of recent times have empowered far too many people to be reversed. According to Stavrianos, "the historical record shows that . . . each major technological breakthrough in the past has been accompanied by a corresponding breakthrough in mass assertiveness and participation rather than by mass subjugation and submissiveness" (Stavrianos 1976, 2). Moreover, these recent gains in individual and collective human empowerment are being shared globally and are not the exclusive preserve of one or a few societies. Stavrianos also states that "the current technological revolution, like the earlier ones, is leading not to a new age of the pharaohs but to greater self-knowledge on the part of humanity. The long process of popular awakening is now reaching its culmination with the twentieth century demand for self-management in all phases of life" (Stavrianos 1976, 24).

Democracy, moreover, is as much a part of human anatomy as autocracy. It is part of humanity's political DNA. When conditions are favorable, it flourishes. When not, it flounders. In some cultures, it is a dominant gene. In others, it is recessive. But it is somewhere in the genetic code. At this point in the development of humanity, with what now appears to be the inevitable forward march of ICT, we feel confident that the 21st century will be ripe for the continued growth of democracy—especially in those cultures where it is dominant and, in them, there will be new and bold bursts of teledemocracy. As for the others, there will be sporadic or incremental gains and a random quantum leap here or there.

In keeping with this line of thought, then, even if there is a present or future major setback due to technological/economic/ecological failures—with incalculable human suffering from Patagonia to Pittsburgh and from Micronesia to Malta—the world will not grovel at the feet of some heroic figure in his gleaming jet who will scapegoat and carpet-bomb other cultures. Instead, people around the world will take matters into their own hands—using decentralized technologies and techniques at local and community levels—to survive for a while and then proliferate anew. New, more appropriate ICTs can be used to help extricate humanity from any quagmire by connecting and supporting diverse communities.

Blame for any human-made disasters may properly be laid at the feet of those who caused them—the owners, managers, or directors of the massive systems that malfunctioned and misfired. Hierarchies will more than likely fall into greater disrepute and nascent forms of self-governance including teledemocracy will ascend. Such would be equally true of horrific events prompted by global ecological failures. The proximate cause of those problems can quickly be identified as the avarice and miscalculations of the super-rich, the social irresponsibility of industrial magnates and financial barons, too much power centralized in top-heavy, rigid, arrogant, and self-serving hierarchies that specialize in group-think and self-congratulation. The solution will lie in the hands and minds of the general public and a truly transformational leadership who know how to use modern ICTs to help us evolve from any post-industrial chaos.

After all, an important role of life-threatening disruptions in the life of the ordinary person or the nation-state is to be a wake-up call, to rouse one from the stupors of business-is-business and politics-as-usual. It is human nature to slip into ruts, to cling to sinking ships until the final reckoning, and to nestle into familiar surroundings and routines. Such is equally true in politics. Governments, regimes, administrations, and even dynasties are extremely resilient—other than when they are the obvious perpetrators of unspeakable suffering and tragedy.

In fact, it takes an awful lot before a public will buck well-fortified political order. At some undefinable point, though, the critical mass coheres and the government is ready to retreat, not with a bang, but a whisper. From the late 1960s through the early 1970s, this almost came to pass in most modern representative democracies. The "best and the brightest" in government were tangled in their own webs of deceit and decrepitude. The turrets and towers of power were about to tumble into the moat. But those who clamored and trumpeted at the foot of the garrison lacked the ultimate weapon to administer the coup de grâce: a sane and well-tested alternative. That arsenal is no longer barren, as Parts I and II amply demonstrate.

If one could time-travel to the end of the 19th century to interview people who were leading the charge to make American democracy more consistent with its high-minded ideology, one would find plenty of potential interviewees around. It would not take long, either, to get a clear picture of their forecast of what America's democracy would be like in the 20th century. After all, this was the heyday of the progressive and populist movements in America and the early days of the women's suffrage movement and a new phase in the African-American civil rights movement too.

It would not have taken a genius to figure out in 1899 what equal rights for blacks and women might look like later in the 20th century: blacks and women having the right to vote without harassment and intimidation; blacks and women being elected as mayors, governors, and even members of the U.S. Congress; blacks and women having equal educational and economic opportunities with white men; and so forth. Yet, in 1899 these ideas were "wild," "radical," and "preposterous"— beyond sober and dignified consideration. These were not acceptable or proper subjects for political or academic discourse in the mansions, country clubs, colleges, and board rooms populated by the American upper crust of that "Gilded Age."

If our time-traveler spoke to the progressive at the turn of the century, here is what they would have said would be the future of the American polity: strong laws against huge corporate monopolies; a national income tax; direct election of U.S. senators; no longer pegging the value of the dollar to the value of gold; national laws protecting the safety and health of citizens and workers; citizens able to vote directly on issues at the state and local levels of governance; women having the right to vote; and so forth.

These were "zany" and "revolutionary" ideas and ideals to the privileged white males who occupied the pinnacles of American political/economic power at the time, yes, but they were also part of concerted political mobilization and local and state experimentation at the time. They, too, were met with derision, disdain, and defensive countermeasures. But these goals and forecasts were consistent with American political ideology and were backed by political action and dedication to furthering the transformation of democracy in America.

In like fashion, we believe that the form and energy of the teledemocracy movements at the end of the 20th century are equally likely to bear fruit—sometime in the 21st century—even though there may be setbacks brought about by political and/or economic crises. Given its explosive growth, as detailed in Part II, it seems that the outline and many details of what will occur in the 21st century are well sculpted by now. It does not take a psychic to make a reasonable prognostication. We do not know the precise time, the exact contours, or the level and tactics of the resistance. We do know many of the features, components, interactions, and trends. And that is what we will do in Chapter 7, lay out the rough draft of an emerging teledemocratic future for the 21st century.

But there is one other important quality to this final chapter. As we have emphasized throughout this book that although we prize our role and standards as empirical political scientists—in the true sense of practicing experimental science—we also are deeply committed to the values of democracy and to what we believe are the more egalitarian, public-spirited, and moral consequences that flow from such a system socially, economically, and politically. Thus, we concede we are not simply reporting our view of the future of teledemocracy as a fact-based trend, like TV weathermen discussing the five-day travel planner. Just as Susan B. Anthony had to act out her desire to see women treated as political equals to men; and just as Governor Hiram Johnson of California went to study Swiss citizens initiatives and then had to weather a hurricane of political opposition before making them part of the California state constitution, so do we see Chapter 7 as a pro-active democratic commitment.

Chapter 7, then, is our best scientific forecast, but we also hope it will become a "self-fulfilling prophecy" in America and any part of the world that might afford a better proving ground. Just as our Web site is designed to both describe and synergize the global democracy movement, so has it been the goal of Parts I and II to describe, and is the goal of Part III to synergize, the future of teledemocracy, this time through the print medium.

7

The Future of Teledemocracy: Entering the Post-Hierarchical Age

The future of teledemocracy and the future of the New Democratic Paradigm are inextricably intertwined. Each may progress at different speeds and in different ways, but each is integral to the other.

The merits of a quantum correction to the Newtonian political thought may engage intellectuals, but they will never be resolved in the public mind without more and more practical, successful, and widely heralded experimentation with new teledemocratic and direct democratic systems. As the future of teledemocracy unfolds, and becomes a greater reality in everyday life, the new theory it mirrors and reflects will become better understood by average citizens. This is because, as we saw in Chapter 2's discussion of quantum medicine, numerous people will already be relishing the fruits of its harvest.

People today, who have incorporated wiser diets, regular exercise, and stress reduction into their day-to-day life, do not need quantum theory to help them reach that level of mental acuity required for such intelligent behavior. But those who practice their individualistic brand of "holistic medicine" can better grasp what is meant by "quantum medicine" when they read about or hear a discussion about it. It will ring bells.

So, too, is the case with teledemocracy and the New Democratic Paradigm. Those who are already experimenting with, or who have taken part in some aspect(s) of it, or who have read about or sampled it on TV will appreciate it and want more of it in their daily lives. They do not need to know about the quantum correction of "quantum democracy" to get there. However, once there, it is much easier to understand, accept, and begin to apply it in new ways. Thus, once understood by a substantial portion of the electorate, it will be easier to generate extra intellectual, economic, and political momentum for further experiments and inno-vations along those lines.

A NEW FORM OF DEMOCRACY IS PROBABLE:
BUT WHAT IS IT?

In Chapter 1, we talked about several incredibly prescient visions of electronically enhanced democracy. In Part II, we defined and described several of the components we have been shaping and honing ourselves for over 20 years and how the work of other teledemocratic experi-menters are best integrated into or are complementary with our models. However, there is a body of futuristic democratic theory that expands on what 21st-century teledemocracy may and ought to include, theory that transcends the limits or integration of any of the empirical work done so far. We will tap into two of the richest veins of that theory in order to expand our discussion of what this new structure of democracy may well involve.

The Theory of Strong, Semi-Direct Democracy

Several leading democratic theorists have been talking about the future of democracy in America and elsewhere for many years now. It is their common view that it will contain several key elements: more direct de-mocracy plus ICT—rather like what we defined as "direct teledemoc-racy" or "quantum democracy" in Chapter 1.

Benjamin Barber

As we noted in Chapter 2, Benjamin Barber pinpointed many of the fallacies and frailties in Newtonian physics that undermine the intellec-tual and empirical foundation of modern "liberal" or "representative" democracy. But he did not stop there. In the concluding chapter of his seminal book *Strong Democracy* (1984), he creates out of whole cloth a pristine system of democracy, replete with a different, but parallel, sys-tem of 21st-century political communications to the one we laid out in Chapter 5 (the authentic, comprehensive ETM model). We might also add that Barber's proposed system is also highly consistent with a quan-tum worldview and with the New Democratic Paradigm.

Barber's system is grounded in hundreds of face-to-face, facilitated town meetings (5,000 citizens in each) throughout the United States. Each of these "neighborhood assemblies" serves many purposes of self-governance, including that of developing agendas, priorities, and policies on local, state, regional, and national issues—but most of all, elevating the quality of civic participation, discourse, and awareness. At the local level, laws passed may be executed locally. However, to deal with issues involving larger polities, Barber is not enamored with the idea of selecting "representatives" to solve these problems—even if they were selected by a clone of the venerable Athenian lottery system, which he advocates.

Instead, he devises a system of "Television Town Meetings and a Civic Communications Cooperative, or CCC." In his view, "strong democracy requires a form of town meeting in which participation is direct but communication is regional or even national" (Barber 1984, 216). Thus, all available ICTs would link these neighborhood assemblies and "have a great potential for equalizing access to information, stimulating participatory debate across regions, and encouraging multi-choice polling and voting informed by information, discussion and debate" (Barber 1984, 219). The CCC would be modeled after the British Broadcasting Company—a "publicly controlled but independent body" whose mandate would be to "promote and guarantee civic and democratic uses of telecommunications, which remain a vital public resource" (Barber 1984, 220).[1]

But Barber does not tarry there either. He realizes that a really "strong democracy" *must* contain direct citizen-powered decision making, like "a national initiative and referendum process." Barber reviews and dismisses the stock Madisonian and Hamiltonian paranoia about rampaging mobs of ragged citizens pillaging the closets of the rich and concludes with a proposal for a multistage process of national initiative and referendum that he believes answers most if not all of the old paradigm reservations. This new system would include "(a) a legislative initiative and referendum process; (b) a mandatory tie-in with neighborhood assemblies and interactive town meetings for the purpose of civic education; (c) a multi-choice format; (d) a two-stage voting process providing for two readings" (Barber 1984, 284–285). He adds also a fifth innovation: "electronic balloting" (Barber 1984, 289–290).

Benjamin Barber, then, has combined the visions of Part I with many of the actual experiments in Part II and added some important elements of citizen-empowerment to produce an all-encompassing picture of 21st-century democracy. His system emphasizes citizen interactivity, people power, and, of course, modern ICTs and randomness at the expense of classic elitism and pyramidal power.

Alvin and Heidi Toffler

Barber's views are strikingly similar to the work of two of the preeminent futurists in the world, Alvin and Heidi Toffler. Starting with their blockbuster book *Future Shock* (1970), where they advanced their theory of why and how people were being overtaken by the dizzying pace of change in the modern world of ICT, the Toffler's have not been shy about advocating what they see as the main remedy for future shock and future political "schlock": *more and better genuine democracy.*

In their subsequent best-seller, *The Third Wave* (1980), they continued to polish their thinking about how the modern world is being battered by a new and troubling "third wave of change," one driven by the information and knowledge revolution. This Information Age is disrupting and dismembering the outdated social order and modes of work closely associated with the "second wave" industrial revolution.

The Third Wave, however, puts political change on the front burner. The Tofflers also decide to be—in their own words—more "prescriptive" than they were in *Future Shock*. Thus, they set up criteria by which to "distinguish those innovations that are merely cosmetic, or just extensions of the industrial past, from that which is truly revolutionary" (p. 22). We engaged in much the same process by clarifying "genuine," "authentic," and "real" ETMs and teledemocracy; and by distinguishing between "reformist" and "transformational" political change (see Chapter 6).

It was in 1980 in *The Third Wave* that the Tofflers coined the term "Twenty-first Century Democracy" or "Semi-Direct Democracy." In their opinion, this completely new kind of democracy would "fundamentally alter" representative democracy because the latter was "increasingly unworkable" (Toffler and Toffler 1994, 435). Like most of us involved in transformational or teledemocratic politics, they did not seek to jettison representative democracy. Instead, they were remodeling it democratically to help make it more accountable to the will of the general public in a time when that has become technologically feasible and a political emergency. Thus, they recommend a cluster of structural changes that would reincarnate 18th-century democracy into its 21st-century descendant.

In their analysis of the failing "majoritarian" system, they note that most industrialized countries today are splintering into many disparate tribes. This makes it increasingly difficult to find solid majorities to support important domestic and foreign policies. They also point out that this fragmentation of interests, coupled with increasing technological muscle to make self-interested demands, places enormously heavy weight on the arthritic representative, hierarchical systems. The Tofflers' diagnosis is that modern Western governments teeter on the brink of "near breakdown."

Thus, they center their recommendations on a number of changes that will help induce authentic consensuses from ever-shifting minorities. Foremost among these are to give voters in initiative and referendum processes better options than "yes-no" or "pro-con." They urge "cumulative voting" similar to the system that protects minority shareholders in corporate elections. They also back the use of random-sampling techniques among small groups within society and recommend that those group discussions be professionally moderated. At this point, one can see many interfaces with what Barber calls "strong democracy."

But the commonalities do not end there. In fact, the Tofflers, like Barber, believe the best way to make national legislatures more representative of the increasingly disparate national community is to choose them via "the oldest way of all," random selection.

This truly democratically selected legislature should be complemented by an entirely new breed of national initiative. To fend off the old argument that such direct democracy would lead to "emotional" results, they recommend a "cooling off" period, perhaps making the same initiative pass public muster twice. They also insist that the public have sufficient time and information upon which to make wise judgments. They write that "spectacular advances in communications technology open, for the first time, a mind-boggling array of possibilities for direct citizen participation in political decision-making." (Toffler 1980, 445).

Repeating their opinion that they are simply trying to repair a degenerated mechanism, the Tofflers state that "the old objections to direct democracy are growing weaker at precisely the same time that the objections to representative democracy are growing stronger. Dangerous or even bizarre as it may seem to some, semi-direct democracy is a moderate principle that can help us design workable new institutions for the future" (Toffler and Toffler 1994, 94).

"Design workable new institutions?" Of course, that has been the central focus of this book up to now and there is an even lengthier roster of relevant and daring experiments than those already examined. The next section will integrate a number of these into what we have already presented and give further proof that the theories of the Tofflers and Barber—being totally consistent with, and part of, what we call the New Democratic Paradigm and teledemocracy—are already well on their way to being implemented, albeit in a piecemeal fashion and on different paths using different tools.

But could it have been any other way? Not according to Kuhn, because that is the way that new paradigms mature. And not according to Auli Keskinen, the leading teledemocratic futurist in Finland, who puts it like this:

In systems terms, teledemocracy is a complex, dynamic, non-linear and multivariate phenomenon. . . . That is why it should be emphasized that there is no "one truth" or "right way" to develop teledemocracy but that many peoples' initiatives and personal understanding are necessary elements of the process . . . essential to produce a truly democratic information society that is most likely to produce the greatest benefits for the broadest base of the society. (Keskinen 1999, 242)

CORE ELEMENTS OF THE TELEDEMOCRATIC FUTURE

At this point, then, we identify the following as the major distinct, but highly interactive, core elements of the New Democratic Paradigm, or a teledemocratic future: (1) the Global Direct Democracy Movement; (2) 21st-Century Democratic Communications Systems; (3) the Modern Mediation Movement; and (4) Transformational Political Organization via the Internet.

Each and every one of these authentic pro-democratic empowerment processes have pragmatic use in all aspects of governance and at all levels of government. Thus they work exceptionally well in helping plan for the future of the polity, for setting grass-roots-inspired public agendas for the polity, for prioritizing and drafting policies with broad public consensuses and last, but not least, for a more efficient and effective carrying out, or public administration, of those policies. They each work well separately, but far better when combined with one or more of the others. Of course, from our point of view, as well as those of Barber and the Tofflers, they would maximize their efficacy when systematically combined in toto. We cannot give exhaustive details on how they are developing and so have chosen what we believe are some of the more interesting and intriguing data and illustrations in each area.

The Global Direct Democracy Movement

Direct democracy, particularly its traditional form of citizens initiatives and referenda (hereinafter referred to as I+R), is burgeoning universally. It should be noted at the outset, however, that direct democracy—as a fundamental form of government—is relatively non-hierarchial, in particular when compared with the various types of representative democracy. For example, in direct democracy, every citizen is equal as a lawmaker. In representative forms, those who are elected to make laws have a superior position to those who elect them. In direct democracy, the flow of information and the deliberative process is lateral among citizens. In the representative form, the flow of information is usually from the candidates and officials to the public, on a downward trajectory. The heart and soul of direct democracy is self-governance among the citizenry, not leaders governing the masses in political pyramid schemes. It is the essence of government of the people, by the people, and for the people.

Therefore, it is our contention that the more direct democracy there is in any system of government, the closer it is to new paradigm thinking about politics and acting in politics. If we are correct that we are now moving toward this New Democratic Paradigm, then we should expect to find expanding surges of direct democracy around the world. In the section that follows, we believe that we can demonstrate that this is surely true. Indeed, new clusters of direct democratic energy are appearing in some of the most likely and unlikely spots and they are starting to connect in both predictable and unpredictable ways.

The Recent American Experience

In the United States, where I+R is presently confined to the state and local level, there is explosive growth in interest, use, organization, and new ideas about how to improve its design. While the idea, advocacy, and practice of I+R in the United States is almost never mentioned in mainstream political discourse—being perilously close to the "censorship" one finds in Communist China today on the subject of starting an opposition party—its growth in acceleration and velocity at the close of the 20th century was phenomenal.

For example, where it is already part of the American political landscape (24 states and countless municipalities), it has reached new acmes of activity of late and it has often been used to outflank the heavily fortified agendas of legislative and bureaucratic elites, particularly when they are in conflict with a general public consensus. This just happens to be one of the key, historical reasons for its very existence, that is, to empower citizens against fallen "public servants," who actually cater to a much smaller group of politically and economically stronger private patrons.

A few examples will suffice. First, there were 41 citizens initiatives at the state level that were on the ballot throughout the United States in 1984. By 1990, that number had grown to 64 and in 1996 it broke the all-time record with 94.

We believe that one of the reasons for this splurge in utilization is multistate initiatives—where the same, or roughly the same, initiative is being considered simultaneously in several states. For example, in 1992, there were 14 different states that had citizens casting ballots on whether or not there should be a limit on the number of terms legislators (including congresspersons) could serve. In 1994, another 12 states passed similar bills via initiatives.

This is not coincidental. An interlocking development is the ability to coordinate these initiatives centrally—in significant part through the Internet (which we will discuss later in this chapter). Thus, U.S. Term Limits, a national organization, helped plan and coordinate these 14 initiatives (all of which passed by an average of approximately 67% of the vote).

Another example of this phenomenon follows: during the 1992–1994–

1996 election cycles, the Humane Society of the United States helped synchronize 12 citizens initiatives in eight states that restricted various types of "inhumane" hunting techniques like using airplanes and electronic communications devices, steel-jawed leghold traps, and bear baiting. (Their record was eight wins and four losses). Meanwhile, the National Coalition Against Legalized Gambling was leading the charge against lotteries and casinos in six states via the initiative process (Varner 1996).

Yet another example of how a well-orchestrated, serial set of statewide initiatives has mounted an effective challenge to an out-of-step, out-of-touch representative democracy at the national level concerns the medical use of marijuana. In 1996, two states (California and Arizona) passed two different citizens initiatives that permitted physicians to prescribe marijuana (and other "controlled substances") to terminally ill patients or to relieve a syndrome of symptoms that many patients say is best treated by marijuana. The U.S. government, adamant in its policy to ban this drug, threatened to revoke the federal license to prescribe any narcotic of any physician who prescribed marijuana pursuant to the new California and Arizona laws.

In 1998, cognizant of this federal reaction and threat, five states in the west (Alaska, Washington, Oregon, Colorado, and Nevada) also passed well-coordinated medical marijuana initiatives by an average of close to 60% of the vote. These citizen-made laws were perfectly clear that physicians need only "recommend" (not prescribe) the drug, allowing individual patients to grow their own for medical purposes. This new wave of citizens initiatives has now compelled the U.S. government to finally say that some national debate on this subject is warranted, and to say it will fund, albeit grudgingly, at least a scintilla of scientific testing of medical marijuana, something it had steadfastly refused to do for decades. Meanwhile, marijuana growing for personal "medical" use is proliferating in these states, as well as in the state of Maine, which passed a similar initiative in late 1999.

Another clear indicator of this quantum leap in the degree of usage is the state of California itself, the leading arena for this kind of democratic politics (with Oregon and Colorado coming up fast on the inside track). After initiatives became a fixture in California's way of doing politics, there was a spurt of them in the early years, with over 30 on the ballot in the 1920s and 1930s. Then there was an ebb in their utilization from the 1940s through the 1970s. However, 44 appeared on the ballot from 1980 to 1989 and there have already been 48 from 1990 to 1997. The success rate has increased as well. From 1911 to 1978—a period of 68 years—Californians passed 42 initiatives. From 1980 to 1996—a period of 17 years—Californians passed 40 of them. In fact, it is so popular in California today that *New York Times* correspondent Todd S. Purnam has called it "a dominant means of setting government policy, not a supplemental one" (Purnam 1998, 1).

A similar pattern is beginning to emerge at the local level as well. Indeed, direct democratic processes are deeply embedded in many municipalities throughout America. But 1998 was a banner year for them, particularly one kind: pro-environmental. It appears that 173 cities and towns across America passed citizen-sponsored laws that improved parks, set aside large tracts of land for conservation, and protected a wide variety of farmlands, historic resources, biological habitats, and so forth (see Myers 1999). This manifested a deepening anxiety about the effects of urban and suburban sprawl upon the quality of life in many communities and the result is a boomlet in citizens initiatives. Why is this the case?

When citizens finally arrive at the dreaded realization that the arteries to their representative government are badly clogged and are the cause of severe political angina, they sadly conclude that bypass surgery is necessary for the survival of the polity. Citizens initiatives re-open the blood supply. That Americans strongly favor empowering themselves along these lines seems to be abundantly demonstrated by this explosion in the usage of the I+R process. It is also clearly indicated by scientific survey data.

The standard type of national public opinion polls unfailingly reveal, over and over and over again, that super-majorities (between 60% and 75% of the American people) support I+R when they are given even a bare bones idea of what it is. The news is at least as good when scientific deliberative polls measure their views on this subject.

As we noted in Chapter 3, when the process was described in detail and citizens were given time to deliberate the issue, about 86% of a representative sample of the people of Hawaii had a positive attitude towards I+R. Alan Kay, using his method of deliberative polling, found that 64% of his national samples were in favor of conducting "national referendums or votes on major issues AND requir[ing] the government to treat a referendum approved by a majority of all registered voters in the same manner as legislation passed by Congress" (Kay 1999, 178).

However, the extraordinary growth of direct democracy in the United States is not just about it being put to greater and more diverse use and about the steady state of positive citizen attitudes about it. That would amount to just more of the same. In the true spirit of thinking along the lines of the New Democratic Paradigm, this movement is also about original thinking, inventing better systems, and the birth of organizations that aim to transform I+R into a 21st-century model.

So, among those most passionately devoted to the expansion of I+R in the United States are some "friendly, constructive critics" who are ever alert to the myriad of *real operational failings* (as opposed to the same old

elitist attacks on the public's ability to participate) in this kind of democracy, particularly as it has evolved in the 20th century. Dr. Kay states
the practical problems with I+R as succinctly and persuasively as anyone:

> We know from such scholars as Thomas E. Cronin (1989) that ref-
> erendums in the US are expensive, time consuming, often heavily
> influenced by special interests. They are frequently captured by
> those who can afford large, often blatantly unfair, advertising and
> public relations campaigns. Referendums typically ask voters to
> judge proposals in the form of exactly worded legislation that are
> extremely complex, sometimes dozens even hundreds of pages
> long. Moreover, the more controversial referendums, particularly
> those that have large economic effects, are challenged in the courts,
> adding to the expense, delay and capriciousness of what finally
> becomes law, if anything. It is no wonder that some consider ref-
> erendums as an inhuman burden on the conscientious voter. (Kay
> 1999, 373)

Thus, an active segment of the modern American I+R movement has
been thinking about how to defend and improve this form of direct democracy in the present and future.

Perhaps the most extensive and thorough investigation of the process,
replete with a full portfolio of improvements to be made, came in a two-
year study of the century-long California experience, co-directed by
Tracy Westen and Robert Stern of the Center for Responsive Government
(CRG) in Los Angeles, California. The title of the study—which was
sponsored by the California Commission on Campaign Financing—says
it all: *Democracy by Initiative: Shaping California's Fourth Branch of Government* (1992).

At the very outset, the authors state that if the trends in California
hold true, then other states that allow initiatives at the state level "will
also begin to see the emergence of 'democracy by initiative' as a new
form of 21st century governance" (California Commission 1992, 1). The
report, however, in no way qualifies as a whitewash of the process. Although it is accurate in reporting how well the process works, it is
equally candid in reporting its blemishes and faults. Although exhaustive
in its review of the pros and cons, there is little that is new here. Its
greatest value, instead, lies in "a comprehensive and interrelated set of
innovative reforms which will enable the electorate, acting through the
initiative process, to function as a more effective and mature part of state
governance" (California Commission 1992, 3).

What this report urges is not to "reform" the system. What they urge
is a brand new system to replace it. From our knowledge of these pro-

cesses, the best way to define their idea might best be capsulized in three little words: *indirect citizens initiatives*. The reader might recollect that this was that oddball hybrid that the largest number of Televoters favored in the very first Hawaii Televote—one that was never mentioned in either the mass media or the debate at the 1978 Hawaii State ConCon, but that was described fleetingly in the Televote brochure.

So how would it work? The essence of this kind of citizens initiative is that it involves the legislature and other government officials in some useful ways that might eventuate in there being no further necessity for the public to vote on that issue at all. The new system starts out by being more citizen-friendly: by limiting the number of words a proposition might include and by extending the period of time it takes to gather names. It also sets up mechanisms to improve the product itself by: (1) requiring public hearings during different stages of the process; (2) by permitting the proponents to improve the wording after the hearings; (3) by having a 45-day "cooling off" period (what the Tofflers recommended) whereby the proponents and legislature can "negotiate compromise legislation"; (4) by allowing the legislature itself to adopt the original or amended initiative—or a negotiated version—as law; (5) by requiring that the pamphlets sent to the voters by the secretary of state be more visually attractive and understandable to average citizens; and on and on. Also, there are many changes that require that citizens be made fully aware of who is funding the various positions.

This study and the report itself should serve as a handy and comprehensive guide to those who want to help improve and develop citizens initiatives anywhere in the world in the 21st century. But there are other ideas out there as well that complement and add to even these extraordinary transformational ideas and recommendations about the citizens initiative process.

One of these has been led by a former U.S. senator from Alaska (1968–80), Mike Gravel. Calling his organization Philadelphia II, Gravel advocates national citizens initiatives (U.S. Initiative)—hardly a novel notion. However, his view as to how to achieve it and run it are well within New Democratic Paradigm parameters.

Gravel believes that the right to national initiative is inherent in the original Constitution itself, particularly in how it was ratified. All that needs to be done in order to institutionalize national I+R, in the view of Philadelphia II, is "self enactment," following James Madison's own idea about the "first principles" of constitutional formation. According to Madison, the people in a democracy are "sovereign" and "were in fact, the fountain of all power, and by resorting to them, all difficulties were got over. They could alter constitutions as they pleased" (Rossiter 1961, 323). Thus, the strategy is to develop a national initiative campaign in 50 states where a majority of those voting in the most recent presidential election would pass a law authorizing the particular kind of national initiative recommended by Philadelphia II. Once this is done, the Constitution would be directly amended by the sovereign people of the United States according to Madisonian "first principles." And what would this new form of national initiative include?

Actually, it is much along the lines proposed by the California Commission on Campaign Financing, mentioned above with provisos that call for only a relatively modest percentage of voters to be required on a petition; a limit on the number of issues that can be voted on in one initiative; a long period of time to collect the signatures (two years); and so forth. Perhaps the most innovative part of the proposal is to establish an entirely new path to getting citizens initiatives on the ballot—by means of an "acceptable public opinion poll."

In other words, the Philadelphia II idea is for Congress to set up something called "the Electoral Trust," which would be a new, largely independent agency of the U.S. government. This agency would authorize, monitor, and authenticate a public opinion polling process that would allow random samples of citizens—after being informed about issues—to put laws up for the general public to vote upon. Therefore, instead of the present system of allowing small groups of citizens who strongly advocate a particular law to be the sole vehicle for putting initiatives up for vote, this proposal allows public opinion pollsters and representative samples of the citizenry to put such issues up for public voting as well. In other words, there will be two avenues by which an initiative gets on the national ballot: (1) the traditional method of citizens' petitions and (2) the new method of scientific public opinion polling.

It should be clear to the reader that we think this is an idea whose time is about to come—particularly if the "acceptable" public opinion poll is administered via a New Democratic Paradigm 21st-century political communications system, which will be described later in this chapter.

Another organization that is a vital part of the new American I+R movement is appropriately called the Initiative and Referendum Institute, or IRI (www.iandrinstitute.org). Founded by M. Dane Waters, a former field organizer for the national term limits movement, IRI is home-based in Washington, D.C. Its general mission is to be a resource organization for the defense and expansion of the I+R process in America for the foreseeable future.

As we have noted throughout this book, democratic movements do not just grow linearly. The karma of their progress is to cope with increased enmity and an at least equally stubborn resistance from their foes. By way of illustration, there are those like political correspondent Peter Schrag (of the *Sacramento Bee*) who believe that the increasing utilization of citizens initiatives in California bears the major responsibility (or guilt) for the steep decline of public education and public social services in that state (Schrag 1998).

But the main arena of the countermovement is not real or virtual book stores. Instead, it is presently mounting battles in two well-fortified bastions of the old hierarchical order: state legislatures and judiciaries at the state and federal level. Thus a barrier of laws is being erected that amounts to a rough and tumble obstacle course for initiatives to traverse before they can even get on the ballot. Once they overcome those hurdles, and succeed in passage (no easy task by itself), they then must run a gauntlet of lawsuits aimed at prolonging their gestation period or aborting them. One of IRI's major contributions to the direct democracy (DD) movement has been to help recruit a coterie of top echelon attorneys. This pro-DD legal SWAT team plans and coordinates legal raids on these restrictive laws and builds legal defenses against court actions designed to undo the legitimate exercise of power by the people. Therefore, in order to prevent or minimize rear-guard erosion of the movement's territorial gains, IRI is headquarters for the pro-DD legal warriors.

On the pro-active side, IRI is an agent of synergy. It sees itself as an educator of the public; a meeting place for advocates and organizers; and a clearinghouse of ideas and new tools of direct democracy. It held a conference in May 1999 that convened nearly 200 such lawyers, political leaders, initiative coordinators, academics, journalists, and assorted and sundry I+R activists and theorists. The feeling among just about everyone who attended was the realization that the movement was far stronger and more advanced that even its most loyal supporters dared dream. Constantly updated news about how the movement is faring can be found on the IRI Web site and many of the Web sites to which it is linked, including TAN+N.

The Worldwide Surge

So much is also occurring along these lines worldwide that it would take an entire book to provide an in-depth depiction and analysis of this movement. In this volume, we will highlight a few prominent developments as samples of their diversity and viability.

Two European nations in which the citizenry partakes of I+R with gusto—first-team players in this kind of political sport—are Switzerland and Italy. In the former, there are actually two styles of citizens initiatives. One is along classic lines, where small groups of citizens sign petitions to get issues on the ballot for other citizens to vote on. The other is more of a body check on the national legislature, to wit, after a law is passed, citizens can petition to print it on the ballot for other citizens to give it a yea or a nay. To put it another way, it is a direct democracy citizens' veto. The Parliament also can offer a counterproposal upon which the public may vote.

Although the Swiss have enjoyed the privilege of direct citizen power for well over a century now, there does not seem to be any slaking of their thirst for it. The level of entry is the requirement that a tiny fraction, 1% to 2%, of the voters are needed to sign a petition to get it on the national ballot. Thus, over time over 450 such votes have been recorded in Switzerland, and, as one British journalist reporting on this Swiss eccentricity noted, "The pace has been accelerating lately" (Beedham 1997, 9). In April of 1999, for example, Swiss voters revamped their Constitution—including (1) the abolition of the gold standard for the Swiss franc; (2) establishing the right to strike; and (3) providing equal opportunities for the handicapped. This is counterevidence to those who claim, with no evidence, that the people get weary of and bleary-eyed from too much civic involvement.

The actual turnout level in almost all of them is relatively low (around 40%) but as we saw above, there are a multitude of available remedies for the malady. So, as Beedham puts it,

> Not long ago there was a splendid moment after most of the political class had shaken a furious fist at the voters' refusal to accept an anti-urban-sprawl planning law. The politicians then discovered that just as much sprawl could be prevented, more cheaply, by a different scheme. Politicians and people may occasionally snarl at each other, but they have learned how to work together. The Swiss will go on doing democracy their direct way. (Beedham 1997, 5)

In Italy, the referendum—where the legislature puts a law up for public vote—is the only type of direct democracy available at the national level. However, it, like the Swiss usage, has been gaining in popularity lately and has been covering an extraordinary range of issues, including abortion; nuclear energy; the concentration of TV network ownership; the personal liability of judges for the consequences of their decisions; and the like. Indeed, back in 1991 and 1993, when the governmental rot reached levels of scandal too horrific even for oft-sickened Italian citizens to stomach, the voters—in the words of Beedham—"torpedoed the country's old political system . . . while the system's two main parties watched ashen-faced" (Beedham 1997, 9).

Thus, in two modern industrialized nations where I+R has been available for many years, citizens are not showing the least inclination to shelve the process and, instead, are resorting to it on a more regular basis and for a wider and more polyglot panorama of issues. Meanwhile, other parts of Europe are catching on quickly with a host of national referenda on major issues of European integration being put to popular vote recently in England, Denmark, Norway, and Sweden. England is also on the verge of one on whether to join the European Monetary Union. But the urge toward more direct democracy in Europe does not stop there. In fact, we believe there is enough data now to assert that there is a storm surge of direct democracy beginning to inundate that continent, reaching into nations where such ideas were barely entertained until very recent times.

In Germany, there is a dynamic movement called *Mehr Demokratie*, which in English means "more democracy." It was founded in 1988 and was known by an acronym IDEE (which means "idea" in German)—but the idea inherent in its full name was "the movement for direct democracy." It was begun by a few young pro-democracy "idealists" (Thomas Mayer is considered by many to be the "founder") with only a few Deutschmarks in their pockets. Yet, today it has matured into a full-fledged national political organization with 10 paid staff members, offices in nine cities and, at the time of this writing, over 2,000 dues-paying members. And, of course, it has its own Web site (www.mehr-demokratie.de).

Much like its comrade movement in America, the leaders of *Mehr Demokratie* hail from an extremely disparate set of political values. Michael Effler, one of its leaders, is a staunch Green, and Thomas Rupp, also a long-term representative, likes to call himself a "conservative." They, like their American direct democracy counterparts, look and sound like the "odd couple," but their surface policy goals and personal styles pale in comparison to their deep bonding on the need to empower the people directly. So, exactly what is *Mehr Demokratie*'s agenda?

First of all, what is not generally known is that the right to indirect citizens initiatives in Germany is common at the state level, being part of state constitutions. So, the agenda of *Mehr Demokratie* is several-fold. Their first major target was the constitution of the southern state of Bavaria and the objective was to change the constitution so as to provide the right of citizens initiatives to the Bavarian people at the city and town level as they had at the state level. Thus, they organized a campaign in Bavaria and in 1995 they scored their first major triumph by changing the Bavarian constitution to reflect their goals. Then they turned their attention to the city of Hamburg, in northern Germany. Here, too, they racked up a surprising victory by amending the city charter to grant citizens the right of indirect initiative in local matters.

Flush with success, and with their movement gaining ever greater visibility and credibility throughout Germany, *Mehr Demokratie* is aiming its sights on a number of other targets, including (1) lowering the petition signature threshold in the *Bundesland* (state) constitutions from 10% of registered voters to 4% to 5%; (2) lessening the percentage of registered voters who must go to the polls to vote on the issue (in other words, making the quorum smaller); (3) lessening the percentage of those who vote "yes" that is needed to pass the initiative; and (4) permitting citizens to vote directly on tax and budgetary issues (which they cannot at present).

However, the "more democracy" movement has an even more ambitious and ultimate objective as well: giving Germany the "most democracy" by instituting *the right of indirect initiative at the national level.* Given *Mehr Demokratie's* overall track record so far, there seems to be a fair chance that Germany, in the early part of the 21st century, will join its neighbor Switzerland in providing its citizens some power of initiative at the national level.

Portugal, however, actually entered into the realm of direct democracy at the national level in 1998. Although there had been a constitutional provision allowing national referenda for many years, the Portuguese finally got their feet wet with two. The first, held in the spring of 1998, called for legalized abortion. The second, coming in the fall of 1998, treated a less controversial, but nonetheless important, issue: decentralizing certain functions of the central government. Both were defeated.

Unfortunately, though, as is proving to be true in many referenda around the globe, the turnout in each was less than a quorum (50% of the registered voters). Under the Portuguese system, this has the effect of making the result nonbinding. Nevertheless, these two experiences have raised the level of consciousness (and perhaps the mass subconsciousness) about DD in Portugal and stoked a great deal of discussion there about how to improve the process and make it more effective. Like the proverbial genie, once DD is let out of the bottle, it is tough to stuff it back in.

Furthermore, we are also aware of other DD movements presently stirring in Denmark, Belgium, and the Netherlands, each with organizations devoted to infusing it into the political life of their nations.

Denmark has already had some experience with national direct democracy by staging three national referenda in 1986, 1992, and 1993— all concerning integration in Europe. This has encouraged some there to want more of the above. Thus, there is the Danish Society for Direct Democracy, led by a business school professor, Marcus Schmidt, the author of *Direkte Demokratie i Danmark* (1993), who personally advocates the kind of random legislatures recommended by the Tofflers as part of their idea for "semi-direct democracy" in the 21st century.

The Society, which goes by its Danish name *Folkestyre*—which means "peoples rule" in English—is not so bold, but it does support the more traditional types of DD as well as electronic voting from the home. It, too, maintains its own homepage on the Web (www.folkestyre.de), publishes a quarterly newsletter, organizes conferences and meetings on the subject, and cultivates relationships with local and national political leaders sympathetic to DD.

To complement the work of this organization, there is a new political party in Denmark called the People's party, and it is led by Pia Kjoersgaard, a member of Parliament who is already a charismatic political figure on the Danish political scene. This group has I+R in its national platform and little by little one can hear more of the political elite supporting such ideas at the national level.

At somewhat earlier stages of development are incipient movements in Belgium, Italy, and Greece—where organizations have begun, Web sites have been set up, and/or agendas have been agreed upon. Belgium, for example, has been undergoing a great deal of political discontent of late, due to a flagging trust between the general public and the political class that occupies all power in its representative government and bureaucracy. There were massive street demonstrations in 1996 against police incompetence, resignations of ministers in 1998 due to corruption, and food poisoning scandals in 1999. During this period, a small group of three or four citizens established the *Werkgroep Implementatie Tijdsgeest* (WIT) in 1995, with a Web site (http://www.ping.be/jvwit/direct democracynow.html). It would appear that they have fertile ground in which to grow.

Belgium provides for nonbinding referenda only at the local level. In addition, there is a requirement that at least 40% of registered voters must cast ballots for it even to be considered as input for the lawmakers. So, WIT wants to change the Belgian constitution to provide more effective DD at the national level, and it has been circulating petitions for some time now. Its goal is to obtain the signatures of 200,000 Belgian citizens, and it was over a quarter of the way to that minimum at the time of this writing. On the other hand, WIT had obtained verbal agreements to support DD in Belgium from four of its major parties, including the Socialist party, the Green party, the Flemish Nationalist party, and the Liberal party. The Christian Democratic Party—which lost power in July 1999—had opposed it. The new ruling coalition then expressed their intention to introduce national referenda, but as WIT saw it in late 1999, there was still strong opposition and the struggle was far from over.

Meanwhile, in the Netherlands, the situation regarding DD is so intense that it recently forced the entire national government to a grinding halt. In May 1999, a vote was taken in the upper house of the national legislature on a bill that granted the Dutch public the right to vote directly, via national referenda, on major social, political, and economic issues. The result was 49 in favor and 25 opposed. However, since a two-thirds super-majority was required for passage, the bill failed. One prominent legislator who led the opposition to national referenda in the Netherlands was quite blunt about his reason: he feared giving the people of the Netherlands so much power over international and European affairs. This caused one of three key political parties to resign from the ruling coalition's cabinet posts and the government almost crumbled. Impassioned negotiations followed and a compromise was reached that gave the Dutch people the power of non-binding national referenda. The rising tide of direct democracy in Holland seems ready to wash away the dike of further resistance.

There are also signs of life for more direct democracy in both Italy and Greece, two ancient practitioners of early forms of democracy. In Italy, the *Associatione Democrazia Diretta* (http://come to/demodiretta) is aimed at adding citizens initiatives to the referendum process already in effect at the national level. In Athens, a fledgling political organization, led by George Kokkas, an Athenian lawyer, is running candidates for local office and for the European Union Parliament on the platform of direct democracy, albeit mainly to get the issue before the public.

Actually, the movement in Europe toward greater integration of its political economy is probably the most pervasive and pressing concern on that continent since the Soviet Union and European communism loomed to the East. Some national elites with Pan-European dreams, however, have been afraid to impose such a threat to national sovereignty on their people. So, they have used the referendum as a major modus operandi to win the approval of the populace for such transnational integration. This has produced decidedly mixed results—with national referenda in Sweden and Norway siding against integration and with a proposed national referendum in the United Kingdom on whether to join the European Monetary Union showing a persistent public sentiment against it.

There are high anxieties in many European countries about ditching their beloved currencies (pounds, crowns, marks) for the transnational "Euro" and there are extremely negative feelings Europe-wide about how much they trust the EU's Parliament, Commission, and bureaucracies ("Eurocrat" being a late 20th-century trans-European epithet). And why not? This goes counter to the general tendencies toward *decentralization* of government, increasing mistrust of distant governments, and a positive feeling about greater citizen participation in self-governance. This is similar to what we saw happening in the United States as well. General publics do not share many of the values and visions of remote and ambitious elites. This is leading in Europe, as well as America, to a decentralized system of multistate—or transnational—referenda on the same or similar issues. This would seem to add impetus for both national and transnational DD movements throughout Europe.

Thus, it is not surprising that we also find a growing movement in Europe called *Eurotopia*. The aspiration of this school of political thinking is to add *transnational I+R* to the EU charter so that the people of the various nations in the EU will have an opportunity to put issues on the ballot or to reverse laws. One of the founders and intellectual leaders of this movement is a Swiss member of Parliament, Andreas Gross. He also runs an organization called the Institute for the Scientific Study of Direct Democracy, which is headquartered in Zurich.

In collaboration with Bruno Kaufmann, a journalist who writes for *Die Zeit* (Hamburg) and is the Northern European correspondent for Swiss National Radio, they co-authored a book called *Transnational Democracy* (Erne et al. 1995). This multi-authored volume contains in great detail the manifesto for *Eurotopia*, the essence of which is to rewrite the constitution of the European Union. At the heart of its recommendations is a formal system of transnational citizens initiatives that permits a certain number of citizens in each member country to petition for a vote of all EU citizens on those issues.

A staunch defender of this position is none other than Benjamin Barber. He argues this point in his book *Jihad vs. McWorld* (1996), where he sees both the advance of religious fundamentalism and global marketism as equal threats to "civil society" everywhere. His solution—as in his prior treatises—is more and better democracy at the global and transnational levels.

> A genuinely public voice—the voice of civil society—can empower those who speak far more effectively than either the officially univocal voice of government or the obsessively contrary talk of the private sector's jabbering Babel. The voice of civil society, of citizens in deliberative conversation, challenges the exclusivity and irrationality of Jihad's clamor but is equally antithetical to the claim of McWorld's private markets to represent some aggregative public good. . . . If civil society is one key to democracy, then global strong democracy needs and depends on a methodical internationalization of civil society. (Barber 1996, 287)

But Europe and America are not alone in seeing fresh sprouts of direct democracy wedging themselves through the dry, cracked surface of representative democracy. Latin America, as well, is showing vital signs that direct democracy—occasionally practiced there—is strengthening.

First and foremost, using nationwide referenda to help calm widespread political resentment and turbulence in Latin America is becoming an acceptable, if not preferrable, tool of governance. In the 1990s, for instance, we have seen political elites in this area of the world defer to the people at large more regularly in order to head off violent turmoil and/or civil war and/or coups d'etat. A few recent examples will show how this is playing out in both Central and South America.

The situation was grim in Ecuador in 1997. The president, Abdala Bucaram, was widely viewed as a failure and the government was tottering toward political bankruptcy. There were raucous public protests and loud demands for him to resign. The Ecuadorean National Congress voted to remove the president from office and replace him with Fabian Alarcon. Alarcon's first move was to call for a national referendum to ratify this action by a *consulta popular*.

Thus, in May of 1997, thirteen propositions were put to the Ecuadorean people for their approval or disapproval. Several million citizens flocked to the polls to make their wishes heard on such momentous issues for their nation. Here were some of the major questions posed and the results: (1) Should the removal of one president and the replacement with the current president be approved by the people? Yes=75%, No=25%; (2) Should a National Assembly be called to devise a new constitution? Yes=68%, No=32%; (3) Should all members of the National Assembly be elected directly by the people? Yes=65%, No=35%; (4) Should the government limit campaign spending and monitor the origin of all campaign funding? Yes=56%, No=44%; (5) Should elected officials be subjected to popular recall because of immorality, incompetence, or illegal activity? Yes=61%; No=39%. The people were invited to participate as decision makers in some of the most important political questions facing their nation. The immediate crisis was alleviated. Direct democracy was the instrument. The people had their say. Its representative system was rescued, at least for the time being, by a healthy dose of a dozen referenda. A vital precedent was set in Equador for Equador and any country in a similar bind.

A similar situation faced Venezuela during the late 1990s. Venezuela, despite a huge reservoir of oil wealth, was on life support. A supermajority of its people were suffering under wretched economic and social conditions. The public was unified only in its beliefs that (1) all the nation's major political parties were corrupt beyond belief; (2) the oil proceeds of the nation had been siphoned into the pockets of large foreign companies and an avaricious handful of their countrymen; and (3) a tiny Venezuelan aristocracy had the government in its hip pocket. This led to an attempted coup in 1992 by a former army colonel, Hugo Chavez, but an overthrow of the government was repelled. Chavez went to prison. The political decline continued unchecked.

Chavez, freed from his imprisonment, ran for president of Venezuela in 1998. His platform was anti-representative democracy and pro-revolution. He spoke of a new day for Venezuela, where the old political clique, posing as representatives of the people, would be deposed from power. He spoke of sharing the oil wealth so that the majority of Venezuelans would themselves be freed from the yoke of poverty. He spoke of a new "participatory democracy" that would replace the evil, "rancid oligarchy" in place. He won handily. His first major move as the new president of Venezuela was to turn to the people via direct democracy.

Chavez scheduled a national referendum for mid-1999. This referendum was the first step in several that were designed to drastically alter the political system. It asked the people of Venezuela whether they wanted a nonpartisan "constitutional assembly of 131 members" to propose a whole new constitution to the people of Venezuela in late 1999—. via yet another national referendum. Eighty-five percent of the people of Venezuela responded that they indeed wanted a new constitution and that a group of delegates should be elected to come up with a new form of government for them to vote on in December 1999 (Rohter 1999). The big day came—right in the midst of Venezuela's most calamitous rainstorm—and 45% still went to the polls—through mud and flood—to vote. Of them, over 70% said "yes" to the new government.

At this writing, no one really knows whether this will turn out to empower the Venezuelan people in a transformation of their representative system to a more truly citizen-based system, one that President Chavez likes to call "participatory democracy." The big question is whether this was actually a "plebiscite" to grant old fashioned Caudillo-style authoritarian rule to the new president and remake Venezuela into what used to be called a "Banana Republic" His critics claim that will happen as surely as night follows day, and the new structure that seems to concentrate excessive power in the hands of the president—while also still expanding rights of minorities—still lends itself to that interpretation. Others hope he will be true to his word. Still, this will be the first time any nation ratified a whole constitution via a formal national referendum in the Information Age. What the public ratifies one day, they may reject in another.

Another example of the expanded use of national referenda in Latin America to handle major structural issues of governance occurred in Guatemala in May of 1999. The 1996 peace plan that halted 36 years of bloody civil war in Guatemala included 47 proposals that were to be put to a vote of the whole Guatemalan population in a national referendum. Included among them were new rights for the Guatemalan Indian population, including the legal right to use their language and wear traditional dress, and severe limitations on the role of the military in domestic matters.

What occurred was predictable. Guatemala's citizenry, being a rural Third World country, is 60% illiterate. Its ruling class is mainly non-Indian and strongly opposed most of the provisions of the peace treaty that were part of the referendum. Thus, there was an extremely low turnout to vote on this extraordinary complex set of propositions (21%) and about 75% of the voters said "no" to everything.

It is quite possible that this is why the political elite went along with the peace plan in the first place. They reckoned they would be able to agree on the peace plan—and look good—by putting the peace accord to a national vote of "all the people" (knowing all along that only a small percentage favorable to their position would actually go to the polls). Once again, though, using direct democracy sets a strong precedent for future Guatemalan politics and it involved far more average people directly in this restructuring process than could have been engaged in any other way. In addition, all these issues must still be resolved inside the new representative political system that now exists in Guatemala, and the general population is far more aware of what occurred than if usual backroom politics had been in effect.

In addition to this recent rash of classic direct democracy in Latin America, there have been several innovative direct citizen empowerment projects there as well. Perhaps the most successful use of sustained direct democracy in Latin America is in the city of Porto Alegre, a metropolis of over a million people in southern Brazil.

The city was having the perennially grave problems of high density urban areas in Latin America: huge pockets of poverty, high crime, inadequate infrastructure, unbearable pollution, endless traffic snarls, and so forth. So, what to do? The idea to bring the entire population into the process seemed worth a try.

Thus, during the 1990s, the mayor's office ceded power over the city budget to a system of open citizen forums—calling the process a "participatory budget." On an annual basis, citizens come to these forums to set priorities and then elect some of their number to determine the exact budget for everything from health policy to capital improvements. One result of this is that the political party that dreamed up this democratic budgeting system (the Workers party) has been re-elected twice to the office of mayor since the participatory budget was instituted. Another result is that this experiment has attracted interest from the World Bank, the United Nations, and other municipalities around the world.

Another attempt at empowering citizens of a major Latin American city has come through the efforts of a group calling itself *Kybernesis*, which started up in the mid-1990s in Peru. Led by some journalists and political scientists, they helped establish a right of citizens initiative in the poorest and most populated section of the capital city of Lima. They also held local forums that were used by the city council as direct feedback on concerns of the residents. Then, *Kybernesis* managed to raise some funds to add an electronic communication system into this area and permit the residents to communicate more easily with one another and with the city council (somewhat along the lines of the Berks County system discussed in Chapter 4). This ETM project was highly publicized throughout Peru, getting widespread media coverage there. The project is still underway. Despite funding and infrastructure deficiencies, they are presently trying to expand their new direct democratic practices into the mountainous and jungle regions of Peru.

There are also some intriguing developments toward direct democracy in Asia, not usually considered fertile ground for such political action or thought.

In the late 1940s, when General Douglas MacArthur helped the Japanese promulgate a national constitution in deference to the American model, no direct democracy was included at the national level. However, as in the U.S. brand of democracy, there was leeway to use it locally. This possibility hibernated for decades until the mid-1990s when political winds of change produced circumstances favorable to its awakening.

By the mid-1990s, Japan was headed into a long-term economic slump. This aggravated a lingering popular disaffection toward its alleged, but poor excuse for, representative democracy. More and more, it seemed to the average Japanese citizen that political officials did not respond to what the citizenry wanted or did not want. Two issues important to many Japanese were the continued American military presence in Japan and the deteriorating ecology. Another two issues close to home with many Japanese were the location of nuclear plants and where to safely dispose of megatons of toxic waste.

Thus, in 1996, direct democracy stirred from its slumber at the local level in Japan. In Okinawa, for example, several referenda were held that showed that the people of Okinawa had reached the limit of their patience with being the gracious host to American bases and troops on their soil. In one, 90% of the voters sent an acrimonious missive to Japanese authorities that the American military machine was no longer welcome in their homeland. This boil on the Japanese body politic continues to fester since the government made only minor, superficial adjustments to abate the public's anger. The U.S. bases remain. The resentments simmer. New protests erupted in late 1999, so it is likely that the future will see uses of direct democracy in this region and on this subject.

On the mainland of Japan, the central government had decided to place a nuclear plant in the small seaside town of Maki, far from Tokyo. The residents of the town used the referendum process and over 60% of the voters told the central authorities where they could not build this facility, that is, in their town. The process and the vote shocked the vaunted Japanese central bureaucracy—exactly the result expected from the use of direct democracy in systems where public administrators completely ignore the will of citizens. This citizen backlash again toxic waste and nuclear power siting in Japan will probably be accelerated by Japan's worst nuclear accident in late 1999 at Tokaimura (French 1999, A-7).

Korea is also showing some early signs of moving into the worlds of teledemocracy and direct democracy. Back in 1996, a group of about 50 members of Parliament—from several different parties—decided to try a teledemocratic experiment. They formed what they called the Cyberparty of Korea and put Seong-Muk Won—a journalist and former foreign radio correspondent—in charge as executive director.

The basic idea was to seek citizen input into policy decisions at the national level through a system of computer conferencing. The Korean Parliament sponsored this "telecommunications forum"—and hundreds of Korean citizens were invited to submit their individual ideas and the results of their cyberconferencing to the decision makers. In addition, Cyberparty maintains a Web site (www.cyberparty.or.kr) upon which it also publishes *The Thread*, the Webzine of New Asia Politics.

So what is the Korean idea of "new Asian politics"? In 1998, Korea elected Kim Dae Jung as its new president. Mr. Kim was an extraordinary choice for this post for several reasons: (1) he had served years of hard time in prison for advocating his democratic political ideals, which strongly criticized the corruption not only of a succession of dishonest presidents, but also of the so-called representative democracy and corporate-run economy in Korea itself; (2) he had been sentenced to death for these beliefs; and (3) he ran on a platform that demanded "comprehensive political reform." The big question, once again, is: What does that mean in practice?

President Kim provided a general answer in his inaugural speech. In it he pointed out that the only way for Korea to overcome its limitations was to "transform" its present representative system into something he called "participatory democracy." He recognized that the old system was totally controlled by large corporate interests and irreparably corrupted. The solution was to find new ways to involve and engage the entire citizenry of Korea in making key decisions for its political economy of the future (Becker 1998, 3).

Finally, two nations "down under," New Zealand and Australia, both practice mild forms of direct democracy at the national level, with the former being the new kid on the block. In 1993, New Zealand passed the Citizens Initiated Referenda Act, which empowered citizens to vote on proposed legislation through a process that might best be defined as "non-binding indirect initiative."

When a group of citizens wants to put an issue on the ballot, they must compose the verbiage for the proposed law and submit it to the Clerk of the House of Representatives. The Clerk then advertises it to the general public and welcomes input. After that, the Clerk consults with the petitioners and other experts and refines it into a final version. The petitioners then have 12 months to get at least 10% of all eligible voters to sign on the dotted line. Once that is done, it goes to the House itself and they must schedule the actual referendum within a year's time. If the referendum is passed by a majority of the voters, the government has the option of accepting or rejecting it. There's the rub. However, as we have previously noted, if there is a strong majority in favor of the new law and Parliament stubbornly resists, those legislators opposed may face grave political repercussions when they run for re-election.

In any event, the citizens of New Zealand had two such initiatives on the ballot in November 1999. Both were passed. One mandated heavier criminal penalties for "home invasions." The other commanded Parliament to downsize itself, from 120 members to a more sleek 99. Clearly, one of these is going to be harder for Parliament to swallow than the other. Time will tell which, if either, they embrace and make as the law of the land.

Australia also has direct democracy at the national level, but it is only in the form of referendum and it is only for changes in the constitution. In its entire history, there have been only 43 such referenda, and a mere eight have passed muster with the citizenry. The latest of these also came in November 1999. The issue: whether to ditch the ancient British monarchy or become an independent, modern republic.

As one might expect, this referendum stirred virulent pangs of emotion among many Australians, but especially over the particular choice that was put to them by Parliament. Instead of simply posing the choice between the monarchy and a republic, Parliament asked the people to vote for the monarchy or for an oddball republic, where the Parliament alone selected the president. Thus, a large number of voters who favored a republic where the voters chose the president themselves were torn. Some were so upset by Parliament's republic that they voted for the monarchy. Others abstained.

The result was twofold: (1) the majority of the voters chose to retain the monarchy; (2) a large reservoir of discontent was created, one that would build pressure for a similar referendum in the future. After all, Fishkin's "deliberative poll" conducted there in October 1999 found that a solid majority of Australians wanted a republic. It is only a matter of time until a more acceptable choice will be put to Australia on this matter.

We have looked at Denmark, Germany, Switzerland, Italy, Belgium, the United States, Venezuela, Ecuador, Guatemala, Brazil, Peru, Japan, Korea, New Zealand, Australia, and trans-European democracy. Is this simply a scattering or smattering of isolated movements, or is it at least the beginnings of a global democratic movement?

As we noted in Chapter 6, we believe that we have seen the start of both a virtual and real-life organizational structure for all these—and many other present and future—democratic—movements to come together and cohere globally. Back in the summer of 1998, we attended and helped organize The First International Congress on Direct Democracy in the Czech Republic. The original idea and impetus for this was the work of a Czech political scientist named Jiri Polak, whose ideas are expressed in his book *The Direct Democracy of Tomorrow* (1996), which he co-wrote with Jaroslav Koci.

The meeting was held in Pribram, a suburb of Prague, and was attended by a potpourri of political leaders, academics, and organizers favorable to direct democracy from 15 nations—many of which have been the sites of the projects discussed above. The outcome was mostly synergistic, a concordance to work together in the future in the ways described in Chapter 6. Since then, as noted in Chapter 6, its Web site on TAN+N has led the global "hit parade" for many months. What this gathering demonstrated was that everyone there saw that they were not solitary players, not isolated, not merely a local or national project. They saw and felt that they were the embodiment of a mutually agreeable and dynamic group from highly disparate cultures. Thus, the final order of business was to set up a committee to organize the Second International Congress on Direct Democracy in Athens in late June of 2000.

As we conclude this book in late 1999, the members of this Continuing Congress have developed what in cyberspeak might be called a *virtual worldwide direct democracy movement*. The dialogue and communication that has followed since Pribram has produced noteworthy results. First, there has been substantial discussion about what direct democracy will mean theoretically and operationally in the 21st century. Second, the main TAN+N Web site—including an e-mail discussion group and message board—has been an excellent tool of continued interpersonal connection and collaboration among the charter members and for attracting and activating new members. Third, the print newsletter (published in Prague) has had similar effects. Fourth, several collaborative projects have already been accomplished or are well along toward completion, including several international conferences and international cooperation on books and articles promoting the global democratic movement.

21st-Century Democratic Communications Systems: Lateral and Interactive

Another area of tremendous growth in the global democracy movement comes in the continued experimentation in and advancement of New Democratic Paradigm, teledemocratic political communications. As we have mentioned in many different contexts in this book, unlike its predecessor systems, this one is not characterized by a centrally controlled, downward stream of information and values. Instead, its heart and soul is a multilateral channel of communication that provides easy interaction between individuals and nodes and that comports with a quantum correction to the dominant Newtonian system of communication.

There are, to our way of thinking, three major components to modern teledemocracy or 21st-century democratic communications: voting from the home; scientific deliberative polling; and ETMs. Although each of these is also a separate and important element in the New Democratic Paradigm, that is, it is a superior empowerment tool by itself, we are linking them in this section because (1) we believe they work best in interaction with one another; (2) many projects inherently include two or more of them; and (3) there are new experiments that try to explicitly link them. What is more, we see them as fitting so well together as a completely new form of interactive, multilateral political communications that would maximize the empowerment of individual citizens within all forms of strong democracy, semidirect democracy, participatory democracy, deliberative democracy, or teledemocracy.

Home Is Where Citizens Think: Voting by Mail, Telephone, and Internet

It is our view that allowing citizens the luxury of voting from their abodes is an extremely empowering experience. As the state of Oregon test proved, voter turnout multiplies at lower cost to the polity. Giving voters weeks to decide and cast their ballots obviously facilitates the participation of working, retired, and disabled people, single parents, just about everyone really.

Might there be a hidden agenda in constraining their electoral participation to one day during the workweek or to one weekend? We think so. Since a so-called democratic elite controls the levers of all contemporary representative systems, it is in their interest to minimize the size of the vote. By doing so they need to raise less money for their campaigns and there are fewer minds to cloud. Moreover, spare time is a perquisite of moneyed and managerial elites—the kind of folks with whom they best identify.

Some critics of home-voting say that citizens need to go to widely dispersed sites in order to gain a sense of being part of an electorate, an electoral community, an active citizenry. Surely they jest. Polling places often have long queues and are insulated systems of highly individualistic, secret voting (in booths or cubicles). There is little if any "community" to these private rites. People try to get in and out of public polling places as swiftly and painlessly as possible. Moreover, in the United States, general elections are almost always held on Tuesdays, which makes it difficult for working people to vote. Transportation is necessary, which presents an obstacle for many poor, disabled, or aged citizens. Voting at sparse and remote polling places is also a problem for single parents with several children. And finally, young people shy away from the experience.

As we noted in Chapter 3, however, voting from the home via telephone and TV can be exciting. We discovered that some families actually turned it into a truly communal experience, waiting in line at home to have their say, even when they knew their votes really packed little to no political punch.

As we have indicated earlier in this book, we have extensive professional experience in electronic "voting from the home" through our work with Televote, interactive TV Town Meetings, and ETMs (Chapters 3 and 4). Our interactions with home-voters have almost always been upbeat. Of course, all our experimental designs have the public's vote communicated to another human being (a telephone interviewer) rather than to a telephone computer system. So, we cannot generalize our results to automated electronic voting from the home, which we concede is less expensive and more "efficient" in terms of speed of tabulation.

So, which is a better way to tally votes from the home: human interviewers or computers? We think both are useful, but for different purposes. In our opinion, automated home-voting systems can be used effectively in ETMs, where the emphasis is on education, discussion, interaction, and massive turnout. It should also be a major part of actual voting for candidates or in referenda or citizens initiatives. (The latter has been the focus of the Voting By Phone Foundation, in Boulder, Colorado [www.vote.org/v/index.htm] for all local initiatives and Olympians Concerned About Democracy [OCAD], who are trying to institute telephone voting as an integral part of local hearings and decision making in Olympia, Washington [www.olywa.net/ocad].) The personal interviewer method would be best used on scientific deliberative samples at home, since it will help maximize the number of respondents who actually participate, thus improving the accuracy of the sample, and can help in facilitating any latent consensuses among them over time.

Most of the home-vote experimentation discussed earlier in this volume has emphasized the speed and efficiency of computers (Nova Scotia Liberal party; Honolulu Electronic Hearing; Reform party of Canada ETM; Bay Voice; U.S. Reform party's presidential nomination; etc.). All these experiments were practical in tallying one vote per phone. We also believe that in order to stimulate a civic discourse in a home that ends in several or many people voting from the same place, this process is best served via an interaction with a human interviewer on the other end of the line.

So, the Oregon mail-vote experiment was a huge success. And the phone-vote experiments for party leaders in several Canadian provinces also increased turnouts dramatically (300% in Nova Scotia) and greatly improved the demographics of the participants. But has anyone ever tried to breach the security of these systems?

In 1992, the Office of the Secretary of State of New Mexico, with the technical assistance of the Sandia National Laboratory (specialists in electronic security for American nuclear installations), tested the integrity of the system in a mock election held in several high schools in Albuquerque, New Mexico. In a memorandum to us, Kathy Flynn, the project's director, stated: "From a technological standpoint, the venture was extremely successful. The participating students had no difficulty following the directions or using the phones, and all the ballots were transmitted without failure. Challenged to test the security of the system, some students tried voting their ballots twice, only to hear a recorded voice tell them that those identification numbers had already been used. Then the system hung up on them."

Ted Wachtel, who has written a lengthy and well-reasoned argument for the widespread use of telephone voting in national referenda, puts it like this: "Voting by telephone . . . would be similar to many business applications already in use on a daily basis. . . . College students register for courses and pay their tuition with credit cards. Bank customers access their accounts and pay bills. They do so by entering touch-tone signals in response to digitized computer voices without any college or bank personnel participating in the process. This technology can easily be adapted to telephone voting" (Wachtel 1992, 76).

Of course, there is no 100% foolproof system for anything. The more one is willing to spend to make it difficult to breach the system, the harder it will be to do so. In any event, the most failsafe system will use numerous methods of voting (mail, voting machines, telephone, and others) and will compel the voters to use complex, multiple personal identification information and numbers. There must be many different kinds of double-checking throughout the system. All methods of voting have been compromised throughout history. There is no reason to suspect that electronic voting is more susceptible to this than any of the other methods.

Those keen on keeping turnout as low as possible point to the fact that in all these systems of home-voting, people may have to cede a degree of privacy and anonymity in their voting, that is, there is a traceable link between your vote and your identification data. Furthermore, a record of this vote may need to be preserved in order to check out the integrity or accuracy of the system.

There are ways to address these problems. For one thing, privacy laws need to be strengthened considerably. Furthermore, unauthorized snooping into voting records could be made a felony—with mandatory jail time—making it illegal for anyone other than election officials to gain access to such information. It should also be made a go-directly-to-jail felony for election officials to disclose anyone's vote except for electoral security checks. Nevertheless, citizens must be told of this trade-off and have the option of going to a secret balloting place somewhere else if they feel the anonymity of their vote is more important to them than the convenience of home-voting. In other words, the security and integrity of home- and electronic-voting has problems, but there are some pragmatic solutions.

But the future of 21st-century New Democratic Paradigm voting-from-the-home will be neither mail-voting nor telephone-voting. It will be courtesy of the Internet—especially after the Web becomes interfaced with home television. This will be commonplace early in the 21st century. So, when citizens can switch on their TV sets and be zoomed into cyberspace, they will have instantaneous capacity to vote online just by pushing buttons on their handset.

Voting online is already quite advanced. One can vote by e-mail, vote in chat-rooms, vote in news groups, vote in Web surveys, and vote on message boards. It can be unsecured or encrypted. Millions and millions of people are "voting" to buy books from www.amazon.com and putting their credit card numbers online to pay for their purchases. In addition, there are already several experiments in the works that will test online political voting and a very recent one that was highly successful.

For example, according to a report in the *New York Times*, the Pentagon and the states of California and Florida are presently experimenting with computer-voting in real life. The Pentagon needs a better way to permit its personnel serving overseas to absentee-vote via the Internet. The state of Florida has plans for a test in the year 2000 (*New York Times*, March 14, 1999, p. A-9)

In March 2000, the Arizona Democratic party added cyber-voting and mail-voting as two new ways registered party members could vote in its presidential primary. These votes would be as binding as those cast at traditional polling places. The main goal was to swell the size of the general turnout. Another was to attract more interest from African-, Hispanic- and Native-Americans.

The party hired Election.com, an experienced innovator in the field of corporate Internet voting. As part of the experiment, computers were located in areas heavily populated by black, Latino, and local indigenous peoples and were staffed by experts to assist voters who were not computer literate. Moreover, computer and mail voters had several days to cast their ballots. The results: (1) computer turnout alone tripled the entire 1996 vote; (2) mail turnout also tripled the 1996 vote; (3) there was much more interest in the minority communities than in past primaries; and (4) there was no hint of electoral fraud.

We believe that as the appeal and success of electronic voting becomes more obvious by its increasing usage, even mainstream politicians will start to use it for their own purposes some high-voltage mainstream political figures will begin to laud its advantages. A recent example is John F. Kennedy, Jr., who in one of the national Sunday newspaper supplements made this case shortly before his untimely and tragic death:

Here's how it might work: At whatever time of day they like, voters could go to a computer wherever they like—at home, at the office or in a public space such as a library. At a website, voters would enter a secure password and see an electronic ballot, including perhaps pictures of and information on the candidates. The votes could be tabulated instantaneously, so that once the polls close, a final count would be immediately available. Such ease and efficiency would appeal most to the group that now votes least: young people. (Kennedy 1999, 7)

Moreover, this movement is spreading globally too. The government of Costa Rica has experimented with and plans to adopt computer voting for its first presidential election of the 21st century in 2002 (Clausing 1997, 1–4). And the government of Austria is presently considering a long-term study of the effect of various types of voting (yes-no, multiple choice, rank-order) on outcomes via the Internet. These are just the early stages of what is bound to become commonplace as 21st-century democracy unfolds. It is a "no-brainer" to see a day in the future when e-voting will be as common—and at least as secure—as e-commerce.

Scientific Deliberative Polling and ETMs: Growth in Number, Sophistication, Momentum, and Staying Power

There has also been increased growth and momentum in the development of scientific deliberative polling and ETMs in the United States and globally throughout the 1990s. This is manifested by (1) the sheer and exploding number of experiments; (2) the cross-national replications; (3) the complexity of their design and innovation in the combination of components; and (4) locating permanent home sites for them.

Jim Fishkin's "Deliberative Poll," for example, is really catching on. He did his first in the United Kingdom in 1994, his second in the United States in 1996, and his 15th in Australia in the fall of 1999 (on whether to remain under the British Crown or become an independent republic). As we did in Hawaii and Dienel does in Germany, Fishkin uses a university as his headquarters.

Ned Crosby's Citizen Jury model continues to draw attention and new sponsors—including Minnesota Governor Jesse Ventura, who supported a Citizens Jury on tax reform in late 1999. Moreover, his Citizen Jury model has been duplicated in other countries. As we noted earlier, the IPPR in London adapted his model numerous times in England, particularly on issues involving the national health service. This caught the eye of Tony Blair, who promised to use Citizen Juries on issues like energy and transportation extensively in the future. It was also tried in Australia as a local citizen planning tool by Lyn Carson, then a councilwoman in a small beach town on the eastern Australia coast (Carson 1995). As a lecturer in government at the University of Sydney, she continues to pursue its study and use in that country.

Another highly successful, long-running model of scientific deliberative polling is The Danish Board of Technology (www.tekno.dk). Its technique is similar to the *Planungszelle* and Citizen Juries along the following lines: Stratified samples of "lay panels" are chosen to discuss and deliberate important issues on the future of governance in depth and over time. As in the Citizen Jury and the Deliberative Poll processes, the citizens have informed exchanges with a number of experts in the area under discussion and the process is facilitated by professionals in the art of coaxing agreement.

There is one big difference between this Danish "consensus conference" model and all the others: It has been a permanent part of the Danish national governmental process and political landscape since 1987. The Danish Parliament, in its wisdom, commissions these citizen panels on a regular basis for the specific purpose of helping them make legislative decisions concerning the ethics and effects of new scientific technologies, that is, genetic engineering, the use of new medical procedures, drugs, and the like.

According to Lars Kluver, the executive director of the Danish Board of Technology, most of the decisions and/or recommendations made by the 18 or so of these lay panels thus far convened in Denmark have been either adopted by the Parliament as is or taken into serious account in their decision making. He also told us by e-mail that a recent survey among national legislators asking them about the consensus panels found that "nearly everybody knew of them and 30% could refer to at least one of them" (April 28, 1998).

In fact, this program has been so successful in getting citizens to think about this important subject matter, that 11 other nations have introduced them in the past few years including Australia, Canada, France, Japan, the Netherlands, New Zealand, Norway, South Korea, Switzerland, and the United Kingdom. Richard Sclove, the executive director of the Loka Institute in Amherst, Massachusetts—which specializes in involving citizens in technological-political issues—held the first Danish consensus board in the United States in April of 1997. His Web site (www.loka.org/pages/worldpanels.html) has an updated listing and linkages to all of them (35 up to the summer of 1999).

Yet another variant on this theme is under way presently in both the United Kingdom and Australia. In Great Britain, where it is called the People's Panel, Prime Minister Blair has had his cabinet randomly select 5,000 citizens to be available for regular polling and focus groups (www.cabinet-office.gov.uk/servicefirst/). In Australia, the mayor of the city of Brisbane invited all citizens to become members of the city council's "community reference group" called "Your City, Your Say." Expecting about 600, over 6,000 accepted. This group is encouraged to come to public hearings and participate in strategic planning sessions, and it gets regular newsletters that contain information on problems and issues, and polling information on the Panel itself, among other things. In other words, it is given lots of data and opinion, participates in deliberative processes, and is routinely polled. It is also included in the city's Web site www.brisbane.qld.gov.au. The mayor claims that some of the city council's projects and budget have already been changed to reflect the views and/or values of the citizens who have participated in this process.

Another component of 21st-century political communications that appears to be thriving is the ETM model of Ron Thomas, a professional architect and city planner who spent the better part of his career designing and testing his notion of "Tele-planning." His first organization was a nonprofit he baptized the Community Design Exchange, located in Seattle, Washington. Under this label, he conceived his unique ETM process, testing it first in Roanoke, Virginia, and Savannah, Georgia, in the late 1980s, and since then in Houston, Texas (1995–96), Racine, Wisconsin (1997–99), and presently in Washington, D.C., Albuquerque, New Mexico, and, starting in Y2K, the Chicago region.

The linchpin of the Thomas-style ETM is to involve all key geopolitical areas within a city in its strategic planning process. He does this by selecting a critical number of neighborhoods and/or communities to hold simultaneous face-to-face meetings. These are supported—and participated in—by local community leaders, once again facilitated by people trained in the skills of consensus building and, most importantly, informed and connected through a variety of TV news shows. For example, at an early stage of the process, all the community discussion groups watch a locally produced and televised documentary on the issue(s) at hand. After group discussions based on that, the final results of these meetings are reported on the late evening TV news. The essence of the Thomas ETM, then, intertwines face-to-face facilitated community meetings with television programming. There are several stages and phases to his Tele-planning process, which usually spans many months.

The results of Thomas's ETMs have been highly praised by the city officials who contracted with him to design and coordinate these processes and, according to them, they have had a significant impact on the strategic planning of their cities. His Wisconsin project, however, was slightly different in that a local corporate-funded foundation put him in charge of a three-year project they called Sustainable Racine.

Surely one of the major challenges for the future in every industrialized nation is how to maintain what has come to be called "sustainable growth." This means that economic growth must be pegged to the capabilities of the natural environment to support such development. It is a modern puzzle that remains by and large unsolved. So, the idea behind Sustainable Racine was to utilize the ETM as a continuing process to develop a long-range community-based plan sensitive to both ecological sustainability and economic growth. The deal gave Thomas three years (1997–2000) to put a community ETM Tele-planning infrastructure in place. This was well underway until something dramatic occurred.

As has often been the case in the development of new paradigm political communications, actual or imminent success led to premature termination. In Thomas's view, the head of the chemical company that had funded the project became alarmed at the direction the community was headed and withdrew support for the project. Community pressures were building in a way that threatened to make the company behave in ways it did not believe to be in its best interests. But as has also been true in the development of new paradigm political communications, when one path leads to a steep cliff, another less precarious one suddenly appears. This came in the form of a parallel ETM project that had been in the works for several years.

Carolyn Lukensmeyer, formerly the chief of staff for the governor of Ohio, served in the White House as a consultant for 1993–1994. (One of her jobs there was to facilitate cabinet retreats.) It was at this point in her career, though, that she decided that something drastic needed to be done to bring the American people more effectively and directly into the national political decision-making process.

Leaving the White House behind, she embarked on a lengthy research trip to find out what had already been done in the country along these lines. She talked to many of the people already discussed in this book, browsing through the shelves of past ETMs, evaluating designs, technologies, and techniques—what worked and what did not.

It became evident to her that what was sorely lacking was some kind of national organization devoted to this cause. So, her first major move in this direction was to obtain funding for a conference to which she invited about 100 people—theorists, experimenters, government officials past and present, foundation people, and citizen activists—who shared the same vision. They convened at Airlie House, Virginia, in 1995 to talk about how this could best be done. The next step was a second conference called Designing for Democracy. It was held at the Wingspread Conference Center in Racine, Wisconsin, and its purpose was to develop a teledemocratic "action plan" to be impemented in specific communities.

The upshot of the Wingspread gathering was the beginning of an entirely new kind of national ETM organization, quite different from the ETMCo hierarchical corporate model. (We should have known such was a liability.) It was, instead, a network that took the name of her founding organization, America Speaks. One of its main components was a trio of local and regional community organizations: (1) Snonet—an Internet-based community services nonprofit in Snohomish County, Washington;

(2) Central Carolina Choices—a community-based planning group for the 14 county region around Charlotte, North Carolina; and (3) a group of Kentuckians in the early stages of setting up a citizen-planning process for their state.

A second key component in the network was the "national resource team," which included Thomas, Becker, Sclove, Lawrence Grossman, Robert Kingston (Kettering Foundation), and Martha McCoy (Study Circles Resources) as well as several experts in Web dialogue and organization. The third element was the central office of America Speaks in Washington, D.C., whose role was to coordinate the network's activities and to maintain network communications mainly via the Internet (www.americaspeaks.org). It was at the Wingspread conference that Thomas was offered the job as executive director of Sustainable Racine on the spot. It was also decided then and there that Sustainable Racine would become the fourth community service organization in the America Speaks network.

What followed was a spurt of cybertalk among the network participants that lasted for several months. After that, the decibel level of America Speaks diminished to a low hum and stayed that way for a while. During this lull, Lukensmeyer reaped a bonanza: the opportunity to become the executive director of that huge ETM project funded by the Pew Charitable Trusts called Americans Discuss Social Security (ADSS) mentioned in Chapter 5. This was a $12.5 million super-project whose aim was to develop nationwide citizen deliberation on the future of the American social security system and to deliver the results to Congress, the president, the mass media, and the American public. After all her research into this area, she realized that she would pioneer the first comprehensive, national ETM in the United States, and would be able to test out the theory that such a system would indeed work wonders nationally in America. After much agonizing, she decided to divert most of her energies and attention to ADSS. America Speaks continued, albeit in low gear.

ADSS, however, was a quantum leap in the design of new democratic communications, due to its scale, complexity, and sophistication in interfacing face-to-face and electronic deliberations. In several ways, it resembled the Ft. Mason model depicted in Figure 5.1. The three major prongs of the ADSS ETM model included a series of conventional (but not deliberative) scientific polls on the subject; paid national advertising (*New York Times, Newsweek, Washington Post*, etc.); and a wide array of methods to stimulate "citizen engagement" (Americans Discuss Social Security 1999, 6). We will limit our discussion here to those elements designed to engage the citizenry in the national dialogue.

At the heart of the ADSS process were the large (from 100 to 600 people), face-to-face forums held all around the country. Participants were not selected via a random process, but efforts were made to make these forums approximate the demographics of the community in which they were held. Several hundred citizens were usually in attendance, although this same process was successfully applied to a gathering of 3,000 people to develop a citywide strategic plan for the District of Columbia in late 1999. However, there were a number of features that elevated the ADSS large forums well above what generally passes as "citizen forums" or "town hall meetings" in America these days.

For one thing, the entire group was broken down into much smaller units sitting around small tables, with 10 to 12 citizens to each group. For another, the usual ratio of who did the most speaking—the "people up front" or "the citizens in the audience"—was reversed with the vast majority of talk coming from the citizens themselves. In addition, the experts simply served as resources for the citizens at the tables, coming to them when requested to answer questions or offer opinions.

Additionally, each table was equipped with two different electronic tools to facilitate the discussion at the table, to link the tables in discussion, and to make the plenary voting anonymous and rapid. One of these was an electronic keypad, which each participant was given. The other was a laptop computer at each table that was used to link to the discussions at other tables and for other statistical and record-keeping purposes.

Another important feature in these forums was that each table was staffed with a trained facilitator. This was an essential factor in getting the participants to listen to one another, to help reluctant citizens speak up, and to focus the group on trying to arrive at mutually agreeable alternatives.

Four times during the project, 10 of these geographically dispersed forums were hooked into a national discussion amongst themselves and with a number of congressmen via video teleconferences. These were unscripted and ran in real time and several of them were broadcast by local cable TV in some of the participating cities, sometimes garnering large audiences and allowing home viewers to call in questions.

Third, ADSS established and maintained a Web site. This Web site contained a broad range of Internet services and resources, including "message boards, information on events, polling results, reform options, and how to contact Congress. An interactive quiz on Social Security and a unique process that allowed users to see how their answers compare to scientific poll results further used technology to educate and engage Internet users in the . . . discussion" (Americans Discuss Social Security 1999, 16). Although no longer on the Internet, there are plans to resurrect it as: www.americaspeaks.org.

There were a host of other innovative features in this project. By way of example, the project went to great lengths to bring young Americans into the discussion by holding forums at 100 college campuses around the country.

Since the Pew organizers expected this particular issue to emerge as a major one only after the presidential and congressional elections of 2000, there is no way at this time to assess the impact, if any, of ADSS on federal decision makers about what to do about the Social Security system.

The ADSS project officially ended on June 30, 1999. Within a few weeks, Lukensmeyer convened a third America Speaks conference in Washington, D.C. A small number of key people who had stayed involved were invited. That meeting, however, constructed the framework for a restructured, renewed, and reinvigorated America Speaks, a more closely knit network that aimed to synthesize the entire American teledemocratic movement into a far more effective force for the 21st century.

The basic idea improved upon what emerged from the Wingspread conference—a network of community-based service and planning organizations plus a coterie of ETM designers and experimenters. There were plenty of new features. First, through an excellent facilitation process devised and executed by Steve Kay, a number of specific tasks were related to the general mission and each of the participating organizations and individuals accepted personal and immediate responsibility for them. These included annual monetary "investment" into the network; developing criteria for "authentic" teledemocratic practices; expanding the network; collaborating on developing projects and obtaining funding for projects for the network; developing a much more extensive Web site; holding annual retreats; and the like. Lukensmeyer agreed to be the chairperson of the board and Thomas agreed to become the new executive director.

One of the most intriguing aspects of this new and novel national ETM organization is that it is driven by an "entrepeneurial" ethic, that is, it seeks to sustain itself by using network resources to raise funding as well as to design and coordinate new and innovative teledemocratic projects in the future. Another is its open door strategy to invite all those who have worked in this area in the past, and are in it now, to join the network. The objective was to pool the sum total of the theoretical and practical experience from the 20th century and marshal it for rapid expansion into the 21st century so as to further edify citizens; cultivate public dialogue; augment interactions between citizens and government leaders and officials; and broaden the base of citizen input in representative systems.

A call for a national organization to support a similar process occurred almost simultaneously in Sweden. Once again it was Tomas Ohlin leading the way, now basing his vision on cumulative knowledge of successful New Democratic Paradigm experiments around the world. In a report, sponsored by a national agency, he proposes a multistep process designed to develop national dialogues on major issues. His recommendations include "new ways to form local communities ... electronic study circles ... Internet for everybody. ... Local online voting should be used to reinforce representative system ... political participation systems must be available for all ... participation with time for careful consideration" (Ohlin 1998, 117–120). Ohlin, like most of the American theorists and experimenters, views these new sophisticated teledemocratic systems as being used primarily to improve the communications system between the public and their representatives.

However, we see a different but equally important utility for 21st-century political communications, one yet to be proposed or tested. This would be to use these systems to mandate a public agenda for a governmental agency or legislature at any level (an electronic version of the Porto Alegre project) or, better yet, to set the table for a referendum and/or citizens initiative.

The reader may recall that we have spoken earlier about the need for public agenda setting in the representative system on several occasions. However, we also believe that there is an equally—if not superior—role in the direct democratic arena as well.

We believe that if scientific random samples of citizens, who actively participate in an authentic, comprehensive ETM process (as described in Chapter 5), were to establish priorities and issues by large super-majorities (75% or better) for citizens initiatives, then (1) the turnout would boom; (2) the influence of big money during the electoral campaigns would diminish; and (3) the percentage of initiatives that pass muster by citizens would surge to new highs. Why would this be so?

The way citizens initiatives are generally run allows a very small group of people who are deeply faithful to their own political agenda to propose that upon which voters must vote—if they can get the required small (usually 2% to 5%) percentage of citizens to sign their petition. Keep in mind that many citizens will put their names on such a petition—even if they do not agree with it—just because they think that the general public should be allowed to vote on it. So, why should such a Lilliputian, highly skewed canvass of people be the *only* ones empowered to put issues on the ballot for the vote of the entire polity? Why not grant this authority as well to random samples of 500 to 1,000, composed of mostly ordinary citizens who have had a shot at a genuine, comprehensive, informed, and mediated deliberation?

At least one major reason why most citizens initiatives fail to win at the ballot box is that most citizens were not consulted prior to the issue being certified for the ballot. Thus even with the best of intentions and a love for direct democracy, organizers of citizens initiatives are yet merely another "special interest group" who arrange public agendas. If a mirror image of the people—doing their civic duty as a jury of peers— overwhelmingly decides that such should be on the ballot instead, there is a much greater likelihood of passage—even with a heavily financed advertising campaign against it.

Our own research, as well as that of Alan Kay and others, reveals there is often a gaping chasm between what entrenched political elites prefer and what the people desire. Kay calls this a "disconnect" (Kay 1998, 1). We would assume that this holds equally true for small counterelites who want the people to vote on their issue as well as for the established elites who feel they already know what is good for the general public.

Thus, we do not advocate eliminating the present method of putting issues on the ballot for the public to vote on. What we do think would be a worthwhile addition to the direct democratic process of citizens initiative is to amend Mike Gravel's prescription of using "acceptable public opinion polls" to authorize national citizens initiatives—with "scientific deliberative polls embedded within a comprehensive Electronic Town Meeting process" (as described in Chapter 5).

We believe, however, that the baseline percentage for authorizing a national initiative should be—after the consensus-building process of the ETM—at least 75% of the random sample being in favor instead of a simple majority. The reasons for this include (1) it will decrease the number of such initiatives to more manageable proportions; and (2) it will greatly increase the probability of passage of each because it will already have extensive and stable support around the country.

We also think that such ETMs should initially be used by the general public to establish priorities for what problems they want to focus on in any given year. Only then should another set of ETMs be run to recommend specific policies to be subject to a general vote. That would be an ideal mixture to promote New Paradigm Democracy in the 21st century.

The Modern Mediation Movement: Non-Hierarchical, Quantum-Style Conflict Resolution

Throughout this book, we have directly and indirectly referenced the worth of "mediation," "facilitation," "consensus building," and "win-win," as important features of the New Democratic Paradigm. This is due to the fact that Newtonian-style methods of conflict resolution, in particular courts and the law, are based on dichotomies like "win-lose," and are theoretically "zero-sum," "winner-take-all" power struggles.

In addition, all Newtonian-based conflict resolution structures are hierarchical, where human beings (sitting on high) inflict their will—their concept of justice based on an alleged logical interpretation of the law—on the disputants. The parties to the dispute have no option other than to voluntarily obey these mandates or be forced to submit to them. Absolute laws, clashing independent interests, great deference to logic, rigidity, and a highly tapered structure are major components of the old Newtonian paradigm.

What we also find is an imperious system meeting its Waterloo, one most citizens find to be as cheery as a hospital operating room. After all, the legal system in almost every country is a monument to "power over," with cloaked judges at the top, sharp-tongued lawyers just below them, and John Q. Citizen groveling at the bottom. It is also a system of conflict resolution that is extremely difficult for the average citizen to decipher, couched as it is in an extraterrestrial lexicon and complicated by rules of combat that often seem to defy the gravity of common sense.

Worse yet, it is a system that is exorbitant, yet cumbersome and clumsy. So, it is not surprising that those who almost monopolize its use are government, large corporations, and businesses. This is why the former chief justice of the West Virginia Supreme Court calls it "a deliberately broken machine" that intentionally excludes the middle-class taxpayers, the very people who actually foot most of the bills for its operations (Neely 1983, 7). Thus, even in America, the world's most litigious society with the cosmos' largest number of lawyers per capita, the legal system is held in contempt by much of the general population.

Walter K. Olsen, a leading observer of the current American court system puts it like this:

> The unleashing of litigation in its full fury has done cruel, grave harm and little lasting good. It has helped sunder some of the most sensitive and profound relationships of human life: between the parents who have nurtured a child; between the healing professions and those whose life and well-being are entrusted to their care. It clogs and jams the gears of commerce, sowing friction and distrust between the productive enterprises on which material progress depends and all who buy their products, work at their plants and offices, join in their undertakings. . . . It torments the provably innocent and rewards the palpably irresponsible. It devours hard-won savings and worsens every animosity of a diverse society. It is the special American burden, the one feature hardly anyone admires. (Olsen 1991, 2)

However, sometime in the mid-1970s, a group of enlightened and far-sighted lawyers, law professors, labor mediators, anthropologists, and community organizers began a movement that breathed a new life and vigor into the long-standing but marginal practice of mediation in America (Auerbach 1984). Mediation, as a nonadversarial mode of ending disputes, had previously been confined in the United States to small religious sects (Mennonites, Quakers), a few ethnic groups (Chinese, Jewish), labor-management relations, and the like. The bright, new idea was to expand this practice systematically throughout American culture as an "alternative" to litigation as the first thing that came to a citizen's mind when he or she got involved in some sort of altercation.

Mediation and the New Democratic Paradigm

Mediation, as practiced throughout the world, is the system of conflict resolution where two parties engaged in some sort of squabble come together informally to confront the problem directly and negotiate a cease-fire and peace plan. The key to its success is the mediator: a neutral third party who helps the parties along in this process. The mediator (or mediators) must earn the trust of the parties to the dispute in order to be of maximum assistance. Neither the "brooding omnipresence of the law" nor the "inalienable rights" of the parties are paramount. Neither the mediator nor the law decides the dispute and neither is above or superior to the parties. It is the parties themselves who are the principal actors and the parties alone who dictate the terms of any settlement.

In other words, where the legal system is almost purely Newtonian in its theory and applications, mediation reflects quantum thought in its theory and practice. There is no hierarchy. There is no higher authority. There are no laws to bind the parties. The parties must develop a lateral dialogue between themselves, communicate their feelings and desires to one another, and they must learn to listen to the needs, feelings, and wishes of the other party. This is what Daniel Yanlelovich, a leading American expert on public opinion, calls "the magic of dialogue" and how it transforms "conflict into cooperation" (Yankelovich 1999). Instead of asserting their individual rights and independence, the parties come to understand how their actions impact upon others and come to grips with their mutual interdependence. Adding a mediator also helps the dialogue along. This method of dispute resolution works best when (1) there is an ongoing relationship between the parties themselves (like among family members, neighbors, partners, members of a community, colleagues, etc.) and (2) lawyers (playing the role of advocate) are absent.

The mediator, unlike the judge, is there to aid the parties, but only as long as both parties maintain an explicit trust in the mediator's impartiality and skill. The ultimate power lies in the hands of the individual citizens. What is just and logical is not a Platonic ideal, Newtonian law of nature, or legalistic construct. In mediation, what is just and logical is—in quantum terms—subjective and hazy. It exists purely in the soul and mind of each party and emerges from the synergy of the soul and mind of each party. Thus, mediation is a truly democratic conflict-resolution process and is the method of conflict resolution most consistent with the New Democratic Paradigm. The reader may recall that, in Chapter 2, we discussed how the Newtonian idea of resolving conflict used "force" and that in a quantum social system, individuals would resolve their differences by coming to understand a sense of interdependence and community among themselves.

Hazel Henderson, as we saw in Chapter 1, is a long-time visionary within the New Democratic Paradigm. In addition to envisioning the uses of electronic technologies to directly empower the citizenry, she has also theorized how these new technologies and software must be democratically deployed to replace the "mechanistic models of eighteenth century representative democracy" in order to "solve our ever-more-complex web of social, cultural, political, and economic problems" (Henderson 1996, 251).

The essence of her argument, though, is that a new system of conflict resolution, one rooted in mediation, is an essential part of the mix:

> We must restructure (the) manipulative, top-down, "big brother" aspects, which currently reinforce hierarchical institutions in both public and private sectors ... by substituting lateral, networked, real-time information flows to allow all parts of a complex system to coordinate and align their knowledge of changing environments and move their activities toward flexible, adaptive responses. (Henderson 1996, 252, 267)

In order to do this, Henderson sees it necessary to use random sample groups of citizens operating from the home (as do we) in order to insulate society's decisions from the bias of big money and power brokers and to ensure the prevalence of "win-win" solutions that are based on "common ground."

We have shown throughout this book that a key "software" in citizen deliberations must be these new, non-hierarchical, consensus-building techniques of conflict resolution, with mediation being the preferred mode. Courts, polarizing policy debates, brawling TV ads, and unmediated free-for-alls are old fashioned ways of presenting information in the hopes of arriving at a reasoned solution. They depend on the superior knowledge of experts and rely on competing positions and competitive posturing as the basis for "intelligent"—albeit unintelligible—decision making.

When using techniques derived from the New American Mediation movement, however, information, facts, and data no longer are understood as being "objective" and/or determinants of a functional decision. Subjective feelings, personal value systems, varying life experiences, and the perceptions of the citizenry are equally, if not more, salient to the solving of the problem. Listening well to the views and values of others is at least as, if not more, important than insisting that one is celestially right and the other is damnably wrong. The aspiration is not illustrious victory. The goal is precious amity, rapport, and solidarity.

It is important to reiterate that such facilitation of authentic democratic input and concordance, as we have seen throughout this book, *must be utilized at all stages of governance*, from start to finish. Auli Keskinen makes this explicit in her concept of "user empowerment":

> If citizens could participate in all phases, starting from the initial phase (preparatory and agenda setting) . . . they would have a much deeper impact. The citizen then could then participate in the deliberative decision-making process, which would not set the partners against each other but, instead, would try to develop alternative solutions to cases . . . in a win-win fashion. (Keskinen 1999, 251)

Thus, mediation is an essential component to the New Democratic Paradigm. It is as theoretically consistent with it as the adversarial system (legal and political) is part and parcel of the old democratic paradigm. That is why we have found it threading its way through so many of the face-to-face experiments already mentioned in Part II, including scientific deliberative polling (the Citizens Juries and "the Deliberative Poll") and some of the ETM experiments as well—particularly those conducted by Ron Thomas and Carolyn Lukensmeyer. And that is why this form of conflict resolution will become an integral part of 21st-century democracy as it continues to reveal itself.

The Electronic Facilitator

Mediation has not only proved successful as an element of the New Democratic Paradigm when used in face-to-face deliberation. There have been a number of successful experiments employing it during electronic conflict resolutions and policy deliberations as well.

Our own personal experience with the efficient power of electronically facilitated peacemaking came in a dispute Becker was asked to mediate between two station managers of the far-flung Peacenet network. The managers lived and worked on two Pacific isles that were thousands of miles apart. Still, they had been at one another's throats for years and the network coordinators in Honolulu were becoming alarmed that their mutual animosity was infecting other station managers in the network as well. So, they asked Becker to play mediator via live, interactive satellite radio from the system's headquarters in Hawaii.

Could that work? Didn't the mediator need to peer into their eyes, scrutinize their body language, maybe even get touchy-feely? Didn't the parties need to glare daggers at one another and hurl invectives with a visible sneer? So went the conventional wisdom. But to bring them together in the same room with a mediator would have cost thousands of dollars (which was unaffordable) and meant leaving the stations unat-

tended for a prolonged period (which was unthinkable). Electronic mediation was the only way to go. What happened flabbergasted everyone.
Despite being drowned out by static at least 25% of the time, we arrived
at a mutually acceptable agreement within an hour. Cost? A few bucks.
Mediation by satellite? No problem.

Actually, this is entirely congruent with the findings of the classic,
pace-setting experiment on moderated multiparty discussion and consensus building by telephone conferencing: Amitai Etzioni's trailblazing
MINERVA project in the very early 1970s. Actually, his team ran two
experiments, one a "laboratory" type using students and the other a
"real-life" experiment using leaders of the League of Women Voters scattered about the state of New Jersey.

What the Etzioni research group found was that mediated telephone
conferencing of small groups produced some excellent results, including
(1) a large majority found it very easy to "gain the floor" in them; (2)
many participants felt that strong personalities were not so intimidating
in a telephone meeting; (3) passive people found it easy to state and alter
contrary opinions; and (4) 13 out of the 16 lab groups reached consensuses of 75% or more.

The Etzioni team came to several useful conclusions about electronic
deliberations vs. face-to-face meetings. One of them was that "electronic
meetings might be somewhat less effective than face-to-face meetings in
terms of people swaying each other, but more conducive to letting people change their own minds" (Etzioni et al. 1975, 69). Another major
finding, consistent with ours, was that "lack of visual communication
did not lead to an uninvolving, rigid discussion" (Etzioni et al. 1975, 71).

As the reader may recall from Chapter 5, our view of the most efficient
ETM process includes many different styles of mediated discussion, that
is, pure face-to-face as well as pure electronic deliberation (particularly
via the Internet). The other type that also works is the face-to-face meeting that uses electronic equipment to expedite open discussion and the
building of a large consensus. We noted earlier that Americans Discuss
Social Security used this technique successfully.

There have been numerous other such experiments—in government
and in the corporate world—all of which have produced enthusiastic,
rave reviews. Perhaps the best use of these enables extremely private
people to vent their feelings in public—anonymously since all the results
of the electronic voting flashed on the screen at the meeting are statistical.
The electronic tally system also permits many more votes to be taken
and generates a momentum toward building agreement that is much
more difficult in large meetings where one relies on counting hands or
sorting paper ballots.

Another advantage to using electronics to facilitate a meeting of the
minds is that it is just about the only way to expand 21st-century de-

mocracy into becoming a global force—at the national and transnational levels. Mediation has proved to be useful at resolving cross-cultural disputes and it has great credibility throughout the world. Electronics has shown its utility in helping forge agreements in large groups. Splicing them together in transnational and/or global matters is doable, particularly in the near future using the Internet with its vast informational sites, its multilateral communications capacities, and its interface with TV. Actually, it is only a matter of time—in the 21st century—when this will be a routine procedure.

The Northern Ireland Experiment in Mediation and Direct Democracy

One of the most innovative and risky experiments in linking mediation with direct democracy in the Information Age was the bold attempt to finally bring closure to the centuries-old blood feud between the Catholics and Protestants in Northern Ireland. This also was the first try at resolving a transnational dispute by combining modern mediation, direct democracy, and electronic communications. Several important prerequisites had to be present for it to have a ghost of a chance to succeed.

First, all the key parties and stakeholders to the dispute had to concur on the process and play pivotal roles in it. Thus, some of the most fearsome factions in the war had to come face to face in the same room and actually listen to one another. Also, the two major countries that were knee-deep in this historic bloodletting also had to join in: the United Kingdom and the Republic of Ireland. Finally, they needed a mediator whom all stakeholders believed to be adroit, unprejudiced, discrete, and trustworthy. This package came in the personage of the former majority leader of the United States Senate, George Mitchell.

The mediation process was tortuous, lasting approximately two years. Like any sound mediation, it was conducted in private. However, in any mediation involving such heavily armed political forces, one where public haggling had been going on for years, the concerned publics were keenly aware of the general nature of what was being negotiated. After the curtain on this seemingly endless mediation was lifted, to everyone's amazement, all the combatants had arrived at a consensus on a whole new form of government for Northern Ireland. This included an innovative set of explicit relations between this brand new Northern Ireland government, the United Kingdom, and the Republic of Ireland. All sides had wrested major concessions from the others. This agreement was as close to a "win-win" situation for everyone as anyone could have hoped for—but it was surely that for the war-weary and war-torn citizenry, Catholic and Protestant, of Northern Ireland. (For a first-hand description of this extraordinary peacemaking process, see Mitchell 1999.)

The next step was to subject this plan for a new form of government to a direct vote of the people in the two most directly involved countries: the Republic of Ireland and Northern Ireland itself. A two-month public discussion period was scheduled prior to this extraordinary transnational referendum. In addition, agreement was reached whereby no TV advertising was allowed on the topic, given the propensity and proclivity of politicians and their political consultants to be negative, surly, and inflammatory. Only face-to-face discussion on the issue was permitted over television on this particularly incendiary question. Finally, the vote was taken and the results showed that a whopping 90% of the citizens of the Republic of Ireland favored the agreement, while a super-majority of 75% of the voters of Northern Ireland were similarly inclined.

So, did mediation + direct democracy + a civilized TV political debate = peace and love in Northern Ireland? It has helped. Since the 1998 referendum, there have been one atrocious act of terrorism (a bombing that killed many people); reports of widespread, savage infighting within the respective religious enclaves (not between them); and heavy foot dragging and/or provocations by some of the most extreme elements, including the Irish Republican Army (IRA) and the Protestant Orange Order.

However, in late 1999, the mediator returned for another round of negotiation, since many citizens were worried that the whole agreement might go up in flames. Once again: success. The majority Ulster Unionist party agreed to start sharing power with the Catholic political leadership even before the Irish Republican Army began to disarm. The actual destruction of IRA weapons was scheduled to begin on January 31, 2000. But what if that did not happen and/or something else causes violence to flare there again?

Even if this worst case scenario comes to pass, the Northern Ireland peace process worked brilliantly, like nothing before it. Imagine what would have occurred if the politics-as-usual method was used, that is, the hierarchy of political leaders coming to an agreement after secret negotiations and then saddling it on the two publics without giving the citizens a final say: instant warfare. Thus this is a New Democratic Paradigm model that can be copied exactly and tried again, particularly in less severe situations than one involving hundreds of years of hate and killing. What is more, an improved version can be invented to help resolve other "hot, hate-filled" conflicts around the world in the 21st century.

After all, there are all those other new, effective methods of citizen empowerment we have been discussing that might be added to its design and make it even harder for extremists to stall or undermine a vast public consensus. Whether or not this new Northern Ireland government takes root and grows—or withers on the vine of extremism—we know that the peace-making process worked well, that it produced a public-friendly interface with direct democracy, and that two national publics performed their roles admirably. The Northern Ireland peace process is a splendid example of what new forms of the New Democratic Paradigm look like in hands-on politics and what they can accomplish even against the greatest of odds. Indeed, in mid-2000, Israel is seriously considering using this process to help validate any land-for-peace deal with Syria.

Transformational Political Organization via the Internet

In Chapter 6 we praised the Internet as a New Democratic Paradigm system of electronic communication, one that has already begun to catalyze the global democracy movement. We also showed how the Internet can and should play a principal role in energizing and informing Televoters at the hub of a comprehensive and flexible ETM process. But there are more direct and immediate impacts that the Internet has for empowering the powerless within the present-day, theoretically representative democratic systems.

First, it serves as a handy communications infrastructure that can pressure these real-life oligarchies into being more responsive to their needs and concerns. Second, it helps organize movements for political structural changes that will compel these obsolescent governments to perform more like actual representative democracies and/or transform them into semidirect, strong democracies as well. Third, its very essence is—according to Fareed Zakaria, the managing editor of *Foreign Affairs*—"disrespectful of tradition, established order and hierarchy" (Lohr 2000, Wk1).

Trying to Limit the Transformational Power of the Internet

That the Internet harbors heroic potential to liberate ordinary citizens from the tyranny of a narrow, downward flow of information through today's mass electronic media (TV and radio) is not a news flash to (1) the few who own and regulate the satellites, broadcast facilities, airwaves, and cable networks and (2) those in the highchairs of political power. So, it is hardly surprising to find politicians and media sages taking aim at this new, but elusive target, the Internet, and mounting an all-out offensive to contain its infinite boundaries and constrain its infinite freedom of communication and organization.

Observe the somewhat subdued glee when the mass media zero in on the sleazy and unsavory aspects of cyberinfoglut, including such calumnies as cyberporn, cyberhate, and cybercrime. Of course, the Net is awash in this kind of slime, but no more so than bookstores, libraries, video stores, and telephone lines. The political fallout in the United States has included some faint-hearted and futile attempts to pass laws against publishing such trash on the Web, that is, the ill-fated Communications

Decency Act (1996), most of which a U.S. court swiftly voided as being blatantly unconstitutional. In truth, government attempts at censoring cyberspace, at least in the United States, are not likely to meet with much success.

In addition to all the text, graphics, and videos that vend this surfeit of smut and bile, there is a virtual firestorm of disgusting and dangerous "flaming" and scheming rampaging through the public "chat-rooms" dotting cyberspace. Some of them make the more scandalous TV talk shows wholesome by comparison. Thus, pressure has been placed on Internet companies that host cyber-chats and message boards to police them.

Recently, American Online, the largest of such companies at the moment, forced one chat-room on Irish politics to bar its cyberdoors because of all the insults, threats, and profanity therein. The panel of U.S. judges that overruled the Communications Decency Act analogized that to permit Internet companies to censor discussions would be tantamount to having telephone companies supervise telephone conference calls. America Online's action was a long stride down that fearsome, slippery slope towards corporate "Big Brotherism"—particularly because it snuffed out a political discussion. The resulting furor mushroomed like an A-bomb. America Online quickly rescinded its cancellation shortly thereafter.

An even worse scenario, though, is when governments cyberspy on their citizens (like most Fortune 500 corporations do on their employees) to see what Web sites they log onto, what they say in their e-mail, and what political organizations they join. Sad to say, this is an ongoing practice. Several national governments are already well down the treacherous path of Internet monitoring, including the People's Republic of China and Saudi Arabia.

These governments have tried to funnel Internet traffic into as few lanes into and out of their countries as possible—so as to beef up their capacity to tailor what information comes into and out of the country by the Internet and pry into what kinds of political communication and organization are in progress. How successful this tactic will be in squelching the free flow of global political information and communication into and out of their nations over the long haul is yet unknown, but it warrants concern. Still, the essentially democratic and chaotic structure of the Internet defies the authoritarianism of even the Chinese communist party: "But control over a multi-headed, constantly morphing creature like the Internet is difficult to achieve, as Chinese censors have already learned. . . . To get to the New York Times on the Web or to sites related to Falun Gong, Chinese who know the proper code can dial a device called a proxy server, which effectively masks the identity of the site being visited" (Rosenthal 1999, A-1). Government cyberprying, however, is a much less serious problem in almost all industrialized nations due to the massive number of conduits already in existence and to their pro-democratic rhetoric, theories, and cultures.

One way that established power elites in industrialized representative democracies try to diminish the power of the Internet to erode their authority is to inundate the Web with cyberpolitics-as-usual. At this writing, it is almost impossible to find a government anywhere, at any level, or a political party or political candidate in any putative representative democracy who does not have a Web site of its own. After all, they are cheap to construct, relatively easy to maintain—and eternal. Furthermore, the fundamental interactivity of the Internet lends them a "virtual halo" of accessibility and responsiveness to the general public. Better yet, they can use the Net to help organize their activities and cut costs.

To further reinforce the old democratic paradigm, the World Wide Web is jammed with every reformist brand of political organization and lobby group imaginable—whether they be environmentalists, polluters, citizen empowerers, citizen disempowerers, feminists, masculinists, pro-choicers, anti-abortionists, rifle lovers, gun haters, ad infinitum. They, too, use it for fund raising, recruitment, announcements, pronouncements, ventilation, self-selected polls, the works. They all use the Internet as a 21st century modus operandi to help maintain the believability and longevity of an 18th-century form of governance, one in which they—as political operatives within the current system—thrive. An early but detailed look at this genre is Graeme Browning's *Electronic Democracy* (1996), complete with an index full of Internet addresses.

Degrees of Political Transformation on the Net

Despite all these attempts to regulate, monitor, and pinch the freedom of the Internet, or clog it up with old paradigm Web sites, there are numerous examples of ordinary citizens using the Net for political transformational purposes. Indeed, there is so much of this already on the Web that we have had to build yet another rating system.

At the lowest level, what we call the *First Degree of Political Transformation*, is the preorganizational type of Web site. This allows previously alienated and solitary disaffected citizens and groups to advertise their information and opinion in cyberlights for one and all to see around the world. Legally, no one can slam their door shut. No one can tell them to shut up and sit down. Once established in a Web site, personal or political, they can continue to supplement what they know or feel, edit their views over time, and upgrade the technology and formatting of their Web site with the newest bells and whistles. What this does is to create a much broader and deeper cybernewsstand, library, and archive of alternative data bases, and transformational ideas and positions that are uplifting and downloadable. This was never plausible when electronic and print publishing and distribution were near monopolies of governments and corporations.

Another advantage at this level is that these individuals and groups of citizens can communicate with one another in a heartbeat and in dyads, triads, or large group sessions via e-mail groups (deferred time), chat-rooms (real time), and soon, via real-time Internet video-conferencing.[2] Data, ideas, and critiques can be exchanged. Best of all, the traditional and pervasive sense of hopelessness, loneliness, and desperation among those well outside the mainstream has been greatly eased. The Internet makes these citizens realize that many others—including those from distant climes and cultures—are at a kindred place intellectually and politically. Movements are no longer dependent on geographic proximity or charismatic personalities.

Just reading and talking, however, though useful unto itself, has its downside: nothing much gets done. So, the next stage or level in the transformational process is to organize, to cohere as virtual communities of transformational political interests. This is the *Second Degree of Political Transformation*, or "Organizational."

The Economist's Frances Cairncross put it like this: "Chatting to strangers becomes easier when based on a shared interest. An important impact of the new forms of communications will be to create new social bonds—'virtual communities' of people linked electronically who meet occasionally for what cyber-enthusiasts call 'face time.' . . . Communities of interest, groups of people scattered around the world, may have more in common with one another than with their next door neighbor" (Cairncross 1997, 242).

The result of this, in her view, is that "free to explore different points of view, on the Internet or on the thousands of television and radio channels that will eventually be available, people will be less susceptible to propaganda from politicians who seek to stir up conflicts. Bonded together by the invisible strands of global communications, humanity may find that peace and prosperity are fostered by the death of distance" (Cairncross 1997, 279). Thus, the Internet is a lethal instrument, one that deals the fatal blow, "the death of distance," between communities of transformational political interest that were previously separated and frail.

But more than huge data troves, e-mail, and cyberlinking are needed to produce transformational change. This leads us to the *Third Degree of Political Transformation*: "Taking direct action within the system" to bring about new policies or to abort those passed without any or sufficient input from the public at large. This latter usage is becoming a swelling tide of change, with numerous examples from all levels of governance.

At the local level, we experienced an interesting illustration recently right where we live, in the state of Alabama. The former governor, a one-time darling of the fundamentalist Christian right wing in America, had decided—along with the chief of the state police—to require all citizens applying or reapplying for driver's licenses to be fingerprinted. This was barely mentioned in the mass media.

Within days, though, an astounding electronic coalition was galvanized into action over the Web. Extreme right-wing political groups allied themselves with the American Civil Liberties Union—their time-honored archenemy. Within a week, e-mails and snail-mails cascaded into the governor's office threatening a host of political countermeasures. Stunned by this sudden avalanche of negative political reaction from the strangest of political cohorts, the governor scrapped the idea.

The usual course of action in this kind of situation would have been for these groups to lobby the legislature, a process that would have taken at least the entire legislative session—if not longer—with faint hope of achieving the desired effect. In addition, it all would have been channeled through professional lobbyists (a costly item)—and in the meantime, fingerprinting would have been well underway and therefore more difficult to stop, with DNA samples probably next on the agenda. Thanks to Level 3 transformational politics, empowering citizens within the present representative framework, individual citizens—from a wide range of political viewpoints but with a common distaste for what they strongly believed to be police-statism—were jolted into direct action against the governor via the Internet.

The Internet is also an ideal instrument to transform the two party system in America so as to embolden and empower the majority of American voters who identify themselves as "Independents" (rather than Democrats or Republicans) to become a more coherent force in the representative politics of the 21st century. Perhaps the first such deployment of this cyberstealth weapon was the 1998 election of Jesse ("The Body") Ventura as governor of the state of Minnesota.

Since "Independent" voters—by definition and practice—do not belong to any organized, hierarchical political party, how can they "organize" to elect a leader or representatives? To do so would be a paradox—one that Green parties, the most transformational of any established political party—tussle with worldwide and forever. Parties that name themselves "Reform"—whether in the United States, Canada, or elsewhere, being true to their name—have no problem with organizing. However, once "Independents" join any kind or name of political party, they become just a part of yet another system-friendly political party. The Internet is a practical solution to both the semantical and real problem.

Ventura, a former professional wrestler, had entered politics by becoming the mayor of a small suburb outside Minneapolis. He was a member of the U.S. Reform party, however, and he decided to run for governor of Minnesota against two extremely well known professional Minnesota politicians. One was the scion of the former vice president of the United States and U.S. senator, and he, as the state's attorney general, had just won a multibillion dollar settlement from the despised tobacco industry. The other was a moderate Republican who was the mayor of a medium-sized city, St. Paul. Yet Ventura won.

One of the chief reasons was the Internet, with its capacity to construct a passing, ephemeral political "organization" for just one election—like a wave becoming a particle and then a wave again. According to some sources, Ventura's campaign did not need to raise much money because of the Web. Most of the huge amount of money needed to run "scientifically managed" political campaigns in contemporary America pays for slick, "attack" TV advertising designed intentionally to keep voters at home. As Lance Bennett puts it, "Political marketing maxim number one: the fewer people voting, the easier it is to sell a candidate" (Bennett 1996, ix).

Ventura did a lot of his "independent" campaigning on the Web, which is inexpensive. He also recruited many of his volunteers in this way, and by using the Web, he attracted the attention and support of a particular demographic group that usually abhors voting in any election: the youth. He also came up with a slogan that tapped into that deep, strong undercurrent in all representative democracies that we have been mentioning throughout in this book: *resentment* against all politicians seen as being dominated by large, well-organized, well-financed, established political parties. His slogan? *"Retaliate in '98."* His original Web site for the 1998 campaign is preserved on the Internet "for historical reference" (www.jesseventura.org/1998intr.htm).

This kind of cyberorganizing of "Independents" and campaigning from the Web worked like a charm. And it is bound to work again and again in the 21st century—not only in state elections, but in local and national campaigns as well. The Internet has the propensity to change the balance in American politics in the 21st century by empowering all those "Independent voters" just waiting for the right person, right group, right programs, and right signals, and for just the right moment. Jim Drinkard analyzed the Internet project (protesting the impeachment of President Clinton) that got 500,000 citizens to sign e-petitions and raised $13 million in a few weeks. He noted how this augured a new age of politics by opening up "the political system in a way not seen in decades, creating new power centers while eroding the influence of the two major political parties and counterbalancing the influence of big money" (Drinkard 1999, 1). Thus, it can (and probably will) transform electoral politics in America and in all industrialized societies by mobilizing individual citizens into ever-changing political convergences ("cyberparties" or "cybercampaigns for individuals") operating from their homes. Its first nationwide debut in electoral politics could occur in the American presidential election of 2000, perhaps via the Reform or Green party or in some new organizational configuration. If not, then soon after.

Can this cyberorganizing of ephemeral political allies also work at the global level? The answer has already come and it is "yes." During 1998, a number of highly placed government officials had been meeting covertly with representatives of some global corporations to negotiate a multinational contract. This concord had a rather innocuous title: "the Multinational Agreement on Investments," or MAI.

The fundamental premise of the MAI was that it would further develop the global marketplace if all nations would pass the MAI as national policy. The policy, in essence, would insulate global corporations from almost all legal liability, within any nation adopting it, for damages caused by their investments in that "market." MAI, then, was a way to make global corporations even less responsible and accountable for torts they may cause and breaches of contract, within any country in which they did business. In the eyes of its detractors, MAI was a euphemism for "the Global Corporation Irresponsibility Act." However, within the MAI group itself, there was dissent—and this led to leaks about what was going on secretly.

As word got out, a group of diverse nongovernmental organizations (NGOs) from many nations around the world decided that it was time for a cyberreflex. Thus, a Web site was set up (www.canadians. org/citizensmai.html) describing the proposed agreement, the process that was underway, who was involved, and their view of the clear and present danger to national, state, and local governments and citizens everywhere. E-mails and cyberchats followed that outlined the plan of action, which included, much like the Alabama anti-fingerprint campaign, a flood of e-mails to well-placed legislators and executives around the world. Wave after wave of cybermissiles left their silos and in short order the MAI talks disappeared (for the time being and under that name). In addition, preemptive demonstration against the most powerful dispute-resolving agency of the global oligarchy, the World Trade Organization (WTO), was held in Seattle, Washington, in November 1999—which was organized globally via the Internet. Called "The Battle of Seattle," it marked a renewal of a new coalition of organized labor and environmentalists . . . and something more.

Michael Elliott, reporting in *Newsweek*, saw it, like this: "The e-generation really came into its own in Seattle. Web sites galore spread the word, told people where to show up and solicited bed and board from sympathetic locals. . . . One of the most important lessons of Seattle is that there are now two visions of globalization on offer, one led by commerce, one by social activism" (Elliott 1999, 37–38).

Once again the Internet served its function of uniting previously unconnected groups to impede major agencies or policies that they considered sinister. This sort of use of the Internet is only going to become more commonplace as a tool for transforming present systems of representative democracy into ones that must take note of what either the general population and/or previously large, but isolated, communities of political interest deem essential. Two Canadian professors who did an in-depth study of the MAI episode stated it like this: "Through adept use of the Internet, those opposed to the MAI were able to open up and strengthen the public spheres which citizens depend upon for active participation in civil society. They did so by opening up public spaces in which citizens engaged in discourse and by making domestic and international institutions of governance more permeable to the dialogue" (Smythe and Smith 1999, 29).

Thomas Friedman is a renowned columnist for the *New York Times*, who (like Francis Fukuyama) exalts in what he perceives to be the inexorable victory of American-style, electronically facilitated corporate and financial globalism (Friedman 1999a). But even he understands the latent power of the Internet as a potential tool to aid such marginal groups as downtrodden Third World labor. What is more, he advocates it. Paraphrasing and modernizing Karl Marx, he says: "Workers of the World, double click" (Friedman 1999b).

Conceding a finite amount of "oppression of the unregulated capitalists," Friedman does not call for "some global governing body to fix the problem." Instead, he foresees a future *global governance via the Internet*. The way this will work, according to Friedman, is that a coalition of some corporations, governmental entities, labor, and universities will erect a Web site that will contain, *inter alia*, universal criteria by which global corporations will be monitored and the results of its investigations will be reported annually. It will also have a logo like a "Good Housekeeping Seal of Approval" that it will award to companies who comply. Companies that earn it can attach such to their products, like clothing. This, in turn, will allow consumers to reject anything without this stamp of fair labor practices. Thus, citizen-consumers will vote with their wallets and the effect will be felt on the bottom lines of those companies that fail to meet these global standards. Essentially, citizen-consumers, with the help of the Internet, will become a major force in global governance, that is, direct democracy, facilitated by the Internet, through the power of the free market (Friedman 1999b). Whether this kind of coalition is the best way to help regulate these corporations is not important. What is important here is the understanding of how the Internet has the capability of regulating what up to now has been unregulatable.

What, then, is the *Fourth Degree of Political Transformation* on the Web? This is the kind that we call "Transforming the System of Government," and it has uses that are pragmatic at all levels of governance.

We have already mentioned how the Internet has been employed at the national level in the United States to informally amend the U.S. Constitution—for all practical purposes—to include a partially decentralized system of direct democracy. At the present time, the exact same initiative could be run in the 24 states that utilize this form of direct democracy.

Of course, one does not need the Internet to do this, as was demonstrated in the 1980s when eight states ran nonbinding citizens initiatives on the nuclear-freeze issue. However, more and more multistate initiatives are appearing on state ballots and the idea of organizing, strategizing, and fund raising for them via cyberspace is becoming better understood and a part of the action plan.

For example, the Internet played a major role in the success of those five medical marijuana initiatives discussed earlier in this chapter. Early on, Americans for Medical Rights uploaded substantial scientific and expert information and opinion on their Web site. Then, they sent e-mails to a wide variety of mass media organizations and reporters describing their campaign and how reporters and editors could quickly retrieve answers to any questions they might entertain. In modern industrial societies, reporters, like other professionals, are drowning in paperwork and welcome any life saver thrown to them to help in their research chores. Thus, the media had a convenient way to educate itself (just click on the URL) and began e-mailing Bill Zimmerman, the executive director of Americans for Medical Rights, their questions and comments. This became an ongoing, informed cyberdialogue between the initiative organizers and the media, thereby lessening the media's reliance on governmental sources, if not their well-conditioned resistance to the propositions.

Another positive use of the Net for this series of initiatives was to help the various state committees agree on the best verbiage in the initiatives in order to (1) minimize an effective legal challenge afterward and (2) help them think through the most effective tactics during their campaigns. Zimmerman believes that the Internet was an extremely helpful tool in the passage of all five state initiatives. Dane Waters, who helped coordinate the 14 state initiatives for term limits in 1992, agrees with Zimmerman. Waters stated that he used e-mail extensively as a means to help with planning, public and media relations, and wording in all 14 initiative campaigns.

Thus, it seems likely that the Internet will multiply the number of multistate initiatives exponentially in the 21st century plus the number of states participating in them. Does it seem unreasonable to assume that we will see 20 or more states running the same citizens initiatives—something like a political "powerball" lottery? If this occurs, it may occasion other states to think again about adopting the citizens initiative process so that they can participate in this new and successful New Democratic Paradigm *decentralized national initiative system*, coordinated and facilitated over the Web. One possible scenario is that in the early part of the 21st century, 30 to 40 states will be featuring I+R and the same issue will be appearing in most of the nation. The big question is whether this will lead to a truly national system of I+R—either via Gravel's idea of a national citizens' vote or via the old-fashioned system of constitutional amendment. One or the other or both will probably be in a "state of becoming" for a good part of the 21st century.

We would be remiss to not mention the furious counterattack emanating from those protecting their power under the old paradigm system. People who worship power guard it jealously and zealously. The ploys are many; the front is broad; the tactics are clever.

The two main counterthrusts are in state legislatures and the courtrooms of both state and federal judiciaries. A much larger percentage of laws passed by citizens are struck down by judges than are those passed by legislatures. Could this mean that they are just more poorly drafted? Yes. But judges, either elected or appointed under the representative system, usually have warm feelings about the very system in which they have been amply rewarded and an unfavorable view of an alternative process that challenges it. Thus, "initiative defense" is becoming at least a cottage industry in the practice of American law.

The most serious spearhead of the counterattack, though, is in the oak-paneled halls of state legislatures. There political elites are busy as bees making laws that impede every step in getting a citizens initiative on the ballot. They are raising the number and percentage of voters that need to sign the petition; adding steps that the organizers must take to clear the petition through officialdom; raising the costs of the process; harassing the workers; and so forth. All this is hypersensitive to the increasing surge of interest and use, but it is being countered by IRI's Web site and regular e-mailings concerning the details of the struggle. Thus, the use of the Internet in the battle for more and better I+R in America has both offensive and defensive components to it—and the headquarters of this melee will be in cyberspace.

Another example of using the Internet in an attempt to change a national political system into a more democratic version of itself came in Mexico in 1995. In this case, the inventor and facilitator of the process was the Zapatista movement—an Indian uprising against the national government and ruling party of Mexico. After some initial military and political successes in their home region of Chiapas, the Zapatista movement bogged down in the mud.

Incredibly, what appeared to be an isolated low-tech, jungle guerrilla group turned to the Internet as an instrument of rejuvenation and empowerment. Among other things, they used the Web to conduct a nationwide survey on what their fellow Mexican citizens wanted them to do in the future and how to do it. Over 1.5 million votes came in via the Net to tell them that the overarching sentiment was that the Zapatistas should not resort to violence to achieve their ends. Instead, what they should do was to help organize a national grass-roots network dedicated to their principles and aims. The Zapatistas took that citizen input to heart.

According to some reports, more than 400 civilian Zapatista committees sprung up throughout Mexico, linked together through an Internet network. Using CD-ROMs, they invited their cyber-followers to come visit them in their jungle hideouts without having to slog through the muddy terrain.

That was 1996. What about the Zapatistas today? Their struggle continues. They remain online, but their cyberpresence has had no visible political impact on Mexico. An excellent portal into their global cyber-movement is called *Accion Zapatista* (www.utexas.edu/students/nave) where one can be updated regularly on its problems and progress. They continue to gain many supporters throughout the country and worldwide, which is probably the main (if not only) reason why the Mexican government has not treated them as violently as the Russian government does the Chechniyans and the Turks do the Kurds.

Two excellent examples of how the Internet helps in organizing new paradigmers at the national and global level have already been mentioned in other contexts: IRI and TAN+N. Each has relied heavily on the Net for its educational and organizational efforts and both will continue to do so into the indefinite future.

THE COMING AGE OF CITIZEN POWER: BEYOND REPRESENTATIVE DEMOCRACY AND COMMUNITY REVITALIZATION

As the 20th century fades into history, there are no end of new books that lay claim to the future. Just about all agree that at this point in time, the world is in a period of unprecedented globalization and Americanization. Then the disagreements begin. Is this good or bad? Is it inevitable and irreversible? Will it end soon or take somewhat longer? Will there be new ideologically based conflicts (hot and cold) in the future, and if so, what will they be: Islamic vs. Western? global vs. nationalistic? pro-U.S. vs. anti-U.S.? Northern Hemisphere vs. Southern Hemisphere? post-industrial vs. neo-Marxist? all of the above? or others?

Our view is what we stated at the outset. We believe that the future contest will continue to be what it has always been: that both the problem and the solution concern the quantity and quality of authentic democracy that will exist in the 21st century. We also said in the first chapter that we believe that genuine democracy will increase in degree and scope, albeit with setbacks.

There will be strong countercurrents. These will include (1) the unabashed elitists whose arguments become less and less convincing in the face of the realities of the Information Age; and (2) the reformers who will try to block real democratic progress by making the most minimal changes in the present system, that is, co-opting the rhetoric and process of democratic transformation while actually resisting any direct citizen empowerment within the system. Their goal is to keep as much power as possible in the hands of those at the top of established hierarchies and as little as possible in the hands, hearts, and minds of those at the base, the citizens.

Another form of resistance comes in the form of the more "liberal" reformers, who see the solution to hierarchy as being the revitalization of geographic communities. After all, they are correct in lamenting the decline of community in America and, in point of fact, much of the industrialized world. Indeed, there is great value in their efforts to restore the benefits of local communities to the social, economic, and political life of the nation. We do not oppose what they do, and we do not believe that it is countertransformational as such.

The difficulty comes in their current inability to see some innate flaws in that approach and in their not being willing to accept direct citizen empowerment through virtual communities as being a powerful complement to their theory and practice.

One of the inherent difficulties they must deal with is that geographic community politics is usually the kid brother of big-time politics-as-usual, that is, a more localized pyramid of power. Community leaders are leaders by just another adjective. Micropolitics-as-usual is just a more personal style of macropolitics-as-usual. If the community's politics is run by a democratic, real-life town meeting process, and/or has a citizens initiative process, that would help. But few do.

Even in some of the new methods of democratic participation that we have described earlier in this book, there is a problem when geographic communities are the sole method of citizen involvement. For example, where the citizens who come to a meeting are either self-selected members of the community or have been recruited through community organizations, the sample is definitely going to be nonrepresentative of the general citizenry, even if the usual demographics appear to make it a representative sample. The reason for this is that a certain "political" type of person will be there and the "apolitical" ones will not. Most citizens do not like to come to political meetings and/or cannot afford to come and/or do not have the energy to come. This can best be overcome through a widespread practice of random selection.

The challenge is to flatten hierarchies as much as possible by engaging all those citizens in the polity who are disgusted with representative politics and are not attracted to community politics. The key to a more truly democratic politics of the future lies in the greater realization and materialization of what we have defined, described, and demonstrated to be bona fide "teledemocracy." Thus, this new politics of the 21st century needs to be consistent with the quantum-corrected New Democratic Paradigm. It must incorporate and deploy its theories, instruments, craft, and findings. If this occurs, here are a few features of the *coming age of direct individual citizen power* that will complement all improvements in representative governance and expansion of normal community politics:

- There will be more community, local, state, provincial, regional, national, transnational, and global direct democratic movements and governance.

- There will be more understanding of the common direct democratic theory that unites them and thus more networking between them.

- These new direct democratic systems will use more scientific deliberative polling, voting from the home, electronic deliberation, and comprehensive Electronic Town Meeting processes. TV set–computers will become home-based, interactive (lateral and two-way) political information and communications systems—eventually assisted by artificial intelligence.

- Simple majority, win-lose systems will give way to broad-based consensus building as the best way for polities to plan, decide, and administer the public sphere.

- The use of random sampling will become more common in empowering citizens in self-governance and in influencing representative governments.

- New forms of electronically based democratic political organization will emerge that are here today and gone tomorrow, for example, "cyberparties," "citizens initiative networks," "cyberpressure groups," and "virtual communities of political transformation." These will transform representative government into a system much less responsive to traditionally organized pressure groups and more responsive to a broad base of its citizenry.

And what will be the long-range consequences of this future splurge of teledemocracy? First, the forces of rampant, market-based globalization will be tempered and tethered as a much broader base of citizens of industrialized nations regain a substantial measure of influence over their national, state, provincial, and municipal governments. The very same modern ICT that drives the current dominance of global financial and corporate power at the expense of traditional national sovereignty will provide the wherewithal to construct a countervailing, truly democratic source of power.

Second, this will lead to domestic policies more geared toward (1) a fairer allotment of wealth and social services; (2) countermovements trying to reverse the severe degradation to the planet's ecology in the 20th century; and (3) a more stable and less turbulent social dynamic. We believe it will also lead to a less chest-beating brand of nationalism and toward a more collaborative sort. It is also possible that advances in teledemocracy will lead to a more citizen-influenced transnational order rather than the strict oligarchy presently under construction.

Third, this new sense of citizen empowerment and influence over the future of this planet will work some positive healing of the human psyche and spirit during the intermediate stages of this Information Age. It will help average citizens become more personally involved in suprapersonal affairs of state and transcend their materialistic, solitary obsessions. Some ancient Athenians understood that an apolitical life was not quite worth living. Citizens who shun politics are helpless and hopeless victims. Teledemocracy is a way to a more socially minded life for everyone in society—toward greater self-esteem through selflessness and making sure citizens are not dwarfed by enormous hierarchies of inaccessible power.

The reason for these beliefs should be more than obvious by now. From our experiences and experiments and those of many others mentioned in this book, we see that informed and deliberative citizenries are far wiser and fairer than any political elite could ever be. The teledemocratic processes examined in depth in this book have corroborated repeatedly that citizens who participate in them are well beyond and above narrowly selfish interests, institutional pressures, and the nearsightedness of elected elites. Moreover, almost universally, they find personal pleasure by joining into these new participatory processes.

How could it be otherwise? Those who hold political power today continue in the tradition of those who have held political power since the Federalists invented modern representative government. They believe that clashing self-interests of elites produce a common good. We know that collaboration among informed representative samples of citizens does a far better job of that. In these processes, thinking about and listening to a diverse panorama of values and experience are the main factors in the decision-making process. In modern representative legislatures, personal political power and the lure of money are primary factors in decision making. Which is more likely to favor a greater equality in the distribution of wealth and protection of the environment, and a greater sense of interdependence with all humans and other living beings on this planet?

When the general public comes to understand this, the way things are done politically will change. The Internet will be the preferred mode of communication to spread the news. It is only a matter of time.

That is why we travel down the same political trail blazed by perhaps the greatest American political thinker and patriot of all time: Thomas Jefferson. If one goes to the Jefferson Memorial in Washington, D.C., and reads his words preserved in stone, one will discover this enduring political wisdom:

> I am not an advocate for frequent changes in laws and constitutions. But laws and constitutions must go hand in hand with the progress of the human mind. As that becomes more developed, more enlightened, as new discoveries are made, new truths discovered and manners and opinions change, with the change of circumstances, institutions must advance also to keep pace with the times. We might as well require a man to wear still the coat which fitted him when a boy as civilized society to remain ever under the regimen of their barbarous ancestors.[3]

We do not end with these words because, sooner or later, any democratic and sustainable future must begin with them.

NOTES

1. For an excellent discussion of why and how a new national system of public telecommunications might be funded, see Lawrence Grossman's *The Electronic Republic: Reshaping Democracy in the Information Age* (New York: Viking, 1995). For a further elaboration on how to democratize a modern system of television, see Edward S. Herman's *Triumph of the Market: Essays on Economics, Politics and Media* (Boston: South End Press, 1995), pp. 213–230.

2. Arena 2000, envisioned by Risto Linturi, is a Finnish project designed to turn Helsinki into a "virtual city" by Y2K, whereby cameras on every computer allow people to teleconference and teletravel anywhere in the city.

3. From a letter to Samuel Kercheval dated July 12, 1816.

Bibliography

Abalos, David. 1993. *Political Transformation and the Latino Family*. Westport, CT: Praeger.

————. 1996. *Strategies of Transformation*. Westport, CT: Praeger.

Abramson, Jeffrey B., F. Christopher Arterton, and Gary R. Orren. 1988. *The Electronic Commonwealth: The Impact of New Media Technologies on Democratic Politics*. New York: Basic Books.

Alaska. Office of the Governor. 1980. *Report on Alaska Television Town Meeting of the Alaska Public Forum*. Juneau: Office of the Governor.

Alaska. State Legislature. Division of Public Services. 1982. *Providing a Participatory Legislative Environment*. Juneau: Alaska State Legislature.

Alaska Legislative Affairs Agency. 1982. *Providing a Participatory Legislature*. Anchorage: AL Division of Public Services.

Americans Discuss Social Security. 1999. *Final Report*. Philadelphia: Pew Charitable Trust.

Arnopoulos, P. J., and K. Valaskakis. 1982. *Telecommunitary Democracy: Utopian Vision or Probable Future*. Montreal: UNESCO.

Arterton, F. Christopher. 1987. *Teledemocracy: Can Technology Protect Democracy?* Newbury Park, CA: Sage.

————. 1993. "Campaign '92: Strategies and Tactics." In *The Election of 1992*, edited by Gerald M. Pomper. Chatham, NJ: Chatham House.

Auerbach, Jerrold. 1984. *Justice without Law?* New York: Oxford University Press.

Bachrach, Peter. 1975. "Interest, Participation, and Democratic Theory." In *Participation in Politics*, edited by J. Roland Pennock and John W. Chapman. New York: Liebern-Atherton.

Baker, Ross K. 1993. "Sorting Out and Suiting Up: The Presidential Nomination." In *The Election of 1992*, edited by Gerald Pomper. Chatham, NJ: Chatham House.

Baldwin, Deborah. 1992. "Push-Button Democracy." *Utne Reader* (September/October): 19, 22.

Barber, Benjamin. 1984. *Strong Democracy: Participatory Politics for a New Age.* Berkeley: University of California Press.

———. 1996. *Jihad vs. McWorld.* New York: Ballantine Books.

Barnet, Richard T., and Ronald E. Muller. 1974. *Global Reach.* New York: Simon and Schuster.

Beall, Donald R. 1993. "Don't Dump Space Station." *USA Today,* June 9, p. 13A.

Becker, Theodore L. 1976. *American Government: Past*Present*Future.* Boston: Allyn and Bacon.

———. 1978. "The Constitutional Network: An Evolution in American Democracy." In *Anticipatory Democracy,* edited by Clement Bezold. New York: Random House.

———. 1981. "Teledemocracy: Bringing Power Back to the People." *The Futurist* (December): 6–9.

———. 1988. Review of *Teledemocracy: Can Technology Protect Democracy?* by F. Christopher Arterton. *American Political Science Review* 82 (December): 1376–1377.

———. 1991. *Quantum Politics.* New York: Praeger.

———. 1993. "Teledemocracy: Gathering Momentum in State and Local Governance." *Spectrum* (Spring): 14–19.

———. 1998. "Participatory Democracy, Teledemocracy and the Future of Politics." *Forum of Democratic Leaders in the Asia Pacific Quarterly* (Spring): 1–3.

Becker, Theodore L., Alvin Clement, Alan McRobie, and Brian Murphy. 1981. *Report on New Zealand Televote.* Wellington, New Zealand: Commission for the Future.

Becker, Theodore L., and Anthony L. Dodson. 1991. *Live This Book: Abbie Hoffman's Philosophy for a Free and Green America.* Chicago: Noble Press.

Becker, Theodore L., and Richard Scarce. 1986. "Teledemocracy Emergent: State of the American Art and Science." *Progress in Communication Sciences,* edited by Brenda Dervin and Melvin Voight. Norwood, NJ: Ablex.

Becker, Theodore L., and Christa Slaton. 1981. "Hawaii Televote: Measuring Public Opinion on Complex Issues." *Political Science (New Zealand)* 33 (July): 52–83.

———. 1985. "Teledemocracy to the Rescue." In *Environmental Sciences: A Time for Decision,* edited by Daniel Chiras. Menlo Park, CA: Benjamin/Cummings.

Beedham, Brian. 1997. "Full Democracy." *The Economist,* December 31.

Bennett, Lance W. 1996. *Governing Crisis: Media, Money and Marketing in American Elections.* New York: St. Martin's Press.

Bezold, Clement, ed. 1978. *Anticipatory Democracy: People in the Politics of the Future.* New York: Random House.

Briggs, John. 1992. *Fractals: The Patterns of Chaos.* New York: Simon and Schuster.

Browning, Graeme. 1996. *Electronic Democracy: Using the Internet to Influence American Politics.* Wilton, CT: Pemberton Press.

Bryan, Frank M. 1989. *Vermont Papers: Recreating Democracy on a Human Scale.* Chelsea, VT: Chelsea Green Publishing.

Burnheim, John. 1985. *Is Democracy Possible?: The Alternative to Electoral Politics*. London: Polity Press

Burns, James McGregor, and Stuart Burns. 1991. *A People's Charter: The Pursuit of Rights in America*. New York: Alfred A. Knopf.

Cairncross, Frances. 1997. *The Death of Distance*. Boston: Harvard Business School Press.

California Commission on Campaign Financing. 1992. *Democracy by Initiative: Shaping California's Fourth Branch of Government*. Los Angeles: Center for Responsive Government.

Callenbach, Ernest, and Michael Phillips. 1985. *A Citizens Legislature*. San Francisco: Banyan Tree Books and Clear Glass.

Campbell, Vincent N. 1974. *The Televote System for Civic Communication: First Demonstration and Evaluation*. Palo Alto: American Institute for Research.

Capra, Fritjof. 1982. *The Turning Point*. New York: Simon and Schuster.

Carson, Lyn. 1995. "Perspectives on Community Consultation." *Australian Planner* 32, no. 4: 217–221.

Carson, Lyn, and Brian Martin. 1999. *Random Selection in Politics*. Westport, CT: Praeger.

Chomsky, Noam, and Edward Herman. 1988. *Manufacturing Consent: The Political Economy of the Mass Media*. New York: Pantheon.

Chopra, Deepak. 1993. *Ageless Body, Timeless Mind*. New York: Crown Publishers.

Clausing, Jeri. 1997. "Costa Rica to Try Online Elections." *CyberTimes* (*New York Times* on the Web), October 22, pp. 1–4.

"The Constitutional Network." 1978. *Rain* (December).

Coote, Anna, and Jo Lenaghan. 1997. *Citizens' Juries: Theory into Practice*. London: Institute for Public Policy Research.

Cronin, Thomas. 1989. *Direct Democracy*. Cambridge, MA: Harvard University Press.

Crosby, Ned. 1996. "Jefferson Center Moves Ahead." *Citizens Jury Update* (Summer). Minneapolis: Jefferson Center.

Dator, James A. 1983a. "Futuristics and the Exercise of Anticipatory Democracy in Hawaii." In *Political Science and the Study of the Future*, edited by William Page. London: Frances Pinter.

———. 1983b. "The Honolulu Electronic Town Meeting." In *The Future of Politics*, edited by William Page. London: Frances Pinter.

———. 1987. "Transforming the Constitution: A Quantum Leap." Paper presented at the Annual Meeting of the American Political Science Association, Chicago.

deTocqueville, Alexis. 1956. *Democracy in America*. New York: New American Library.

Dewey, John. 1957. *Reconstruction in Philosophy*. Boston: Beacon Press.

Dienel, Peter. 1998. "Planning Cells: The German Experience." Paper presented at the Institute of Public Policy Research International Conference, London, United Kingdom, July.

DiZerega, Gus. 1991. "Integrating Quantum Theory with Post-Modern Political Thought and Action: The Priority of Relationships over Objects." In *Quantum Politics: Applying Quantum Theory to Political Phenomena*, edited by Theodore L. Becker. New York: Praeger.

Downs, Anthony. 1957. *An Economic Theory of Democracy*. New York: Harper and Row.

Drinkard, Jim. 1999. "One Click Can Reach Millions." *USA Today*, August 31, 1999, p. 1.

Elgin, Duane. 1991. "Conscious Democracy through Electronic Town Meetings." *Whole Earth* (Summer): 28–29.

Elliott, Michael. 1999. "The New Radicals." *Newsweek*, December 13, 1999, pp. 36–39.

Erne, Roland, Andreas Gross, Bruno Kaufmann, and Heinz Kleger. 1995. *Transnationale Demokratie*. Zurich: Realotopia Verlagagenossenschaft.

Etzioni, Amitai, Kenneth Laudon, and Sara Lipson. 1975. "Participatory Technology: The MINERVA Communications Tree." *Journal of Communications* (Spring): 64–74.

Ferguson, Marilyn. 1980. *The Aquarian Conspiracy*. Los Angeles: Tarcher.

Fishkin, James. 1991. *Democracy and Deliberation*. New Haven, CT: Yale University Press.

French, Howard W. 1999. "Death Stirs up Opposition of Japanese to Atom Use." *New York Times*, December 23, 1999, p. A-7.

Friedman, Thomas. 1999a. *The Lexus and the Olive Tree*. New York: Straus and Giroux.

———. 1999b. "The New Human Rights." *New York Times*, July 30, p. 20.

Friedrich, Carl. 1943. *The New Belief in the Common Man*. Boston: Little, Brown, and Co.

Fromm, Erich. 1955. *The Sane Society*. New York: Rinehart.

Fukuyama, Francis. 1989. "The End of History." *The National Interest* (Summer): 1–18.

Fuller, R. Buckminster. 1971. *No More Secondhand God*. Garden City, NY: Doubleday.

Goodwin, Barbara. 1992. *Justice by Lottery*. Chicago: University of Chicago Press.

Grossman, Lawrence. 1995. *The Electronic Republic: Reshaping Democracy in the Information Age*. New York: Viking.

Halpern, Manfred. 1998. "A Theory for Transforming the Self: Moving beyond the Nation-State." In *Transformational Politics: Theory, Study, and Practice*, edited by Stephen Woolpert, Christa Daryl Slaton, and Edward W. Schwerin. Albany: State University of New York Press.

Hawking, Stephen. 1988. *A Brief History of Time: From the Big Bang to Black Holes*. New York: Bantam Books.

Henderson, Hazel. 1970. "Computers: Hardware of Democracy." *Forum* 70 (February): 22–24, 46–51.

———. 1996. *Building a Win-Win World: Life beyond Global Economic Warfare*. San Francisco: Berrett-Kohler.

Hobbes, Thomas. 1985. *Leviathan*. London: Viking Penguin.

Hoffman, Abbie, Jerry Rubin, and Ed Sanders. 1972. *Vote*. New York: Warner Paperback Library.

Honolulu Advertiser. 1977. Editorial. "ConCon and Openness." March 2.

Jefferson, Thomas. 1984. *Jefferson Writings*. New York: Literary Classics of the United States.

Johnson-Lenz, Peter, and Trudy Johnson-Lenz. 1992. "Using Our Differences Creatively." *Bulletin of the Institute for Awakening Technology* (Fall).

Jones, Larry. 1997. "Educated Opinion." *Electric Perspectives* (January/February): 9–17.

Kay, Alan F. 1998. *Locating Consensus for Democracy: A Ten-Year Experiment*. St. Augustine, FL: America Talks Issues Foundation.

Kennedy, John F., Jr. 1999. "Bold Ideas for a Better America." *USA Weekend*. June 13, pp. 6–7.

Keskinen, Auli. 1995. *Teledemokratia*. Helsinki: Painatuskeskus.

———. 1999. *Towards User Empowerment*. Tampere, Finland: Studia Politica Tamperensis, No. 6.

Kidder, Rushworth M. 1988. "Making the Quantum Leap." *Christian Science Monitor* (June): 13–17.

Kiel, L. Douglas. 1994. *Managing Chaos and Complexity in Government*. San Francisco: Jossey Bass.

Kim, Dae-Jung. 1998. "Words of Kim Dae-Jung: Call for Reconciliation." *New York Times*, February 26, p. A-8.

Korten, David. 1995. *When Corporations Rule the World*. San Francisco: Berrett-Koehler.

Kramer, Jane. 1999. "Living with Berlin." *The New Yorker*, (July 5), pp. 50–64.

Kuhn, Thomas. 1970. *The Structure of Scientific Revolutions*. Chicago: University of Chicago Press.

Landau, Martin. 1961. "On the Use of Metaphor in Political Science." *Social Research* 28: 331–353.

Lippman, Walter. 1921. *Public Opinion*. Reprint. Glencoe, IL: The Free Press.

Lohr, Steve. 2000. "Welcome to the Internet, the First Global Colony." *New York Times*, January 9, p. Wk1.

Madison, James. 1961. "Federalist Paper #10." In *The Federalist Papers*, Alexander Hamilton, James Madison, and John Jay. New York: The New American Library.

Mansbridge, Jane. 1983. *Beyond Adversary Democracy*. Chicago: University of Chicago Press.

Marrow, Alfred F. 1969. *The Practical Theorist: The Life and Work of Kurt Lewin*. New York: Basic Books.

McLaughlin, Corinne. 1993. *The Inner Side of World Events*. New York: Ballantine Books.

McNeill, William. 1975. *The Contemporary World*. Chicago: Scott Foresman.

Michael, Donald. 1968. "On Coping with Complexity." *Daedalus* (Fall): 1179–1193.

Mills, C. Wright. 1956. *The Power Elite*. New York: Oxford University Press.

Mingus, Matthew. 1998. "Quantum Theory and the Philosophy of Henryk Skolimowsky: Co-creation and the Spiral of Understanding." Paper delivered at Conference on Public Administration Theory, Colorado Springs, CO.

Mitchell, George J. 1999. *Making Peace*. New York: Alfred A. Knopf.

Munro, William Bennett. 1928. "Physics and Politics—An Old Analogy Revisited." *American Political Science Review* 23 (February): 1–10.

Myers, Phyllis. 1999. *Livability at the Ballot Box*. Washington, DC: Brookings Institution.

Naisbett, John. 1982. *Megatrends*. New York: Warner Books.

Neely, Richard. 1983. *Why Courts Don't Work*. New York: McGraw-Hill.

Ohlin, Tomas. 1971. "Local Democracy in the Telecommunications Age." *Svenska Dogbladet* (August 8): 1.

———. 1998. *Samhallsdialogen*. Stockholm: Kommunikations Forsknings Beredningen, Rapport, No. 6.

Olsen, Walter K. 1991. *The Litigation Explosion: What Happened When America Unleashed the Lawsuit*. New York: Truman Talley.

Olsson, Anders. 1999. *Elektronisk Demokrati*. Stockholm: SOU, No. 12.

Osborne, David, and Ted Gaebler. 1992. *Re-inventing Government*. New York: Penguin Books.

Overman, Samuel. 1991. "Policy Physics." In *Quantum Politics*, edited by Theodore L. Becker. New York: Praeger.

Polak, Jiri, and Jaroslav Koci. 1996. *The Direct Democracy of Tomorrow*. Prague: DD Publishing House.

Purnam, Todd S. 1998. "Ballot Initiatives Flourishing as a Way to Bypass Politicians." *New York Times*, March 31, p. 1.

Rohter, Larry. 1999. "Power Quest Drives Leader as Venezuela Goes to the Polls." *New York Times*, April 25, p. 4.

Rosenthal, Elizabeth. 1999. "Web Sites Bloom in China, and Beijing Weeds." *New York Times*, December 23, p. A1.

Rossiter, Clinton (ed.). 1961. *The Federalist Papers*. New York: New American Library.

Rummel, R. J. 1977. *Field Theory Evolving*. Beverly Hills: Sage.

Sabin, George. 1961. *History of Political Theory*, 3d ed. New York: Rinehart and Winston.

Sartori, Giovvanni. 1994. *Comparative Constitutional Engineering*. New York: New York University Press.

Satin, Mark. 1979. *New Age Politics*. New York: Dell.

Savolainen, Reijo and Ari-Veikko Anttiroiko. 1999. *The Communicative Potentials and Problems of Teledemocracy*. Tampere, Finland: University of Tampere, Local Government Study, No. 6.

Schlesinger, Arthur J., Jr. 1986. *The Cycles of American History*. Boston: Houghton Mifflin.

Schmidt, Marcus. 1993. *Direkte Demokratie i Danmark*. Copenhagen: Nyt Nordisk Forlag Arnold Busck.

Schrag, Peter. 1998. *Paradise Lost: California's Experience, America's Future*. New York: The New Press.

Schubert, Glendon. 1983. "The Evolution of Political Science: Paradigms of Physics, Biology, and Politics." *Politics and the Life Sciences* 1: 97–110.

Schwerin, Edward. 1995. *Mediation, Citizen Empowerment and Transformational Politics*. New York: Praeger.

Slaton, Christa Daryl. 1992. *Televote: Expanding Citizen Participation in the Quantum Age*. New York: Praeger.

Smythe, Elizabeth, and Peter J. Smith, 1999. "Globalization, Citizenship and Technology: The MAI Meets the Internet" Paper presented at the "CIPA '99" Conference, Tampere University, Tampere, Finland, August.

Southern California Association of Governments. 1983. *Report on the Los Angeles Televote*. Los Angeles: SCAG.

Stavrianos, L. S. 1976. *The Promise of the Coming Dark Age*. San Francisco: W. H. Freeman.

Stolberg, Sheryl Gay. 1999. "Sham Surgery Returns as a Research Tool." *New York Times*, April 25, p. 3.

Tehranian, Majid. 1979. "Development Theory and Communications Policy: The Changing Paradigms." *Progress in Communications Sciences* 1: 120–166.

Theobald, Robert. 1978. "The Deeper Implication of Citizen Participation." In *Anticipatory* Democracy, edited by Clement Bezold. New York: Random House.

Thomas, Ron. 1997. "Teleplanning: Using Television as an Interactive Democratic Planning Tool." *Planning Casebook*. Chicago: American Certified Planning Association.

Toffler, Alvin. 1970. *Future Shock*. New York: Random House.

———. 1980. *The Third Wave*. London: William Collins.

Toffler, Alvin, and Heidi Toffler. 1994. *Creating a New Civilization*. Atlanta: Turner.

Tribe, Laurence H. 1991. "The Curvature of Constitutional Space: What Lawyers Can Learn from Modern Physics." In *Quantum Politics*, edited by Theodore L. Becker, Chapter 8. New York: Praeger.

Uphoff, Norman. 1992. *Learning from Gal Oya*. Ithaca, NY: Cornell University Press.

Van Natta, Jr, Don. 1999. "Pollings Dirty Little Secret: No Response." *New York Times*, November 21, Wk1.

Varner, Bill. 1996. "Citizens Initiate a Record 94 Ballot Questions." *USA Today*, October 17, 1996.

Vaughn, C. E. 1915. *The Political Writings of Jean Jacques Rousseau*. Cambridge: Cambridge University Press.

Wachtel, Ted. 1992. *The Electronic Congress*. Pipersville, PA: The Piper's Press.

Woolpert, Steven, Christa Slaton, and Edward Schwerin. 1998. *Transformational Politics*. Albany, NY: SUNY Press.

Yankelovich, Daniel. 1999. *The Magic of Dialogue: Transforming Conflict into Co-operation*. New York: Simon and Schuster.

Zohar, Danah. 1990. *The Quantum Self*. New York: Morrow.

Zohar, Danah, and Ian Marshall. 1994. *The Quantum Society*. New York: Morrow.

Index

About the Authors

TED BECKER is Professor of Political Science at Auburn University. The author of eleven earlier books, including *Quantum Politics* (Praeger, 1991), he is also a political activist trying to link teledemocracy, direct democracy, and environmental sustainability.

CHRISTA DARYL SLATON is Director of the Masters in Public Administration program and Professor of Political Science at Auburn University. Among her earlier publications is *Televote: Expanding Citizen Participation in the Quantum Age* (Praeger, 1991).